AMERICAN FOREIGN ENVIRONMENTAL POLICY AND THE POWER OF THE STATE

American Foreign Environmental Policy and the Power of the State

STEPHEN HOPGOOD

OXFORD UNIVERSITY PRESS
1998

Oxford University Press, Great Clarendon Street, Oxford OX2 6DP

Oxford New York

Athens Auckland Bangkok Bogota Bombay
Buenos Aires Calcutta Cape Town Dar es Salaam
Delhi Florence Hong Kong Istanbul Karachi
Kuala Lumpur Madras Madrid Melbourne
Mexico City Nairobi Paris Singapore
Taipei Tokyo Toronto Warsaw
and associated companies in
Berlin Ibadan

Oxford is a trade mark of Oxford University Press

Published in the United States
by Oxford University Press Inc., New York

British Library Cataloguing in Publication Data
Data available

Library of Congress Cataloging in Publication Data
Hopgood, Stephen.
American foreign environmental policy and the power of the state /
Stephen Hopgood.
Includes bibliographical references.
1. Environmental policy—United States. 2. Environmental policy—
United States—International cooperation. 3. United States—
Foreign policy—1993– I. Title.
GE180.H66 1997 363.7'00973—dc21 97-31036
ISBN 0-19-829259-7

1 3 5 7 9 10 8 6 4 2

Typeset by Best-set Typesetter Ltd., Hong Kong
Printed in Great Britain
on acid-free paper by
Bookcraft (Bath) Ltd
Midsomer Norton, Somerset

Acknowledgements

As will be painfully obvious to the initiated, the book which lies before you began life as a doctoral thesis. Although extensively revised and updated, it has been an impossible task to rid the text completely of that lack of sophistication so characteristic of graduate work. Those bits worth salvaging owe their survival largely to the efforts of Andrew Hurrell and Byron Shafer. As my supervisor, Andrew has been a remarkably knowledgeable reader and critic, whose guidance and advice improved my work immeasurably. Byron, despite having no formal responsibility for me, devoted much time and patience to my academic development. If the published book is very different from my submitted thesis I hope neither feels it is for the worse. Latterly, Yuen Foong Khong has also been an influential guide to the mysteries of both international relations and academic publishing and I thank him warmly. All three of these scholars are fellows of Nuffield College, Oxford, where I spent four years as a graduate student. It proved the ideal environment for undertaking research and I am grateful to the wardens, fellows, and staff of the college for all their help and support. I would also like to thank the staff and fellows of Queen's College, Oxford, and my head of department at the School of Oriental and African Studies, Tom Young. Gratitude is also due to all those who gave their valuable time to be interviewed and a full list appears in the Bibliography.

This book would not have been possible were it not for the kindness of many friends and colleagues from both Oxford and London. I would especially like to thank Daniel Attas, Yael Boverman, Bob and Geri Dallek, Christopher Lake, and John Sidel, the latter a latecomer to the project who soon became both a valued friend and fellow-worker. Rebecca Mosley put a great deal more into this than she got out and I am unable to properly express my gratitude. I would also like to thank Dominic Byatt, Sophie Ahmad, Cecilia Garcìa Peñalosa, Penny Moyle, John Darwin, Anthony Jarvis, Robert Mason, Caroline Thomas, my sister Mandy Hopgood, and the Hovaguimians: Andre, Veronika, Catherine, and Alexandra, and two anonymous reviewers for

Oxford University Press. Gillian Peele, of Lady Margaret Hall, Oxford, has been the source of much good advice for which I thank her wholeheartedly. I am also extremely grateful for the generous financial support I received from the Economic and Social Research Council, the Cyril Foster Fund (Oxford University), the Goodhart Fund (Nuffield College), and from SOAS for a research trip to Washington, DC.

Helen Jenkins has contributed so much to my life in so many ways. Her sympathy and sensitivity have sustained me and, but for her love, generosity, and tolerance, I would never have finished. Our joint piece of work—Eleanor—will neither know, nor doubtless care, very much about this book but she should be aware, if only for the sake of posterity, that she provided a constant source of perspective about social science. Finally, my parents, Anne and Mark. Their support for me has always been unconditional and it is only through their achievements, and with their love, that I have been able to prosper. I hope they are as proud of me as I am of them. It is to all these members of my family that I dedicate this book.

Stephen Hopgood

Oxford
June 1997

Contents

List of Abbreviations

BDT	Biodiversity Treaty
CAPE '92	Consortium on Action to Protect the Environment, 1992
CCMS	Committee on the Challenges of Modern Society [of NATO]
CEQ	Council on Environmental Quality
CFC	Chlorofluorocarbon
CITES	Convention on Trade in Endangered Species
EC	European Community EU European Union (after Nov. 1993)
ECOSOC	Economic and Social Council
EPA	Environmental Protection Agency
ESA	Endangered Species Act, 1973
FAO	Food and Agriculture Organization
GATT	General Agreement on Tariffs and Trade
GEF	Global Environmental Facility
ICSU	International Council of Scientific Unions
IMF	International Monetary Fund
INC	Intergovernmental Negotiating Committee
IPCC	Intergovernmental Panel on Climate Change
IPE	International Political Economy
ITTO	International Tropical Timber Organization
IUCN	International Union for the Conservation of Nature and Natural Resources
NATO	North Atlantic Treaty Organization
NEPA	National Environmental Policy Act, 1969
NGO	Non-Governmental Organization
NIPCC	National Industrial Pollution Control Council
NRDC	Natural Resources Defense Council
NWF	National Wildlife Federation
ODA	Overseas Development Assistance
OECD	Organization for Economic Cooperation and Development
OES	Office of Oceans and International Environmental and Scientific Affairs, State Department

OMB	Office of Management and Budget
TFAP	Tropical Forestry Action Plan
UNCED	United Nations Conference on Environment and Development
UNCHE	United Nations Conference on the Human Environment
UNCTAD	United Nations Conference on Trade and Development
UNDP	United Nations Development Programme
UNEP	United Nations Environment Programme
UNESCO	United Nations Educational, Scientific and Cultural Organization
WCED	World Commission on Environment and Development
WHOEP	White House Office on Environmental Policy
WIPO	World Intellectual Property Organization
WMO	World Meteorological Organization
WWF	World Wildlife Fund

Introduction

It may seem perverse to be arguing for the relevance of the state in the era of the global village, an impression reinforced when international environmental politics constitute the subject matter. Few, if any, issues pose such complex problems both for the autonomy and sovereignty of states. Nevertheless, it is the argument of this book that an analysis of foreign environmental policy-making contributes significantly to an understanding of exactly how the growth of non-state actors and of awkward transnational issues impacts upon the state itself, the core institution for traditional theories of international relations. This project has two dimensions: a focus on explanations of foreign policy in the context of theories of the state and international relations, and an empirical assessment of how one state in particular has formulated its foreign environmental policy since 1965.

In the last thirty years, environmental politics have emerged as a major new issue on the international political agenda.[1] Although environmental problems had been the subject of both national and international discussion before, events since the 1960s have represented a qualitative change. Prior to this, concern had focused largely on fears about the exhaustion of natural resources and the side-effects of industrial development. In 1909, for example, US President Theodore Roosevelt called a world conference on conservation (it was later cancelled by President Taft). Acid rain had been diagnosed as early as the seventeenth century and, in the

[1] Among the growing number of introductory guides to international environmental politics are Andrew Hurrell and Benedict Kingsbury (eds.), *The International Politics of the Environment* (Oxford: Clarendon Press, 1992); Caroline Thomas, *The Environment in International Relations* (London: RIIA, 1992); John McCormick, *The Global Environmental Movement: Reclaiming Paradise* (London: Belhaven Press, 1989); Matthew Paterson, *Global Warming and Global Politics* (London: Routledge, 1996); John Vogler and Mark F. Imber (eds.), *The Environment and International Relations* (London: Routledge, 1996); Ian H. Rowlands, *The Politics of Global Atmospheric Change* (Manchester: Manchester University Press, 1995); and Gareth Porter and Janet Welsh Brown, *Global Environmental Politics* (Boulder, Colo.: Westview Press, 1991).

decades after 1920, attempts were made to protect some wildlife, most notably migratory birds.

Despite these early efforts, however, environmental concerns were still viewed primarily as local, or occasionally national, issues. While it is fair to say, therefore, that environmental problems as such were not new, it is important to acknowledge that the advent of large-scale multilateral negotiations represented a substantial change. In this sense, 1967, the year in which the first major UN conference was called, marked the beginning of the era of international environmental politics.[2]

Several issues have come to exemplify the extent to which the different nations of the world are linked by their shared environment. These include climate change, ozone depletion, the destruction of tropical rainforests, and the loss of species biodiversity. In each of these areas the national policies that states pursue have important implications for others, not just their near neighbours but also distant countries with whom they have few if any dealings. It is often not possible to solve one's own environmental dilemmas because activities elsewhere may be worsening the atmosphere, or the oceans, as fast as one's own remedial measures can take effect. Hence, the contrast between an international system divided into separate states and the 'ecosphere'. As a World Commission on Environment and Development put it: 'The Earth is one, but the world is not.'[3] The environment thus shares with several other contemporary issues—the spread of disease, economic globalization, terrorism, refugee flows—the sense of an asymmetry between sovereign political institutions and the international nature of the problem.

For this reason, the state is under scrutiny both conceptually and empirically. For some, persistent failures to fix on an acceptable definition of 'the state' render it a relatively useless conceptual tool.[4] For others, it is the empirical evidence of state decline which

---

[2] For an excellent overview of the origins of modern environmentalism, see McCormick, *The Global Environmental Movement*, ch. 1.

[3] World Commission on Environment and Development, *Our Common Future* (New York: Oxford University Press, 1987), 27; see also Andrew Hurrell, 'International Political Theory and the Global Environment', in Ken Booth and Steve Smith (eds.), *International Relations Theory Today* (Cambridge: Polity Press, 1995), 132.

[4] Yale H. Ferguson and Richard W. Mansbach, *The Elusive Quest: Theory and International Politics* (Columbia, SC: University of South Carolina Press, 1988), 112, 142.

seems most convincing. Consider, for example, Edward Morse's argument from the 1970s:

The linkages between domestic and foreign policies constitute the basic characteristic of the breakdown in the distinction between foreign and domestic affairs in the modernized, interdependent international system.[5]

Or, as Keohane and Nye argued in 1977: 'Domestic and foreign policy become closely linked. The notion of national interest—the traditionalists' lodestar—becomes increasingly difficult to use effectively. Traditional maxims of international politics—that states will act in their national interests or that they will attempt to maximize their power—become ambiguous.'[6] In relation to the environment, for example, the gap between domestic and foreign policy is perceived to have receded, privileging accounts which stress that 'large-scale earthkeeping activities' will 'break down the distinction between the "domestic" world of "internal" or intrastate affairs; and the world of "foreign" interstate relations'.[7] One influential account describes this situation as 'postinternational politics', a 'transformation' to a world where: '. . . the state-centric system now coexists with an equally powerful, though more decentralized, multi-centric system'.[8]

According to David Held and Anthony McGrew, the 'common thread uniting this particular school of thought is the assumption that increasing global interconnectedness is transforming the nature and role of the state in the global system.' They continue:

In essence, this 'transformationalist' literature portrays the modern state as trapped within an extensive web of global interdependence,

---

[5] Edward L. Morse, 'The Transformation of Foreign Policies: Modernization, Interdependence, and Externalization', (originally in *World Politics*, 22/3 (1970), as repr. in Richard Little and Michael Smith (eds.), *Perspectives on World Politics*, 2nd edn. (London: Routledge, 1991), 172. See also Edward L. Morse, *Modernization and the Transformation of International Relations* (New York: Macmillan, 1976).

[6] See Robert O. Keohane and Joseph S. Nye, Jnr., *Power and Interdependence: World Politics in Transition* (Boston: Little, Brown, 2nd edn., 1989 (1977 originally)), 8.

[7] Daniel Deudney, 'Global Environmental Rescue and the Emergence of World Domestic Politics', in Ronnie D. Lipschutz and Ken Conca (eds.), *The State and Social Power in Global Environmental Politics* (New York: Columbia University Press, 1993), 284.

[8] James N. Rosenau, *Turbulence in World Politics: A Theory of Change and Continuity* (New York: Harvester-Wheatsheaf, 1990), 11.

heavily permeated by transnational forces, and increasingly unable to fulfil its core functions without recourse to international cooperation.[9]

In other words, the distinction between the state and the international system, a constituent and perhaps even a necessary feature of the mainstream study of international relations, is eroded. If the argument for a permeable state is convincing, one may legitimately look to these new transnational forces as critical, rather than merely evident, parts of an explanation for the making of foreign policy itself. One cannot make claims for the 'internationalization' of domestic policy if state elites simply continue to make foreign policy as they did before, apparently oblivious to the changing world around them. Interdependence, and its 'successor concept', globalization have to make good on their promise to provide satisfactory alternative explanations for state choices in the international sphere.[10]

Arguments for the diminishing national–international distinction concentrate their fire on the declining efficacy of the state along two dimensions, described by Mark Zacher as 'the two central features of the traditional Westphalian system'.[11] First, the state's loss of effective control, or 'autonomy'. Second, its loss of sovereignty, or authority. As Ken Conca has suggested, arguments in the ecology–sovereignty debate have tended towards one of two positions: sovereignty may be eroded by environmental developments, or it may even be enhanced (through the greater problem-solving capacity provided by international collective action).[12] Hence, the relationship between sovereignty, and its 'twin', autonomy, needs to be problematized.

For some, the two are analytically distinct. Janice Thomson, for example, argues that state control—autonomy—has 'waxed and waned enormously over time' while sovereignty—'ultimate politi-

[9] David Held and Anthony McGrew, 'Globalization and the Liberal Democratic State', *Government and Opposition*, 23/2 (1993), 279–80.

[10] For this claim about globalization as a 'successor concept', see R. J. Barry Jones, *Globalisation and Interdependence in the International Political Economy: Rhetoric and Reality* (London: Pinter, 1995), 3.

[11] Mark W. Zacher, 'The Decaying Pillars of the Westphalian Temple: Implications for International Order and Governance', in James N. Rosenau and Ernst-Otto Czempiel (eds.), *Governance without Government: Order and Change in World Politics* (Cambridge: Cambridge University Press, 1992), 61.

[12] Ken Conca, 'Rethinking the Ecology–Sovereignty Debate', *Millenium: Journal of International Studies*, 23/3 (1994), 701–11.

cal authority'—has persisted.[13] Samuel Barkin and Bruce Cronin, by contrast, maintain that sovereignty, as a 'social construct', has always been subject to interpretation and thus is not a constant but a variable. They suggest that changes in sovereignty—which they argue is reformulated and reinterpreted in the light of the interrelations between states in a states system—can 'greatly affect the ways in which states are constrained or enabled to act in their international relations'.[14] As Naeem Inayatullah and David Blaney suggest with their title, 'Realizing Sovereignty', and in their initial discussion, there is a difference between the state's possession of formal sovereignty and its capacity in reality to actually influence its own destiny.[15]

Others have sought to distinguish *formal* from *operational* sovereignty: the former is a constant reflecting the state's legal supremacy, the latter a variable giving states the capacity for alienation required for resolving collective action problems through international institutions. The relationship between this variable sovereignty, and autonomy, is unclear, although it may be that the necessity of yielding some operational sovereignty is indicative of a failure of state capacity.[16] As Conca suggests, one implication which may be drawn from this is that 'sovereignty' may be lost at the same time as the state gains capacity from its newfound ability to solve more problems by alienating authority to a collective.[17]

There is little doubt that in quantitative terms flows of commodities and people are greater now than in any previous epoch

[13] Janice E. Thomson, 'State Sovereignty in International Relations: Bridging the Gap between Theory and Empirical Research', *International Studies Quarterly*, 39 (1995), 214; see also Charles R. Beitz, 'Sovereignty and Morality', in David Held (ed.), *Political Theory Today* (Cambridge: Polity Press, 1991), 241.

[14] J. Samuel Barkin and Bruce Cronin, 'The State and the Nation: Changing Norms and Rules of Sovereignty in International Relations', *International Organization*, 48/1 (1994), 109–10.

[15] Naeem Inayatullah and David L. Blaney, 'Realizing Sovereignty', *Review of International Studies*, 21 (1995), 3–4; see also Robert H. Jackson, *Quasi-States: Sovereignty, International Relations and the Third World* (Cambridge: Cambridge University Press, 1990).

[16] Marc A. Levy, Robert O. Keohane, and Peter M. Haas, 'Improving the Effectiveness of International Environmental Institutions', in Haas, Keohane, and Levy (eds.), *Institutions for the Earth: Sources of Effective International Environmental Protection* (Cambridge, Mass.: MIT Press, 1993), 415–17.

[17] See also Alexander Wendt, 'Collective Identity Formation and the International State', *American Political Science Review*, 88/2 (1994), 393.

(although by some measures not that much greater than in the late nineteenth century). This 'global society' paradigm is described by K. J. Holsti as follows:

The standard position is that trade, technology communications, tourism, and the vast network of transnational relations between private citizens, associations, and companies has reached a point of such density that today there is already the framework of a world society based on a global economy.[18]

In relation to the environment, more specifically, Paul Wapner describes a perceptual shift, the emergence of an 'ecological sensibility' or a change in 'the governing ideas that animate societies'.[19] Ultimately such accounts give rise to arguments for an emergent world society; this is especially true in sociology where the discipline's core focus on 'society' is under pressure from 'trans-societal perspectives'.[20] In short, boundaries are being blurred, and even eradicated, conceptually and empirically. Hence, the collapsing national–international distinction leading to what James Rosenau calls 'the tattered authority of the state'.[21] Or, as Joseph A. Camilleri and Jim Falk have argued:

Theorists of widely diverging ideological persuasion have recognized the declining efficacy of state action, and the emergence of issues, relationships and institutions that dissolve the national-international divide.[22]

[18] K. J. Holsti, *The Dividing Discipline: Hegemony and Diversity in International Relations* (Boston: Allen and Unwin, 1987), 52. Holsti also remarks that: 'The old dichotomy between domestic and foreign policy has broken down,' (p. 55). On the 'global policy agenda', including the environment, see Marvin S. Soroos, *Beyond Sovereignty: The Challenge of Global Policy* (Columbia, SC: University of South Carolina Press, 1986).

[19] Paul Wapner, 'Politics Beyond the State: Environmental Activism and World Civic Politics', *World Politics*, 47 (1995), 322. This echoes Benedict Anderson's description of the relationship between material and perceptual change in the emergence of 'national' consciousness (*Imagined Communities* (London: Verso, 1991, rev. edn.), 22). See also John Gerard Ruggie, 'Territoriality and Beyond: Problematizing Modernity in International Relations', *International Organization*, 47/1 (1993), 157, where he considers the idea of 'social epistemes'.

[20] See Mike Featherstone and Scott Lash, 'Globalization, Modernity and the Spatialization of Social Theory: An Introduction', in Mike Featherstone, Scott Lash, and Roland Robertson (eds.), *Global Modernities* (London: Sage, 1995), and Martin Shaw, *Global Society and International Relations* (Cambridge: Polity Press, 1994).

[21] Rosenau, *Turbulence in World Politics*, 107.

[22] Joseph A. Camilleri and Jim Falk, *The End of Sovereignty: The Politics of a Shrinking and Fragmenting World* (Aldershot: Edward Elgar, 1992), 39.

As we can see, however, the precise nature of the relationship between autonomy and sovereignty is far from clear. States may have lost autonomy, they may have lost sovereignty, or both, or neither. Sovereignty, as authority, may fluctuate over time and place; autonomy, as an index of coercive power, may continue to exist when sovereignty has gone. What is certain, however, is that the two concepts, assuming they are analytically separable, operate in some kind of interdependency. The argument and evidence in this book has more to say about autonomy—understood as 'state capacity'—than sovereignty. It focuses on the extent to which state officials can implement their own preferences and finds that they remain surprisingly empowered even in relation to international environmental issues.

They also retain, at least in the American case, a jealous grip on their sovereignty. As we will see, US officials continually stressed how limited a role international institutions ought to play, how tightly they should be monitored by states, how few were the issues appropriate to international settlement, and how dominant the 'domestic' sphere should remain over the 'foreign'. No other substate, transnational, or international institution was or is in any position to make a bid for this kind of authority, given that what states actually do is hugely complex and multifaceted.

In preference to the idea of declining sovereignty in many accounts, one might often read 'tarnished legitimacy' instead—a weakening of the shared *perception* of a populace that its state has the right to do what it does based on its functional efficacy (that it *should* do it because it *can* do it). But sovereignty is about more than perception. As Gianfranco Pogge has argued, power is more effectively exercised when it demands compliance through a perceived obligation ('authority'), rather than explicit coercion, but still the 'threat' of force—the means for which the state famously monopolizes—still lies behind authority. Sovereignty is ultimately the state's to relinquish.[23]

The argument in this book leads towards a conclusion about sovereignty but only through an analysis of the continuing power of the state, its autonomy. In maintaining that significant state autonomy is in evidence in the making of American foreign

[23] Gianfranco Pogge, *The State: Its Nature, Development and Prospects* (Cambridge: Polity Press, 1990), 6–7.

environmental policy, one is drawn first to the conclusion that, in some sense, it is not fatal for the state if sovereignty is lost when autonomy remains. As Pogge suggests, this makes governing hard, but possible. However, one is also forced to consider that, if autonomy remains, scepticism may be in order about just how much sovereignty has *really* been displaced.

If one conflates autonomy and sovereignty, an opportunity presents itself to highlight the prominent role of non-state actors, to demonstrate their infiltration into the policy-making process, and thus to argue that their small parcel of influence is synonymous with an equal increment of sovereignty. The 'people' will now look in part to these societal and international actors for answers, perceiving them to have some 'authority'. Sovereignty is thus no more than the popular recognition of superior functional performance.

If one separates the two, however, doubt is cast on this notion. The works of non-state actors may be ubiquitous: providing crucial strategic information, lobbying for and publicizing alternatives, highlighting backsliding, raising resources independently of the state, facilitating interstate co-ordination. Yet, this undoubted influence does not, necessarily, reflect the acquisition of any sovereignty. States still retain their role as the holders of decison-making authority, often using societal actors to enhance their capacity and designing institutions to entrench it. In the long run, perhaps, sovereignty does come to follow capacity but it is usually a painfully slow process, and eventually no doubt a violent and revolutionary one, making a mockery of contemporary arguments that it has, in some measure, seeped from the clutches of the state.

The argument in this book goes even further, however. It constitutes an explanation for foreign policy which shows that capacity, too, has largely remained with the state, and that the 'multicentric system' is more a sideshow of the policy process than a central player in deliberations. To the extent that these societal forces are important, they serve as the raw material for struggles between state officials who possess different ideas about what the state ought to be doing. They create the 'political context' for intrastate debate, leaving the locus of policy explanation firmly within core national institutions. The state thus retains autonomy, and even more so, sovereignty, over policy choice.

The impression that the state lies at the mercy of societal

pressures—rather than being a powerful shaper and user of these forces—relies on an understanding of the state as an essentially *territorial* entity devoid of agency. For this reason, the preceding discussion prefigures to some extent a deeper one about the appropriate conception of 'the state' in use in theorizing about international relations. Boundary crossing there may be in abundance but a more sophisticated conception of the state serves to render much of this raw data less persuasive.[24]

This *territorial* state is highly familiar to international relations theorists. Nevertheless, a different picture of state capacities exists, one which conceives of the state as having the ability to 'act'. What one discovers is the state absorbing and channelling and reorienting societal and international forces, not a reactive but also a proactive entity. In this respect, states as 'actors' have not only been able to accommodate elements of the environmental critique but also to turn them into new power resources. The domestic–international distinction is still problematized but within the context of an active state.

This last point is worth stressing. The argument presented throughout this book is not that impermeable boundaries surround 'the state', 'society', and the international 'system' either as concepts or political entities. There is a pressing need to analyse the ways in which domestic and international politics interact but this must be done through a more sophisticated treatment of the role the active state plays in this process. Domestic and international politics are, in this sense, refracted through the state. As we will see, there is a conceptual tendency to see a boundary between domestic and foreign policy where all that is not one is the other. Even the 'transformationalist' literature—in seeking to prove the erosion of this boundary—gives credence to its prior existence. But, as Chapter 1 makes clear, such an image only makes sense with a particular, territorial, conception of the state. Adopting an alternative conception of the state as an 'actor', in both the domestic and international realms, necessitates a re-examination of the implications of 'postinternational' politics.

This is facilitated by a 'vertical' analysis—looking at the interaction between society, state, and international system in a single

---

[24] Held and McGrew in 'Globalization and the Liberal Democratic State' (p. 281) argue: '. . . the transformationalist literature has so far failed to provide a convincing or coherent account of the modern liberal democratic state itself'.

country—so that one can see the extent and depth of the political linkages which are a crucial element in the case against the state. There are few systematic accounts of the actual impact that international environmental issues have had on the process of foreign-policy making over time, and thus claims about the declining capacity of the state stand in need of careful assessment. By relying heavily on primary research, we can shed light on exactly how these 'new' international issues, and the political forces which engage with them, have affected the state. Detailed analysis of foreign environmental policy—especially because of the issue's chronic rather than acute nature, along with its complexity and uncertainty—is also necessary for the evaluation of competing explanations within international relations.

The choice of the United States as a case-study also requires explanation. There are at least six good reasons for studying the formation of American foreign environmental policy over the years since 1965. First, the United States remains the most powerful actor in the international system, and is therefore as good a place to start as any, and a better place than most.

Second, *domestic* environmental politics in the United States have been remarkably extensive throughout the period on which this study concentrates. There are many large interest groups, with high memberships and huge financial resources, and they have secured significant legislative successes. Third, the United States has been one of the most prominent participants since the formative years of international environmental negotiations.

Fourth, the degree of openness in the American political system is conducive to an analysis of the impact of societal and international developments on foreign policy. There is high visibility and apparently good accessibility for domestic and transnational groups. Fifth, and related to this point, the United States is widely seen as having a 'weak' state in the sense that there is a considerable degree of penetration by societal groups into the core of the governing institutions. It strengthens the claim for the continuing importance of state autonomy, therefore, if even a weak state can be shown to retain a meaningful degree of independence.

Finally, the crucial role of the American national experience in the evolution of international relations theory makes it a highly appropriate case for analysis of the impact that environmental politics have made. Having provided much of the 'data' for theorizing about war and peace since 1945, it is only proper that it should be the object of study in this non-traditional area, and that insights from the literature of international relations should be assessed against evidence from the discipline's principal case (however unreflective its selection has often been).

These reasons are encapsulated by the following observation about negotiations on global warming:

There is little question but that the climate change issue presents a difficult foreign policy challenge to the United States. The US is in the unenviable position of being at the same time the world's largest emitter of carbon dioxide and other greenhouse gases, the recognized leader of the international system, and the home of the world's most influential environmental organizations. The US therefore has no place to hide from the climate change issue at home or abroad and is universally perceived as both the largest part of the problem and the largest part of the solution.[25]

The empirical material for this project is drawn from American preparations for two major conferences held on the international environment, the first in Stockholm in June 1972, the second in Rio in June 1992. These events constitute excellent points at which to assess the evolving impact of international environmental politics. Stockholm took place at the very beginning, and the preparatory process proved to be something of a voyage of discovery for all concerned. By the time of Rio, twenty years later, much had changed. A wealth of experience had been accumulated by states and non-governmental organizations, public awareness was a great deal higher, and the establishment of the United Nations Environment Programme (UNEP) meant the institutionalization of environmental issues in a permanent international forum.

Chapter 1 presents the book's central arguments. Beginning with an account of how the state might be reconceptualized in international relations, it provides a substantive explanation for American foreign environmental policy which focuses strongly on the continuing power of the state and on a particular conception of its relationship with societal and international pressures. This

---

[25] William A. Nitze, 'A Failure of Presidential Leadership', in Irving M. Mintzer and J. A. Leonard (eds.), *Negotiating Climate Change: The Inside Story of the Rio Convention* (Cambridge: Cambridge University Press, 1994), 187. Whether this position really is 'unenviable' is, of course, debatable.

approach is contrasted with the arguments of both pluralists and realists (and, to a lesser extent, Marxists).

The chapters which follow deal with preparations for the two conferences, and US participation in each. Chapter 2 deals in detail with policy formation for Stockholm. Much of this material is original, both interview and archive, and presents the story of US preparations for the first major environmental conference in more depth than has hitherto been provided. Chapter 3 deals with the conference itself, its aftermath, and with the subsequent developments in environmentalism in the United States. This deals with the growth of professional lobbies, increased membership in interest groups, congressional activism, and with the retrenchment the movement faced in the Reagan years. It ends with the calling of the Rio conference.

Chapter 4 analyses in detail the story of US policy development for all aspects of the pre-Rio process: three conventions (on climate, biodiversity, and forests), an 'Action Plan', and a Declaration or 'Earth Charter'. This chapter contains detailed primary interview material provided by key players in the intrastate process, and by environmentalists on the outside. Chapter 5 then provides a brief account of the conference itself, its aftermath in the last months of the Bush administration, and, finally, an interim assessment of foreign environmental policy under the Clinton administration.

The final chapter serves as a general conclusion. It also contains some speculation about what, if anything, has fundamentally changed in the making of American foreign environmental policy over three decades of international environmentalism. Although the analysis of foreign *environmental* policy is my sole concern, authors in other areas, such as foreign economic policy, have argued a slightly stronger case for the integration of societal influences and some consideration is given to this in conclusion. However, the specific claims made are based on an analysis of one issue-area only, the environment, across the twenty-five years between 1967 and 1992.

The account of state autonomy given in this book has both strengths and weaknesses, and I leave it to others to point out the latter, as they surely will. The case for the state presented throughout this book is therefore made in forthright and clear terms in the belief that this enhances the opportunity for constructive criticism.

If at times nuance and subtlety are the casualties, it is to be hoped that the project of constructing more theoretically informed explanations for foreign policy—and thus for international politics—will be the eventual beneficiary.

1

American Foreign Environmental Policy and the Power of the State

Given that the state has been the foundational concept for theorizing about international relations it is remarkable that so little has actually been written about what this state might look like and how it might operate.[1] This reflects two separate factors: the centrality of the American historical experience to theories of international relations, and the belief that what is special about international politics is what happens outside, and between, *sovereign* states.

It has become a commonplace to argue that there is, in any meaningful sense, no state in the United States and to explain the absence of such a concept from much American social science as a result.[2] Yet this observation only refers to one meaning of 'the state', that which we might label *institutional*. This 'state', familiar to sociologists and comparativists alike, refers to 'a set of administrative, policing, and military organizations headed, and more or less well co-ordinated by, an executive authority'.[3] It does not exclude a much broader understanding which conceives of the state as *territory* (thus encompassing everything that lies within it). J. P. Nettl illustrates this distinction by referring to the difference between 'the British state' and 'Britain as a state'.[4] It also explains why the United States can be both a 'weak' and a 'strong' state: the American state is said to be weak; America as a state is conspicuously powerful.

The absence of an 'institutional' conception in most international relations theory has contrasted with other areas of political

---

[1] See Fred Halliday's *Rethinking International Relations* (London: Macmillan, 1994), ch. 4, for a good general introduction to this issue and Anthony Jarvis, 'Societies, States and Geopolitics: Challenges from Historical Sociology', *Review of International Studies*, 15 (1989), 281–93.

[2] See J. P. Nettl, 'The State as a Conceptual Variable', *World Politics*, 20/4 (1968), 561, and Graham K. Wilson, *Interest Groups* (Oxford: Blackwell, 1990), 134.

[3] Theda Skocpol, *States and Social Revolutions* (Cambridge: Cambridge University Press, 1979), 29.

[4] Nettl, 'The State as a Conceptual Variable', 564.

science and sociology where the state was recently 'brought back in'.[5] Thus Theda Skocpol could claim, in 1985, that: '. . . not long ago the dominant theories and research agendas of the social sciences rarely spoke of states', while, a year later, Robert Keohane argued of 'political realism' in international affairs, that: 'Approaches using new concepts may be able to supplement, enrich, or extend a basic theory of state action, but they cannot substitute for it.'[6]

In other words, there are two 'states' here. One an internal actor, a complex of institutions and practices which derives power—at least in theory—from a monopoly over the means of coercion; the other, a totality, a geographical, national-territorial entity comprised by a physical space and resources, society, government, and people.[7] The institutional state and its relations to its 'own' society have formed the core of sociology while the interactions between territorial states—especially the observation that their sovereign equality generates an anarchic structure—has dominated international relations theory.[8] Even a renewed focus on societal forces in the 1970s, encouraged by a shift in emphasis away from traditional military security, soon gave way to the neoliberal–neorealist debate which abstracted from 'internal' state:society relations altogether perpetuating a grim attachment to the image of the state as a 'black box'.[9]

---

[5] See Timothy Mitchell, 'The Limits of the State: Beyond Statist Approaches and Their Critics', *American Political Science Review*, 85/1 (1991), 77–82, and Paul Cammack, 'Review Article: Bringing the State Back In?', *British Journal of Political Science*, 19 (Apr. 1989), 261–90.

[6] Theda Skocpol 'Bringing the State Back In: Strategies of Analysis in Current Research', in T. Skocpol, Peter B. Evans, and Dietrich Rueschemeyer (eds.), *Bringing the State Back In* (New York: Cambridge University Press, 1985), 4; Robert O. Keohane, 'Theory of World Politics: Structural Realism and Beyond', in R. O. Keohane (ed.), *Neorealism and Its Critics* (New York: Columbia University Press, 1986), 159.

[7] Halliday, *Rethinking International Relations*, 78–9. Marvin Soroos argues that 'for reasons of style' he uses 'nation', 'nation-state', 'country', and 'state' interchangeably thereby guaranteeing confusion (*Beyond Sovereignty*, 78).

[8] See Kenneth N. Waltz: *Theory of International Politics* (New York: McGraw Hill, 1979), 88.

[9] See David A. Baldwin (ed.), *Neorealism and Neoliberalism: The Contemporary Debate* (New York: Columbia University Press, 1993). Stephan Haggard and Beth Simmons have advocated an analysis of 'the interaction between domestic and international games and coalitions that span national boundaries' while still appealing for a return to the core insight of the interdependence literature, that 'growing interdependence means the erasure of the boundaries separating

In the work of Kenneth Waltz, for example, the functions performed by territorial states are considered so similar they are only distinguished by differential capabilities. Waltz argues: 'International politics consists of like units duplicating one another's activities.'[10] Regardless of the internal nature of 'states', the peculiar character of their *institutional* stateness, Waltz is struck by similarities between the functions states perform in the external world and thus 'state' becomes a shorthand for the totality of the 'inside' of a bounded territory. One of the keenest observations which Waltz in particular draws from this is that a theory of international politics is not a theory of foreign policy.[11]

This strong formulation leaves the locus of explanation firmly at the international structural level, it is true, but in attempting to account for state behaviour by reference to the 'international system' alone, such arguments are unavoidably subject to comparison with alternative, foreign policy, explanations, pitched at the state-level but making claims to account for the *same* state behaviour. Waltz is explicit in arguing that '. . . the theory does not tell us why state X made a certain move last Tuesday'.[12] Thus he provides no plausible way of analysing the interaction between theories of international politics and theories of foreign policy.[13]

Historical sociologists have, on the whole, fared better in terms of integrating international and social forces, a task greatly facili-

international and domestic politics'. The empirical material presented in this book suggests that, in studying US foreign environmental policy, undertaking the first casts doubt on the validity of the second (Stephan Haggard and Beth A. Simmons, 'Theories of International Regimes', *International Organization*, 41/3 (1987), 513 and 516).

[10] Waltz, *Theory of International Politics*, 97.

[11] Ibid. 121–2.

[12] Ibid. 122.

[13] See Andrew Linklater, 'Neo-Realism in Theory and Practice', in Booth and Smith (eds.), *International Relations Theory Today*. In criticizing Waltz, Linklater argues: 'Either the system determines the principal moves which states make, in which case foreign policy analysis is a residual enterprise, or states can profoundly influence the system, in which case reductionist and systemic theories deserve equal standing' (p. 253). Waltz was forced to concede the importance of some theory of the state. He accepted that: 'Structures shape and shove. They do not determine behaviors and outcomes, not only because unit-level and structural causes interact, but also because the shaping and shoving of structures may be successfully resisted' ('Reflections on *Theory of International Politics*: A Response to My Critics', in Keohane (ed.), *Neorealism and Its Critics*, 343).

tated by a more sophisticated conception of the state.[14] However, this approach has usually drawn inspiration from the work of Weber and Hintze, and thus—in analysing the interlinkages between the state's economic and military functions—has often appeared suspiciously neorealist in its conception of the external constraints imposed by a system-of-states.[15]

Nevertheless, given that foreign policy analysis *necessarily* involves comparison between internal and external sources of state behaviour, an opportunity is presented by the institutional state which is denied by its territorial variant. This institutional state can usefully be conceived as an actor at both the domestic and international levels in a way the territorial state cannot, and thus 'state-centric' theorizing appears a powerful way to provide integrated explanations for modern political developments which do not sit comfortably within the exclusive labels 'domestic' and 'international'.[16] As Fred Halliday argues: 'The most significant theme for International Relations pervading this literature is that the state is seen as acting in two dimensions, the domestic and the international.'[17]

This state 'lives' at the intersection between societal and international forces. In other words, such approaches promise—facilitate—a richer and more satisfying account of the interaction between societal, state, and international politics.[18]

[14] For example Charles Tilly's *Coercion, Capital, and European States, AD 990–1992* (Cambridge, Mass.: Blackwell, 1992, rev. edn.); Skocpol, *States and Social Revolutions*; and Michael Mann, 'The Autonomous Power of the State: Its Origins, Mechanisms and Results', in M. Mann (ed.), *States, War and Capitalism: Studies in Political Sociology* (Oxford: Blackwell, 1988).

[15] Jarvis, 'Societies, States and Geopolitics', 290–1.

[16] This idea of the state has been profitably employed by adherents of the two-level games approach, for example. In the words of Peter Evans: 'The image of the state leaders as "Janus-faced", forced to balance domestic and international concerns, stands at the core of the integrative approach making it "state-centric", not in the realist sense of emphasizing nation states as units but in the sense of seeing chief executives, and state bureaucracies more generally, as actors whose aims cannot be reduced to reflections of domestic constituent pressure' (Peter B. Evans, 'Building an Integrative Approach to International and Domestic Politics', in Peter B. Evans, Harold K. Jacobson, and Robert D. Putnam (eds.), *Double-Edged Diplomacy: International Bargaining and Domestic Politics* (Berkeley: University of California Press, 1993), 401–2). Evans was, of course, a co-editor of *Bringing the State Back In*. We look in more detail at this approach later on.

[17] Halliday, *Rethinking International Relations*, 84.

[18] Jarvis argues: 'Not only is International Relations required to have a theory of the state, it is now also required, more precisely, to be a theory of the fit between societies, states and geopolitics' ('Societies, States and Geopolitics', 283).

Notwithstanding this, the territorial dimension of the state does not simply evaporate. On the contrary, territoriality—and the sovereignty which is historically consequent upon it—constitute a core part of the state's resource base. As Michael Mann has argued, for example, the institutional state draws power from its position as the sole legitimate authority over a delimited territory in contradistinction to other agglomerations of social power.[19]

Territorial control, manifested for example in border patrols, immigration policies, and in the legitimate scope of the activities of domestic police forces, is a key constitutive element in the historical development of the state's power. It is this link between authority and territory which suggests the nature of the challenge posed by international environmental problems: they subvert the capacity of states *as institutions* to control some of the key natural resources (i.e. air and water) of states *as territories*. The emergence of the idea of sovereignty—which Ruggie has argued amounted to a property right over a particular territory[20]—entailed first of all the sovereign's and subsequently the state's rights in relation not just to the people within a given area but also the natural resources contained within it.[21] As we have seen, this arbitrary process of resource allocation created obvious disjunctures between elements of the natural world—rivers, forests, seas—and the political communities which administered and exploited them.

Sovereignty also entailed certain obligations or duties. In the classic Hobbesian sense the state was to be legitimated functionally as a provider of both internal and external security. State obligations have far outstripped this minimal role as 'nightwatchman', however, and the state has come to be seen as indispensable to the provision of collective goods in many other areas, of which basic subsistence, including clean air and water, is one (which is not to say it is in reality feasible for many states to provide for these resource elements of 'territory'). Yet the possible implications for sovereignty are clear, especially for states which derive their

[19] Mann, 'The Autonomous Power of the State', 15–16.
[20] John Gerard Ruggie, 'Continuity and Transformation in the World Polity: Toward a Neorealist Synthesis', in Keohane (ed.), *Neorealism and Its Critics*, 143–8. See also Pogge, *The State: Its Nature, Development and Prospects*, 22.
[21] Ken Conca points out that the declarations of principle from Stockholm and Rio both reaffirm the state's right to dispose of its own resources as it sees fit, something on which both North and South could agree; 'Rethinking the Ecology–Sovereignty Debate' (p. 709). See also Beitz, 'Sovereignty and Morality' (p. 243).

political authority from the claim that they can, and indeed are, providing these goods.

Environmental degradation problematizes the boundaries of territorial states, denying them the use of unadulterated natural resources, impinging on the basic requirements of liveable exist-ence, and threatening unpredictable and potentially hazardous climatic changes. The relationship between the *institutional* and *territorial* states is thus emphasized, firmly establishing the need to theorize the linkages between the state and its 'external' world.

The equally vexed question of the relationship between state and society reveals itself to be a similar disagreement about the appro-priate conceptualization of the state: institutional or territorial. Thus debates in this area of political science and sociology since the 1970s have revolved largely around the question of state *autonomy*—the capacity of the state to formulate and implement its own objectives. The question becomes: can the state be under-stood in any meaningful sense as an 'actor'—as possessed of agency—in the political process?

If the answer is 'No', the institutions of government simply pro-vide the location where competing social groups battle over the allocation of resources. Thus the state serves as an 'essentially passive' arena for the playing-out of societal pressures, acting as 'a disinterested referee for competing groups'.[22] The state is just 'a cash register that totals up and then averages the preferences and political power of societal actors'.[23] The most common exponents of such a view are pluralists who 'insist on the reality and impor-tance of multiple channels through which citizens can control their political leaders and shape the development of public policies'.[24] The state becomes a 'weathervane' which 'simply mirrors or re-sponds to the balance of pressure group forces in civil society'.[25] The state has no interests of its own.

[22] G. John Ikenberry, David A. Lake, and Michael Mastanduno, 'Introduction: Approaches to Explaining American Foreign Economic Policy', in Ikenberry, Lake, and Mastanduno (eds.), *The State and American Foreign Economic Policy* (Ithaca, NY: Cornell University Press, 1988), 8.
[23] Stephen D. Krasner, 'Review Article: Approaches to the State, Alternative Conceptions and Historical Dynamics', in *Comparative Politics*, 16/2 (1984), 226–7.
[24] Patrick Dunleavy and Brendan O'Leary, *Theories of the State: The Politics of Liberal Democracy* (London: Macmillan, 1987), 23.
[25] Ibid. 43.

Hence, when a state 'acts' internationally, it does so as the totality of its internal social and economic processes as resolved through the political process. If the state has no interests, its goals internationally must be set by the outcomes of societal competition and so the state becomes a kind of representative. It simply is 'the state', the international legal label for societies when they deal with each other. Thus we have 'America as a state' rather than 'the American state' in action. This state is a familiar shorthand for the totality of its internal processes.

The alternative formulation gives the power of agency to the state, allowing *its* actions to enter into the explanation, and endowing it with the capacity to develop and try to implement its *own* preferences—to advance its *own* interests. Thus, it becomes 'an important intervening variable between social and international forces'.[26] In Stephen Krasner's formulation, the state is conceived of as 'a set of roles and institutions having peculiar drives, compulsions, and aims of their own that are separate and distinct from the interests of any particular societal group'.[27] These 'roles and institutions' refer us to a group of key posts within the central decision-making machinery rather than to the specific individuals who occupy them. In the United States, Krasner confirms, these posts include 'the President' and 'the Secretary of State' plus institutions such as 'the White House' and the 'State Department'. These institutions of the state have certain characteristics which unite them (both by form and function):

What distinguishes these roles and agencies is their high degree of insulation from specific societal pressures and a set of formal and informal obligations that charge them with furthering the nation's general interests.[28]

This formulation has two central implications; firstly, it is to the 'offices', rather than to the individuals who occupy them, that the duties and obligations and powers adhere; and secondly, if bona fide parts of the state are 'insulated' from society, then institutions without a high degree of insulation must be located outside the state.

[26] Ikenberry, Lake, and Mastanduno, 'Introduction', 10.
[27] Stephen D. Krasner, *Defending the National Interest: Raw Materials Investments and American Foreign Policy* (Princeton: Princeton University Press, 1978), 10.
[28] Ibid. 11.

This 'state' captures not just the permanence of the administrative skeleton but also the permanent status of those bureaucrats who implement national decisions through the legal, economic, and social apparatus. This reflects two central elements in the history of the Western state: the growth of a bureaucracy charged with the maximization of more than simply self-interest, and the idea of depersonalization. The depersonalized state, a state of structure—institutional, normative, and precedential—was a core conceptual development during the transformation from absolutism in Western Europe.[29] The relationship between agency and structure within the state still lies at the heart of arguments between instrumental and structural Marxists, for example, as well as touching upon the very essence of what makes the state a distinctive phenomenon. In Nettl's words:

If the notion of state is to be at all meaningful, and not merely a ragbag synonym of government, it must be divorced from and even *opposed* to personal power—not in the legal but in the political sense.[30]

In using the phrase 'ragbag synonym of government', Nettl highlights the core tension between accounts which stress the role of the institutional state and those which have dominated foreign policy analysis. The distinction is largely the absence, in the latter case, of a concept of 'the state' at all, a fact which reflects the roots of foreign policy studies in the postwar United States where, as we have seen, 'the state' as a concept did not flourish. In other words, foreign policy explanations came to look a lot like pluralist accounts except with foreign policy as their focus. Some writers perceived no discernible distinction between the processes of innovation in domestic and foreign policy.[31]

The work of prominent foreign policy analysts has thus tended to display a relatively broad list of potential variables with little hope

---

[29] See Quentin Skinner, 'The State', in Terence Ball, James Farr, and Russell L. Hanson (eds.), *Political Innovation and Conceptual Change* (Cambridge: Cambridge University Press, 1989), and J. L. Holzgrefe, 'The Origins of Modern International Relations Theory', *Review of International Studies*, 15 (1989), 11–26.

[30] Nettl, 'The state as conceptual variable' (p. 563, italics in original).

[31] See Nelson W. Polsby, *Political Innovation in America: The Politics of Policy Initiation* (New Haven: Yale University Press, 1984), 150. Polsby—a 'domestic' political scientist—claims that it is difficult to argue '... that there is something about foreign policy innovation as a process or activity that plausibly groups these cases together and separates them from policy initiation in other subject areas' (p. 147). Thus no role for innovatory sources outside the territorial state is allowed.

for establishing a systematic explanatory hierarchy.[32] To concentrate on James Rosenau's work, which has remained central to the field, one can see through all the attempts at 'pre-theory' the difficulties inherent in organizing one's variables without some sense of permanence about either the outcome of struggles between social groups, or the institutional matrix within which these struggles take place. Without some structure, in other words.

In his remarkably influential article on 'pre-theories' of foreign policy, Rosenau argues for '. . . the need to develop an explicit conception of where causation is located in international affairs'.[33] In order to construct a 'pre-theory', Rosenau isolates five sets of variables: individual, role, governmental, societal, and systemic. The third variable—reflecting the absence of a concept of the state—comes down to 'executive–legislative relations' while the societal variable is defined in the following fashion:

The major value orientations of a society, its degree of national unity, and the extent of its industrialization are but a few of the societal variables which can contribute to the contents of a nation's external aspirations and policies.[34]

In the same volume of collected works, Rosenau argues that internal factors leading to foreign-policy initiation include 'elections, group conflicts, depleted oil reserves, geographic insularity, demands for higher tariffs, historic value orientations, a lack of societal unity, executive–legislative functions and so on, through all the diverse factors that contribute to national life and can thereby serve as sources of foreign policy'.[35]

In terms of his five sets of variables, one needs, Rosenau agrees, to determine their '*relative potencies*', assessing 'which . . . contributes most to external behaviour'.[36] Rosenau then develops the idea of 'issue-areas' and also criticizes 'the tendency of researchers to maintain a rigid distinction between national and international political systems in the face of mounting evidence that the dist-

[32] See e.g., Charles W. Kegley and Eugene R. Wittkopf, *American Foreign Policy: Pattern and Process*, 4th edn. (New York: St Martin's Press, 1991).

[33] James N. Rosenau, 'Pre-theories and Theories of Foreign Policy', in Rosenau, *The Scientific Study of Foreign Policy* (New York: The Free Press, 1971), 107.

[34] Ibid. 109.

[35] Rosenau, 'Comparative Foreign Policy: Fad, Fantasy or Field?', *The Scientific Study of Foreign Policy*, 80.

[36] Rosenau, 'Pre-theories', 109.

inction is breaking down'.[37] Throughout this description of what Rosenau calls 'philosophies of analysis', the term 'state' is never used. In classic pluralist style he mentions 'the political system' or 'national society'. Yet many of the issues which Rosenau seeks to problematize—the relations between the international and the national, between social values and foreign policy, about penetrated and non-penetrated national societies, and about issue selection and promotion—would prove much more comprehensible were a concept of the institutional state to be invoked.[38]

Rosenau's later work, still influential, makes more of the collapsed national–international distinction in terms of 'postinternational politics', a pluralist perspective which accepts that states exist while denying their centrality and hinting at their demise.[39] No differentiation is made between conceptions of the state despite the fact that it is clearly the contemporary experience of the territorial states of the states system which now drives his argument. The world can be envisaged as divided into two systems, one of 'sovereignty-bound states', another a 'multicentric system' of sovereignty-free actors. The state now becomes just 'one type of politically relevant entity'.[40] In other words, sovereignty now becomes a bind, not a resource.

Rosenau's argument that the state has lost autonomy due to 'the increasing obscurity of the distinction between foreign and domestic affairs' disguises a failure to distinguish between the territorial and institutional states.[41] Both 'states' are present in this account, as the following quotation makes clear:

The units of states active in the multi-centric world are those bureaucratic ministries and agencies that are below the state's top leadership and thus do not need to be preoccupied with the responsibilities of sovereignty, a circumstance that renders them responsive to the decision rules of the multi-centric world, even if they have to reverse themselves on those occasions when they report to their superiors in the state-centric world.[42]

---

[37] Ibid. 117.
[38] One immediate advantage might be more theoretically sophisticated cross-national comparison.
[39] Rosenau, *Turbulence in World Politics*, 6. Rosenau claims the modern world is marked by an explosion in the 'personal skills' of individuals which has eroded the state's competence (pp. 13–15, 130). On p. 127 he talks of subgroups actually being able to 'paralyze governments', hence his essential pluralism.
[40] Ibid. 11, 36.
[41] Ibid. 127.   [42] Ibid. 100 n. 16.

This deeply unconvincing description of the burgeoning relationships between state and non-state actors, and between intrastate
officials, sees those at 'the top' running both the institutional state
and acting on behalf of the territorial state while their underlings
are busy making deals with non-state actors and thereby rendering
tenuous, to say the least, their adherence to the roles they inhabit
within the institutional state. (One wonders, however, what the
value of such contacts is for non-state actors if junior officials trying
to structure the agenda in their favour jettison these efforts so
readily.) Rosenau's work, while frequently provocative, pays scant
attention to the relationship between the institutional state and its
social and international environment, and thus underplays the extent to which the state can and does dominate these relations.

In 1987, the prolific Rosenau did acknowledge the pressure to
think about the state at the same time as betraying his ambivalence
about its value for explaining political developments:

... with issues of political economy now occupying a central place on the
global agenda, the role of the state, its limits, scope, and autonomy, has
emerged as a prime consideration in the conduct of foreign affairs. For
students of foreign policy this development presents a challenge because
for several decades they have not been inclined to treat the state as a
substantive concept, preferring instead to equate it with the actions of
governmental decision makers and thus to bypass the questions of its role,
competence and autonomy. For better or worse, such an inclination is no
longer tenable if foreign policy analysts are to bring their work into harmony with the many observers for whom the state's place in the processes
of political economy has become pivotal.[43]

As Rosenau suggests, the need for such a conceptual shift in
foreign-policy studies was explicitly recognized by those working in
the tradition of international political economy (IPE) in the 1970s.

---

[43] James N. Rosenau, 'Introduction: New Directions and Recurrent Questions in
the Comparative Study of Foreign Policy', in Charles F. Hermann, Charles W.
Kegley, Jnr., and James N. Rosenau (eds.), *New Directions in the Study of Foreign
Policy* (New York: Harper-Collins, 1987), 3. As Bruce E. Moon argues in the same
volume: 'The lack of a consistent viewpoint on the nature of the state and the bases
for its behaviour can be traced to the absence of a theoretical paradigm. In its place,
the Rosenau (1966) pre-theory has served as a guiding light for nearly two decades,
but by simply organizing classes of explanatory factors by levels of analysis it has
encouraged *ad hoc* and atheoretical analysis' ('Political Economy Approaches to
the Comparative Study of Foreign Policy', in Hermann, Kegley, and Rosenau (eds.),
New Directions, 36).

In dealing with the interaction between economic and state actors at both the domestic and international levels, it became hard to sustain the idea that the state was not an active participant in the process. It was in IPE, therefore, that the adoption of a more sophisticated conception of state:society relations was undertaken. Peter Katzenstein, for example, explicitly argued for a transcending of the 'clear-cut distinction between domestic and international politics' in order to facilitate analysis of their interaction.[44] Katzenstein acknowledged that states may 'organize the societies they control' and he described on-going societal:state interaction in the following manner:

The governing coalitions of social forces in each of the advanced industrial states find their institutional expression in distinct policy networks which link the public and private sector in the implementation of foreign economic policy.[45]

Even this formulation has a distinct 'plural' edge, and Katzenstein's account rejects the idea of any significant autonomy for the state, stressing state:society 'networks' both for the formulation and implementation of policy. Nevertheless, it moves in the direction of the idea of an institutional state enjoying a patterned and regularized relationship with the social and international. Although Katzenstein explicitly rejects pluralist and bureaucratic politics approaches, there are nevertheless strong similarities with what remains one of the most influential modern works on American foreign policy and the classic text on bureaucratic politics, Graham Allison's *Essence of Decision*.[46]

For Allison, policy was the outcome of a constant bargaining process conducted by senior personnel both within and outside government.[47] This model suggests there is:

---

[44] Peter J. Katzenstein, 'Introduction: Domestic and International Forces and Strategies of Foreign Economic Policy', in Katzenstein (ed.), *Between Power and Plenty: Foreign Economic Policies of Advanced Industrial States* (Madison, Wis.: University of Wisconsin Press, 1978), 4.

[45] Ibid. 18–19.

[46] Graham T. Allison, *Essence of Decision: Explaining the Cuban Missile Crisis* (Boston: Little, Brown, 1971); see also, Allison and Morton H. Halperin, 'Bureaucratic Politics: A Paradigm and Some Policy Implications', in Raymond Tanter and Richard H. Ullman (eds.), *Theory and Policy in International Relations* (Princeton: Princeton University Press, 1972).

[47] The use of the term 'bureaucratic' obscures the fact that Allison was talking about senior officials in non-government institutions as well, and that his argument

...no unitary actor but rather many actors as players—players who focus not on a single strategic issue but on many diverse intra-national problems as well; players who act in terms of no consistent set of strategic objectives but rather according to various conceptions of national, organizational, and personal goals; players who make government decisions not by a single rational choice but by the pulling and hauling that is politics.[48]

This formulation was explicitly designed to undermine a 'rational' or 'black box' approach to explaining foreign-policy decisions. Allison's emphasis on the importance of the intrastate process, and on the game-like nature of policy struggles, reintroduced the idea of 'politics'. What his argument lacked, however, was a clear account of either the state or of state–society interaction. He makes some mention of non-state actors but says little about how these actors affect the process. The bureaucratic model has little to say about this deep relationship over time and thus provides only a partial picture of the interaction which produces public policy.[49]

Although work on US foreign economic policy showed more interest in the state, a degree of ambivalence persisted, reinforcing the idea that there is no state in the United States beyond the pluralist-territorial. John Odell's explanation for US international monetary policy, for example, rejects arguments which rely on the structure of government, and bargaining between officials, settling in the end for the importance of conditions external to the territorial state and of the role of ideas as sources of change, that is

---

bears some relation to the idea of policy 'communities' or 'networks' (addressed in the next section). For example, he claims: 'The apparatus of each national government constitutes a complex arena for the intra-national game. Political leaders at the top of the apparatus are joined by the men who occupy positions on top of major organizations to form a circle of players' (see *Essence of Decision*, 144). He names congressional influentials, the press, and important interest groups as members of this circle (pp. 164–5). Thus 'bureaucratic' seems to describe a very political style of decision-making rather than just the activities of bureaucrats and politicians.

[48] Ibid. 144.

[49] Allison also underplayed the structural dimension to intrastate struggles which meant that, once entrenched, certain groups could obtain a stability in policy, thus: 'The battles may be fought anew each time, but the distribution of power resources ensures that the gains flow in a persistent, if slightly wavering, direction'; Lawrence Freedman, 'Logic, Politics, and Foreign Policy Processes: A Critique of the Bureaucratic Politics Model', *International Affairs*, 52/3 (1976), 447.

'changes in reigning ideas help produce changes in policy content'.[50]

What Odell does not do, however, is give an account of the intrastate process and it is unclear, as a result, how—or rather 'on what'—the various pressures he delineates are supposed to act. It is one thing to accept an important independent role for ideas which are not reducible to an underlying interest,[51] quite another to provide a convincing explanation for the ways in which these ideas are traded and fought over within the state. Ideas about international power and market conditions may matter, but who or 'what' responds to these international constraints? Societal groups playing out their competing interests in the 'cash-register' state (domestic politics), or state officials possessed of ideas but also institutional responsibilities and opportunities (bureaucratic politics)? Neither of these can simply drop out of an explanation for foreign policy unless one adopts the pluralist-territorial conception of the state as an essentially passive entity.[52]

More recent approaches, involving many of those associated both with historical sociology and with rational choice theories of state action, have explicitly and fruitfully adopted the institutional state as a means to provide an integrated analysis of factors in operation at the domestic and international levels. The most successful centres on the idea of 'two-level games', a 'conceptual framework for understanding how diplomacy and domestic politics interact'.[53] Proponents of this approach use the metaphor of 'two-

[50] John S. Odell, *U.S. International Monetary Policy: Markets, Power and Ideas as Sources of Change* (Princeton: Princeton University Press, 1982), 58. See also John S. Odell, 'Understanding International Trade Policies: An Emerging Synthesis', *World Politics*, 43, (1990), 139–67.

[51] Ibid. 150.

[52] Odell does argue that: 'All but the most extreme policy situations seem highly complex and uncertain, policy-makers typically disagree among themselves as to diagnosis and prescription, or later analysts uncover evidence and reasoning that support more than one plausible interpretation of the national interest' (*US International Monetary Policy*, 62) leading to the idea of 'policy learning' (p. 367). It is in stressing institutional factors within the state, and an essential link to domestic politics, rather than just 'ideas', that the account offered below differs. See also Peter A. Hall's work on domestic economic policy: *Governing the Economy: The Politics of State Intervention in Britain and France* (Cambridge: Polity Press, 1986), esp. ch. 1.

[53] Robert D. Putnam, 'Diplomacy and Domestic Politics: The Logic of Two-Level Games', *International Organization*, 42/3 (1988), 430. This is the original article on which the 'two-level games' approach, extended in *Double-Edged Diplomacy*, was based. A second approach is Thomas Risse-Kappen (ed.), *Bringing Transnational*

level games' to describe the process by which a 'chief of government' (COG) bargains simultaneously in the domestic and international spheres, making 'moves' which have effects both at home and abroad. This approach concentrates on the process of bargaining, rather than on the formation of policy, but there are instructive similarities.

The statesman is the focus from the outset and, in *Double-Edged Diplomacy*'s conclusion, Peter Evans describes 'the constrained but still relatively autonomous chief executive' as the 'fulcrum for an integrative analysis'. Indeed, he adds: 'This "state-centric" vision emerged out of the cases almost in spite of the project's preconceptions.'[54] In addition, the importance laid on the interactive nature of politics is worth stressing. As the introduction states: 'The two-level-games approach recognizes that domestic policies can be used to affect the outcomes of international bargaining, and that international moves may be solely aimed at achieving domestic goals.'[55]

This approach still fails, however, to adequately theorize about intrastate processes, leaving out of account an important dimension of interactive explanations. In the original article, Putnam was well aware of the shortcomings of 'state-centric' literature in failing to appreciate the diversity of views within the state, arguing that 'it is wrong to assume that the executive is unified in its views', and concluding that this approach was 'an uncertain foundation for theorizing about how domestic and international politics interact'.[56]

In his own analysis, however, he assumes that each country is represented by a 'chief negotiator'. This composite figure is the only one who appears at both game boards and, although initially restricted to representing the views of constituents only, Putnam later allows this negotiator to have independent preferences (and

Relations Back In (Cambridge: Cambridge University Press, 1995), where the authors attempt to show how, perhaps unsurprisingly, 'variation in domestic structures accounts for differences in the policy impact of transnational coalitions and actors' ('Introduction', 33).

[54] Evans, 'Building an Integrative Approach', 401.

[55] Andrew Moravcsik, 'Introduction: Integrating International and Domestic Theories of International Bargaining', in Evans, Jacobson, and Putnam (eds.), *Double-Edged Diplomacy*, 17.

[56] Putnam, 'Diplomacy and Domestic Politics' as reprinted in the appendix to *Double-Edged Diplomacy*, p. 435.

thus to manœuvre for a preferred outcome).[57] At no point, however, is factionalism within the state discussed, even though Putnam's main empirical example has such a feature as a vital part of his analysis. In explaining the outcome at the G7 economic summit held in Bonn in 1978, Putnam argues that 'agreement was possible only because a powerful minority within each government actually favored on domestic grounds the policy being demanded internationally'.[58] In other words, the differentiation of the state is a key part of the explanation.

The references to 'COGs' and then 'statesmen' mask the absence of a sophisticated conception of the state and how it works *internally*. As Peter Evans suggests: 'While in many cases the referent for "COG" is an individual leader, it often makes sense to conceptualize the COG as a (relatively small) group of decision-makers within which particular decisions are generated with varying degrees of collective input.'[59] *Double-Edged Diplomacy* is, however, strong on insights about the central negotiator trying to mould and use societal preferences to gain preferred outcomes, a significant conceptual advance for foreign-policy analysis.

There are, of course, a series of meta-theoretical issues surrounding the relationship between 'levels of analysis' like society, state, and international system. For R. B. J. Walker, for example, the idea of privileging this 'statist' reading, and the inside/outside ontological disjuncture it embodies, is already to accept the most profound 'reification of modern political discourse'.[60] He argues:

As a specifically liberal account of a world of individuals, states and anarchies, it renders all other political categories—of class, race, gender, capitalism, modernity, and so on—entirely superfluous.[61]

It is not clear, however, that this admonition applies equally to both the territorial and institutional states. In the case of the former, it has long been clear that one of the advantages historical sociologists enjoyed with their 'institutional' state was the capacity to analyse movement, social and economic forces which were dynamic, fluid, inherently transnational. Forces, that is, which were

---

[57] Ibid. 438, 456.   [58] Ibid. 432.
[59] Evans, 'Building an Integrative Approach', 428 n. 2.
[60] R. B. J. Walker, 'Social Movements/World Politics', *Millenium: Journal of International Studies*, 23/3 (1994), 670.
[61] Ibid. 671.

impossible to explain within a dichotomous state/non-state picture of the world. Thus revolution and capitalism, and the spread of ideas and practices associated with them, have been a staple for sociologists but almost completely absent from the literature on international relations.[62] Those who have been most prominent in contemporary arguments about globalization tend to be sociologists for a similar reason. The idea of the state as an actor, promoting *and* frustrating the dynamic of change, makes it an option to analyse what happens when political concentrations of social power interact with the economic and ideological in a way inconceivable within the sovereign territoral state framework. The state is no longer 'frozen' and becomes, rather than a border, a bridge (a 'bridge' with a gatekeeper, however).

As a result, the theoretical and empirical argument which follows in the second part of this chapter is, in the end, an argument for a 'state-centric' approach as the best hope for allowing us to construct a theory of foreign-policy making—and hence a theory of international politics—which allows the societal and international to interact. That is, by integrating them into an answer for the question: by what process does the state come to identify its interests? How does the state, in other words, come to conceive of itself? The sections which follow shed light on this question in relation to the formation of American foreign environmental policy.

THE SCOPE OF THE STATE

In the argument which follows, a picture of the *institutional* state and its linkages to societal and international forces is developed. The first step—in the following section—is to describe this state in very broad terms; subsequent sections consider the differentiation of the state and the role played by individuals; existing explanations for society–state–international relations; and the process by which societal and international factors work themselves into the intrastate process.

The concept of 'the state' for which I want to argue is similar to the image of national public officials using their skills and experi-

---

[62] See Halliday, *Rethinking International Relations*, 124.

ence to 'confront, puzzle out, and form judgements about substantive societal problems and the effectiveness of the available options for dealing with them'.[63] This image gives a strong sense of the power of agency, of individuals in positions of authority able to make choices which advance their conceptions of the 'national' interest.

What is special about these officials is the degree to which they have the *capacity* collectively to undertake these judgements according to their own preferences, to be *autonomous*, in other words. They occupy 'offices' which comprise the structure of the state and which transcend the tenure of any one set of specific individuals, thereby distinguishing the occupants from the duties and responsibilities which attend the 'offices of state' at all times. These roles are open to manipulation but they nevertheless present *any* incumbent with certain powers and particular obligations within which he or she is forced to manœuvre.

To stress this point: the state is comprised by individuals— possessed of *both* ideas and interests—who are at once constrained and enabled by the duties and powers associated with the offices they hold. They are expected to fulfil certain key functions—a duty incumbent upon them—and it is in this expectation, the acknowledgement that they have the authority to act *on behalf of* the territorial state, the totality, to act both 'inside' and 'outside', that their power lies.

Skocpol, for example, envisages state autonomy in the following manner: 'States conceived as organizations claiming control over territories and people may formulate and pursue goals that are not simply reflective of the demands or interests of social groups, classes or society.'[64] In short, state officials 'select' the national interest. The *reality* of a society 'choosing' is the essence of the pluralist account in contradistinction to state-centric arguments where the state chooses 'on behalf of' its society, a society which can try to lobby and threaten and pressure and infiltrate and bemoan and bribe and cajole, but which none the less does not have the power and responsibility associated with sovereignty, and so is in no position, in the final analysis, to choose. The state may work hard to legitimate this view, emphasizing and institutionalizing its

[63] Eric A. Nordlinger, *On the Autonomy of the Democratic State* (Cambridge, Mass.: Harvard University Press, 1981), 33.

[64] Skocpol, 'Bringing the State Back In', 9.

essential role as the only bridge between the territory inside states and the anarchy of interstate relations. It thus renders itself indispensable.

Within the state apparatus one finds both agency and structure, a continuous and flexible interchange between individuals and their institutional environment. The opportunity to formulate policy choices which have society-wide consequences, and which define the 'national' interest, is the core of the power these state officials enjoy. This account is similar to that offered by Martin Hollis and Steve Smith:

Foreign policy is made, in our view, by persons in various offices, who need to juggle with the imperatives of office, to display skill in negotiation and readiness to concede one point for the sake of another, to ride the horses of role-conflict, and to interpret a changing situation with a mixture of impartiality and commitment.[65]

In this sense, Krasner is right about the essential importance of 'roles and offices' but wrong in his assertion that *insulation* alone is the key to the boundaries of the state. His narrow concentration on the State Department and the White House, for example, excludes Congress from consideration. Indeed, at one point he even counterposes 'the state' and 'the legislature'.[66] Congress, he rightly argues, has a different constituency from the president's national electorate, and an institutional structure which fragments and disperses power thus allowing societal groups to gain access. Nevertheless, Congress is still an institution with universal and centralized decision-making powers which can, and often does, pass legislation which is 'separate and distinct from the interests of any particular societal group'.[67]

Eric Nordlinger, in contrast, defines members of the state as 'those individuals who are endowed with society-wide decision-making authority'.[68] He extends the sweep of the state in deliberate fashion:

---

[65] M. Hollis and S. Smith, *Explaining and Understanding International Relations* (Oxford: Clarendon Press), 165.

[66] Krasner, *Defending the National Interest*, 63.

[67] See also John Gerard Ruggie, 'Review of *The National Interest* by S. D. Krasner', *American Political Science Review*, 74 (1980), 296–9.

[68] E. A. Nordlinger, *On the Autonomy of the Democratic State* (Cambridge, Mass.: Harvard University Press, 1981), 11.

Although the executive and/or bureaucracy have been said to constitute the 'core' of the state, this in itself does not warrant a definition limited to them alone. Since we are concerned with all authoritative actions and all parts of the state as they relate to one another and to societal actors, the definition should include all public officials—elected and appointed, at high and low levels, at the center and the peripheries—who are involved in the making of public policy.[69]

The nature of the issue under consideration conditions the involvement of what we might see as the 'core' (or narrow) and the 'peripheral' (or extended) state, resembling the argument of Aaron Wildavsky who distinguished one president from the 'two' presidencies.[70] In domestic affairs, the incremental nature of change and the need for societal support for a policy leads into coalition building and to much greater involvement for Congress. In foreign affairs, in contrast, the more rapid speed of change, the greater complexity, the higher stakes, and the expectation placed upon the executive to 'act', all limit the involvement of peripheral state actors in the process. Indeed core state officials may use the 'redefinition' of domestic issues as foreign issues as an explicit strategy to increase their policy-making autonomy.[71]

Congress is more 'porous' than the executive to the activities of both business and environmental lobbies. As later empirical material will show, environmental interest groups have had success in domestic politics by working through Congress (and the courts). They have had less success in foreign policy, however, not just because they have less access to the 'narrow' state, but also because the more permeable state institutions, especially Congress, are also less involved in the making of foreign policy.

For example, the State Department has a high degree of insulation from societal pressure. With no specific constituency to which it is answerable domestically, societal groups representing the environment and business rely on the State Department itself to grant access, and officials have little experience of, or interest in, these kind of inputs. In other words, the obligation to act on behalf of the

---

[69] Ibid. 9–10. Public officials are those involved in policy-making itself as opposed to public 'employees' who hold publicly funded positions but are not involved in 'authoritative decisionmaking'.

[70] Aaron Wildavsky, 'The Two Presidencies', in Wildavsky (ed.), *The Presidency* (Boston: Little, Brown, 1969).

[71] Ikenberry *et al.*, 'Introduction', 13.

whole territory is a key source of *non-accountability*. The idea that there could be *a* constituency interest is denied and inaccessibility is legitimized as a central feature of the process of formulating a truly *national* interest. A specific constituency means a special interest which is antithetical to the whole notion of a national interest. The Department's specific mission is to protect and promote the 'national' interests of the United States. These are formulated quite legitimately, however, with little direct or continuing reference to the positively expressed views of the populace at all.

Thus the State Department combines physical insulation with a representative function. As suggested, potential autonomy of this sort can be more or less evident depending on the nature of the issue and on which parts of the state are involved.[72] Autonomy may vary over issues, and it certainly varies over time. Its 'use' may also entail an increase in societal opposition which leads to parts of the state being 'captured'. As Skocpol concludes: 'In short, "state autonomy" is not a fixed structural feature of any governmental system. It can come and go.'[73]

INSIDE THE CORE STATE

Given the preceding argument, a central question which arises concerns the internal differentiation of the core state. We have already seen Nordlinger's formulation, the idea of policy-making as a puzzle. Consider the following description of factionalism within the foreign-policy elite (*and* the general public), in which John Vasquez isolates an 'accommodationist' and a 'hard-line' position. The former, he argues:

. . . can be defined as an individual who has a personal predisposition that finds the use of force, especially war, repugnant, and advocates a foreign policy that will avoid war through compromise, negotiation, and the creation of rules and norms for nonviolent conflict resolution. Conversely, a hard-liner can be defined as an individual who has a personal pre-

---

[72] Crisis decision-making, for example, limits the search for alternatives and the breadth of consultation (see Polsby, *Political Innovation in America*, 150).

[73] Skocpol, 'Bringing the State Back In', 14. Skocpol's point is more ambitious but the principle is the same—that state autonomy depends on circumstances and is therefore not a constant but a variable.

disposition to adopt a foreign policy that is adamant in not compromising its goals and who believes in the efficacy and legitimacy of threats and force.[74]

Each faction adopts *a* 'foreign policy' (through 'predisposition', circumventing any explanation for preference formation), and this is designed to secure *the* national interest. The precise relationship between means and ends remains uncertain, however, and yet this space holds so much promise for challenging and thought-provoking work on foreign policy. Is there one, assumed, national interest, and many foreign policies designed to achieve it, or is one's foreign-policy stance effectively dictated by one's conception of the national interest (they are essentially synonymous)?

It is in the process of the formulation of ends, of choices about what the state should be trying to achieve, in other words, that the essential role state officials play in constructing the national interest is to be observed. A focus on structure, to the detriment of agency, in international relations, has fuelled the notion that empirical toil is fundamentally misconceived (history with a small, rather than a large 'h'), a tendency reinforced by the lack of theoretical sophistication in much work on foreign policy. Too often the failure to analyse how 'states know what they want' has led to the *means* of 'power' and 'wealth' being mistaken for *ends*.[75] In making a post-structuralist critique of neorealism, for example, Richard Ashley maintains:

... neorealism joins all modes of historicism in denying the historical significance of *practice*, the moment at which men and women enter with greater or lesser degrees of consciousness into the making of their world.[76]

[74] John A. Vasquez, 'Foreign Policy, Learning and War', in Hermann, Kegley, and Rosenau (eds.), *New Directions in the Study of Foreign Policy*, 374.

[75] See Martha Finnemore's thought-provoking *National Interests in International Society* (Ithaca, NY: Cornell University Press, 1996), 1–2. Finnemore would, of course, reject my approach (single-country, agentic), my conclusions (the determining role state officials play in constructing the national interest), and my assertion that international relations currently has too much structure and not enough agency. It is not clear, however, that a 'vertical' analysis of the sort attempted here fails to accommodate factors in operation outside the state, providing that state is conceived of as more than just a sovereign territorial entity (see Finnemore, p. 10). Finnemore does not differentiate the state throughout most of her analysis although she does on occasion refer to 'state actors' without greater specification (i.e. p. 40). See also Peter J. Katzenstein (ed.), *The Culture of National Security* (New York: Columbia University Press, 1996).

[76] Richard K. Ashley, 'The poverty of Neorealism', in Keohane (ed.), *Neorealism and Its Critics*, 290 (his italics). See also Alexander Wendt, 'Anarchy is What States

In the making of American foreign environmental policy, state officials argued about what *they* thought policy should be. Some were *sceptics* who maintained that international environmental problems were scientifically unproven, and that costly remedial action was therefore unnecessary. They simply did not believe in the environmental critique. Others within the state were clearly *activists* (in the sense that they wanted a more pro-environmental foreign policy adopted), and they used their resources to try to get their preferences enacted. There was no agreement in this instance on ends, on a national interest over and above the policy struggle between competing officials.

Policy choice—what the state actually chose to do—is thus necessarily explained by a focus on this intrastate process. In Eric Nordlinger's words, it reflects the 'parallelogram (or resultant) of the public-officials resource-weighted preferences', (a conception of what might be meant by 'resource-weighted' is developed in the next section).[77]

There appears to be, prima facie, similarities between such an explanation and Allison's bureaucratic politics paradigm. Allison's notion of a clash between 'the power and skill of proponents and opponents' as a central part of foreign-policy explanations is very similar to Nordlinger's.[78] However, although this kind of competition within the core state is important for Allison, he places too much emphasis on 'roles' rather than the personalities of those who occupy them in explaining the origin of preferences.[79]

In other words, state officials compete with each other over their conceptions of the national interest—their *own* ideas about what should be done—from which are derived their policy prescriptions about the issue at hand.[80] Sceptics do not *believe* in the environmental critique and seek to steer the state away from concessions;

Make of It: The Social Construction of Power Politics', *International Organization*, 46 (1992).

[77] Nordlinger, *On the Autonomy of the Democratic State*, 8.
[78] Allison, *Essence of Decision*, 145.
[79] Hollis and Smith, *Explaining and Understanding*, 148, 151 n. 10.
[80] The category of 'ideas', broad and notoriously malleable, doesn't seem to me amenable to the clear distinction between 'world views', 'principled beliefs', and 'causal beliefs' posited by Judith Goldstein and Robert Keohane. The claim that 'sustainable life depends on averting the greenhouse effect' may be based on a causal belief but in order to prompt action it must have a principled component. The question is, are these really 'separate' ideas? To say 'the atmosphere requires attention' is still to invite the question 'why'? The answer lies in claims about the

activists, committed to environmentalism of varying degrees, work to embroil the state in a progressive foreign-policy stance. For the sceptics, the preferred option is non-engagement, for the activists, constructive commitment.

These officials do not operate as delegates for societal interests of one sort or another. They do not come into the core offices of the state determined to put an amorphous 'business' view, or that of the 'environmental lobby' (and, of course, both these societal agglomerations actually break down in practice into factions which may have *competing* interests). What they have are beliefs and opinions, ideas about the world, which make them highly sympathetic to some interests rather than others.[81] Such beliefs emerge out of their engagement with these issues and their proponents societally, no doubt, but 'joining' the state alters their status.

In other words, they may be in office in the first place because of, say, their environmental credentials, but once on the 'inside' they have to face much more complex calculations which involve committing the totality of the territorial state to a particular course of action. Thus they find themselves in a competitive environment with others, at more junior and senior levels, who conceptualize the relation between certain issues and 'the' national interest differently. They are now forced to compete at the level of ideas. These ideas form a kind of web which encompasses whole swathes of societal interests. To advocate signing a treaty to limit national carbon-dioxide emissions has long-lasting implications for all

value of human life. Often, as they accept, the deeper justification for principled beliefs lies in reality with 'world views' but they argue that as more than one set of principled beliefs may be adduced from the same source, the distinction holds. Nevertheless, the dispute always reverts ultimately to interpretations of the world view from which the principled beliefs are drawn and so the latter remain a residual category (see Judith Goldstein and Robert O. Keohane, 'Ideas and Foreign Policy: An Analytical Framework', in Goldstein and Keohane (eds.), *Ideas and Foreign Policy: Beliefs, Institutions, and Political Change* (Ithaca, NY: Cornell University Press, 1993), 8–11).

[81] An example of principled ideas (or world views) in action comes from a comparison of the religious beliefs of Bill Clinton's interior secretary, Bruce Babbitt, and Ronald Reagan's, James Watt. Babbitt's environmental philosophy stressed the notion of stewardship drawn from the story of Noah's Ark; Watt, downplaying the need for conservation in 1981, argued: 'I don't know how many future generations we can count on before the Lord returns' (see Jack Anderson and Michael Binstein, 'Biodiversity Breakfasts', *Washington Post* (6 June 1993), p. C7).

manner of societal groups in different ways. The ideas define the likely impact on involved interests, and their configuration (for or against), not the other way around.

Yet it is hard to prevail within the state through force of argument alone. In the actual process of policy-making, these officials use many strategies to improve their positions. In argument, for example, what they seek to do is marshall those societal interests—the quantifiable—to their defence. They do this by publicizing and asserting the wide range of social and international groups which will be affected, which have expressed an interest, which have been supportive and so on. This is the only way to 'prove' that one's own conception of the national interest has a material currency which can be weighed. Ideas have independent explanatory power in this sense: they define the relevant interests and how those interests are in turn to be dealt with.

Thus, the integration of societal and international factors takes place along two dimensions. First, by helping to place sympathizers within the state and trying to provide staunch support and ammunition for these sympathizers once 'inside' (i.e. agenda-setting, publicity), and second, as collections of societal and international interests which can be assembled in defence of the idea, the conception of the national interest, which state officials, now possessed of a partial stake in the state's autonomy, seek to advance. The next two sections look at this process in more detail.

PLURALISM, REALISM, AND MARXISM

We now have a picture of the autonomous state whose officials, separated from their sectoral societal responsibilities, struggle over conceptions of the national interest.[82] These officials are able to use an array of resources to press their cases, showing how their conception of the national interest not only meets the demands of important societal coalitions but also of international actors as well. This section looks at how the interaction between society, state, and international system can be theorized, first, by briefly considering three sets of existing explanations: pluralist,

---

[82] As Lawrence Freedman argues of intrastate struggles, 'the random clashes of fragmented, selfishly motivated actors are, in fact, reasonably patterned and linked to conceptions of the national interest' ('Logic, Politics and Foreign Policy', 449).

realist, and Marxist; then by outlining a contrasting state-centric argument.

As we have seen, the essentials of *pluralism* are: a principal focus on societal groups as the main factors in explaining policy; a stress on the importance of this societal competition to the democratic process; an accent on the fragmentation of power; and, finally, an emphasis on the multiple ways in which access can be gained, and influence exercised, in the policy-making process.[83]

On international environmental issues there exist many potential sources of influence: domestic groups, transnational groups (Greenpeace, Friends of the Earth, the World Wildlife Fund), scientific research bodies like the International Union for the Conservation of Nature and Natural Resources (IUCN), and international institutions like the UN and, more specifically, UNEP. It is this plethora of well-resourced and permanent organizations which informs the pluralist explanation for foreign environmental policy.[84]

The most 'plural' picture is one in which competition between differently resourced groups is responsible for explaining policy.[85] Multiple access, long-term relationships between groups and government departments, and the central role of societal groups not just in agenda-setting but also in affecting policy choice, all means that the most 'independent' role envisaged for the state is as a group or collection of groups itself, with government departments lobbying for their own options against *competing* societal groups.

This view of the deep and overlapping links between government and society is also found in the literature on policy 'networks'

---

[83] Martin J. Smith, *Pressure, Power and Policy: State Autonomy and Policy Networks in Britain and the United States* (London: Harvester-Wheatsheaf, 1993), 15–18.

[84] Although these groups and organizations have different characteristics, they are most distinguished by location. Domestic interest groups have opportunities which are not open to UNEP, and vice versa. What these different bodies share, however, is a similar goal: to force states to enact pro-environmental policies. They are all 'non-governmental' sources of pressure in this sense.

[85] Andrew McFarland terms this rather 'naïve' view 'group theory' in distinction from pluralism. He also maintains that its proponents, like Robert Dahl (in *Who Governs?* (New Haven: Yale University Press, 1961)), were 'quite aware of the possibility of independent action by the state'; see McFarland, 'Interest Groups and Theories of Power in America', *British Journal of Political Science*, 17 (1987), 137.

and 'communities' (despite being seen as to some extent a departure from pluralism). 'Policy communities' are stable, highly integrated and closed relationships between a few privileged groups and governments. At the other end of the continuum, 'issue networks' are open, unstable, and non-interdependent, with groups moving in and out regularly and with the issue itself defining the criteria for membership.[86] In an influential article on issue networks, for example, Hugh Heclo concluded that '. . . any neat distinction between the governmental structure and its environment tends to break down'.[87]

Although pluralist authors have mainly concentrated on the domestic realm, we saw earlier that there is little indication that foreign policy should be viewed very differently. This reflects, of course, the adoption of a non-active conception of the state. To stipulate a meaningful distinction between the making of domestic and foreign policy is hazardous for pluralists because it suggests that the usual society-led domestic process does not translate into the foreign-policy sphere at the same time as the territorial state obviously 'acts' abroad. If societal competition does not explain these actions, what does? The only real answer is the 'other' state, the institutional one, which must then be conceived of as an actor. Hence, the question arises: why does this state have agency internationally and not at home, and why does it not use the power derived from 'foreign' resources to act domestically? For many, it clearly does do precisely this.

A prominent example of international pluralism has centred on what are called 'epistemic communities'. These are 'networks of knowledge-based experts' which help states define interests through the information and analysis they provide. This expertise moulds the way state officials understand problems, 'as represented by those to whom they "turn for advice under conditions of uncertainty"'.[88] This argument gives quite some weight to the activities

[86] David Marsh and R. A. W. Rhodes 'Policy Networks in British Politics: A Critique of Existing Approaches', in Marsh and Rhodes (eds.), *Policy Networks in British Government* (Oxford: Clarendon Press, 1992), 13–15. See also J. J. Richardson and A. G. Jordan, *Governing Under Pressure: The Policy Process in a Post-Parliamentary Democracy* (Oxford: Blackwell, 1985), 25.

[87] H. Heclo, 'Issue Networks and the Executive Establishment', in Anthony King (ed.), *The New American Political System* (Washington, DC: American Enterprise Institute, 1978), 106.

[88] Peter M. Haas, 'Introduction: Epistemic Communities and International Policy Coordination', *International Organization*, 46/1 (1992), 2.

of these experts, who are in the main, but not exclusively, scientists. As a new issue emerges, or decision-makers are faced with uncertainty, they turn to specialists for interpretation of the information—largely technical—and guidance. Peter Haas claims, in a special issue of *International Organization*.

As demands for such information arise, networks or communities of specialists capable of producing and providing the information emerge and proliferate. The members of a prevailing community become strong actors at the national and transnational level as decision-makers solicit their information and delegate responsibility to them.[89]

In a conclusion to the same special issue on epistemic communities, Haas and Emanuel Adler place the approach in its context within international relations, stressing the extent to which the state is undermined by these plural forces:

Before choices involving cooperation can be made, circumstances must be assessed and interests identified. In this regard, to study the ideas of epistemic communities and their impact on policymaking is to immerse oneself in the inner world of international relations theory and to erase the artificial boundaries between international and domestic politics so that the dynamic between structure and choice can be illuminated.[90]

The pluralist case rests on the primary importance of non-state forces, and in the foreign environmental policy process there is no shortage of candidates. A multitude of different actors is involved in providing information and in lobbying for specific choices but this high visibility overstates the real impact that societal forces have had. For example, even though information matters, and is used as part of the intrastate negotiation, it only filters in at a relatively low level and—most importantly of all—the decisions made in core state institutions are made in terms of general political arguments, not because one or other scientific analysis seems more convincing.

State officials use arguments about this kind of material to press for their own preferences, but they also interpret and reorient it; they are active participants who do more than simply relay societal

---

[89] Ibid. 4.
[90] Emanuel Adler and Peter M. Haas, 'Conclusion: Epistemic Communities, World Order, and the Creation of a Reflective Research Program', in *International Organization*, 46/1 (1992), 367.

concern and argue about alternatives framed elsewhere. There is not much evidence of high-level non-state access at all, and plenty about the dissatisfaction of groups with their role in the policy process. Influencing agendas, and providing information and publicity, still remain potent weapons but they do not substitute as an explanation for the policy-making process within the core state.

The central and enduring *realist* insight is that the pursuit of power is the principal motivation for states, and that states are really the only actors of note in the international system. According to Joseph Grieco:

Realism has three basic assumptions. First, states are the major actors in world affairs. Second, the international environment severely penalizes states if they fail to protect their interests or if they pursue objectives beyond their means; hence they are 'sensitive to costs' and behave as unitary-rational agents. Third, international anarchy is the principal force conditioning the external preferences and actions of states.[91]

In order to survive and thrive in this system, states are more or less 'forced' to pursue power.[92] In its modern variant, neorealism, this power-seeking behaviour is explained solely in terms of the way the international system is organized (into separate entities), and the distribution of power within it. States remain the most important actors, and the system they comprise the crucial factor in explaining their behaviour.[93]

International co-operation is therefore always transient and superficial in the sense that it does not alter the basic absence of trust which characterizes the system. What may change is the ranking of states (X may rise and Y may decline). Furthermore, the anarchy is self-fulfilling, containing a tendency towards preservation by ensuring that no one power can turn the anarchy into a hierarchy.[94]

What the *state-centric* account shares with realism is an emphasis on the importance of the state. Indeed, realism is often described as

[91] Joseph M. Grieco, *Cooperation Among Nations: Europe, America, and Non-Tariff Barriers to Trade* (Ithaca, NY: Cornell University Press, 1990), 3–4.
[92] On the differentiation of realist arguments see Michael Doyle, 'Thucydidean Realism', *Review of International Studies*, 16 (1990), 223–37.
[93] As another prominent realist has claimed, '. . . the state is the principal actor in that the nature of the state and the pattern of relations among states are the most important determinants of the character of international relations at any given moment' (Robert Gilpin, *War and Change in World Politics* (Cambridge: Cambridge University Press, 1981), 18).
[94] Waltz, *Theory of International Politics*, 66.

a 'state-centric' theory. There, however, the similarities end. If the pluralists stress the fragmentation of power, and realists accentuate the possession and acquisition of power by the state, both reject any conception of the state which would conceive of it as an actor in any meaningful sense.[95] Realists also argue that domestic societal factors are largely irrelevant in explanation because it is the international system which accounts for state behaviour.[96] They therefore privilege the relationship between the state and other states above all else, explicitly rejecting plural influences as important determinants of state behaviour but also rejecting the idea that the state as an *institutional* entity 'acts'.

The state-centric argument advanced here differs from realism in several respects. First, a state 'centric' approach is precisely that because the state is the focus for an explanation, rather than the whole of it. Societal factors remain highly relevant in accounting for foreign-policy outcomes as we will see. The second dimension of the state-centric/realist demarcation is on the question of what happens *within* the state. For realists, the negotiations and arguments in which state officials engage are much less important as an explanatory factor than the distribution of power within the international system. The state thus constitutes an epiphenomenal starting-point for analysis.

In contrast to this position, the empirical material in the chapters which follow suggests that it is essential to know what actually happens within the state in order to understand why particular options were pursued. Relying on a systemic explanation framed in terms of the pursuit of power fails to account for the way decisions were actually made. Not only this, it also proves inadequate on its own terms; that is, the empirical material suggests the state did not even act *as if* it were pursuing power as a unitary rational entity responding to the logic of international anarchy.

[95] Krasner's work *Defending the National Interest* is to some extent an exception although his core claim is still that: 'The distribution of power in the international system is the critical variable in determining the broad foreign-policy goals sought by American central decision-makers' (p. 15).

[96] As Ole R. Holsti has argued: 'Because the central problems for states are starkly defined by the nature of the international system, their actions are primarily a response to external rather than domestic political forces. At best the latter provide very weak explanations for external policy'; O. R. Holsti, 'International Relations Models', in Michael J. Hogan and Thomas G. Paterson (eds.), *Explaining the History of American Foreign Relations* (Cambridge: Cambridge University Press, 1991), 60.

The third distinction centres on the motivations of state officials. If one accepts that the 'black box' of the state can be opened to reveal the workings of the policy process, one may still find that those centrally involved in decision making are, in fact, motivated by realist concerns (as Krasner suggests). They might see environmental issues as a means by which to enhance power and increase security. The chapters which follow show some instances when these concerns are attributable to officials. But these are always subject to a countervailing outlook from others about the importance of co-operative action on environmental issues, about the need for remedial action to take place, and about the desirability of playing a full and meaningful role in the unfolding international process. There is no realist consensus, therefore, but a realist viewpoint shared by some, not all, officials.

The realist and pluralist visions differ from a state-centric approach most importantly in terms of their conception of the state but also in two other areas: the key actors in foreign policy, and the prime motivations for policy choice. For pluralists, transnational and societal forces are vital, for realists and for state-centrism, states still dominate, although 'different' states. As for motivation, pluralists highlight the ways societal groups infiltrate the policy process to advance the wishes of their supporters, trying to change outcomes through the provision of information, by setting agendas, and most strongly by trying to pressure government into making the choices they, the societal groups, want. Realists, on the other hand, stress the drive for power in the international system as the key to foreign-policy choice. A state-centric approach accepts an important role for societal pressure, thereby rejecting the realists, yet maintains the primacy of the state, countering the claims of the pluralists that non-state forces undermine the independent explanatory importance of central state officials.

As for *Marxism*, one variant of this 'third tradition' involves a strong emphasis on the relationship between state and society. Instrumental Marxism's picture of the policy-process does not differ in surface appearance from that provided by the pluralists. At heart, instrumental Marxists claim that state actions represent the dominance of ruling class interests within the social and, most significantly, economic spheres. This economic power is cashed-in to provide political spoils which further advance ruling class interests. In other words, business and industry—the institutions of capitalism—use their power and influence to achieve rewards in much the same way as other pressure groups. However, their power and influence gives them an edge which they can fashion into an entrenched position in the policy-making process.

Thus the state represents the directly expressed views of the capitalist class making it an account in the plural tradition because of the primary role it accords to societal factors. The question becomes: which (not whether), societal influences explain policy? In the case of instrumental Marxism, the answer is usually capitalists. This explanation clashes with a state-centric account on both a general and a specific point. Generally, because societal factors are not as important a factor in explaining policy outcomes as the state, and specifically, because there is relatively little evidence to suggest appreciably more impact for business—in securing the particular policy choices it sought—than environmentalists. On the latter point, it is simply not enough to argue that the outcome in certain cases (but by no means all), was nearer to the commercial than the environmental position. Where this was the result, the question *why* still remains a live one.

There is also the argument for structural Marxism with which to contend. Its emphasis on the state certainly weakens one objection to its adequacy as an explanation. Structural Marxism stresses the degree to which the state may undertake action which appears to be *against* the interests of capitalists but which is, in fact, designed to ensure the long-term future of capitalism itself. An example is the introduction of social reforms. The state solves various collective action problems and saves the capitalists from themselves.

The main difficulty with such accounts is the near impossibility of successfully attributing the actions the state takes to such a particular cause. It is possible to show when the state seemed to act against the interests of capitalists, but this simply provides evidence for a variety of explanations for policy formation. Perhaps it was a concern with the long-run survival of capitalism, perhaps the state was just unresponsive to society, maybe the 'naïve' pluralist picture is accurate and business loses on some occasions and wins on others, or maybe it is none of these.

For example, how is one to interpret the different stands taken by opposing officials? It is hard to know exactly what would be appropriate in terms of capitalism's long-term future. Perhaps, resisting regulation will damage the environment so badly it will stimulate social revolution. Or, alternatively, following the environmentalists' line may restrict business so much that the economy begins to falter and the efficacy of the system is put in doubt.

Officials rarely argued from either of these apocalyptic viewpoints, but they did disagree substantively demonstrating that 'the state' was, in reality, seriously internally differentiated. If one adopts restrictive assumptions about unitariness and rationality, to avoid this puzzle, one is thus required to demonstrate, as with the realists, that 'the state' did act *as if* it were pursuing capital's long-term interests. Notwithstanding the fact that the argument thus far has given serious weight to the views and actions of individuals within the state apparatus, how can one settle the question of which policy choice was the right one? This is even harder if one can't ask the officials what they thought they were doing because they may well have been serving an end of which they themselves were unaware.

The state-centric approach advocated here differs from the foregoing accounts along three dimensions. First, the idea of the state which is adopted bears a similarity only to the way Marxists have used the concept. Second, this state is internally differentiated hence individuals and their own ideas matter, as does the struggle for policy choice: state actions cannot be reduced to either an international systemic stimulus or the determining role of domestic economic forces. Third, societal forces are integrated in an unusual way, serving partly to promote individuals into the state but then as a kind of implicit support which these state officials use to bolster their positions. Given new opportunities and constraints, state officials cease to be in any crude sense delegates for societal or international interests. The following section fleshes out this dimension of a state-centric account.

POLICY CONTEXTS

These *policy contexts* are made up of the political forces which circle the state both at home and abroad. They serve to create the basic conditions of choice, drawing in effect a map of the terrain which state officials have to negotiate. Contexts do not constitute an 'objective' set of pertinent circumstances, however, because officials possess the ability not only to try to alter them, but also to reconfigure them, often unpredictably, by the simple act of resolving part or all of a policy question.

The principal elements within the context are the activities of other major actors and the profile of other relevant issues. For example, domestic interest groups try to create enough publicity on a particular foreign-policy issue such that the state addresses the problem in a way conducive to that group's desired goal. There are, usually, countervailing pressures as well, both sides working through Congress, the media, or the courts, to try to resolve things in their favour. The result is a political 'terrain' or 'landscape', a set of societal arguments and pressures which present state officials *individually* with different opportunities and constraints. Activists will use the pressure exerted by environmental groups to argue, for instance, that it makes electoral sense to act.

Sceptics, on the other hand, will accentuate the arguments of societal groups better suited to support their preferred options. What they argue is, 'we ought to do this *because* business thinks it a good idea', while what they really mean is 'we ought to do this, *and* business thinks it a good idea'. It is, crucially, a two-stage process. Societal pressure gives the particular issue under consideration a certain set of characteristics and implications. Environmental issues matter in many ways: costs, voters, public relations, support or otherwise of prominent societal forces, sympathy or antipathy of other states, moral and competitive considerations. The state is not simply a collection of officials who each pursue one or other of these concerns. Some, activists, think action should be undertaken; others, sceptics, are resistant. Both will argue about the effect of each course of action on key contextual elements: how will different sets of voters react, how will international allies line up, how will public opinion respond? They use their perspective on each of these considerations to bolster their advocacy for or against certain policy choices.

The impact of the environment on other issues is a central consideration. How will a choice one way or the other on climate change, for example, affect trade, regulatory reform, energy policy, general economic growth, GATT negotiations, relationships with allies, dealings in international institutions, understandings with important congressional figures, and so on? State officials use either the negative, or positive, impact of environmental choices to try to sustain their bid for what they consider a desirable policy.

The idea of contexts allows us to integrate the activities of actors in operation at both the societal and international levels and to show how they make an impact. Non-state organizations provide information which state officials can use to substantiate their claims, and they provide corroborative pressure by adding their support to an official's position. The setting of agendas is also important, although not necessarily positively. If environmental groups succeed in getting the question of compensation for species destruction, for example, discussed in an international-treaty negotiation, then they create a particular dilemma for forces within the state as it is by no means clear such a development works *in favour* of intrastate environmentalists. The link with a contentious issue like 'compensation' may, for example, strengthen the arguments of sceptics by enabling them to show that acquiescence would have unacceptable costs. For this reason it is unwise to draw a direct line from societal pressure to state action, or even to use the existence of societal pressure to explain the preferences of activist officials, without examining in detail the content of the intrastate process itself.

Direct pressure on activist officials by environmentalists is unnecessary because they are broadly in agreement on a more positive stance towards international environmental issues already. Those who are sceptical, on the other hand, are unlikely to be persuaded by direct action by societal groups opposed to them. Attempts at personal lobbying (except in rare cases and at the *highest* level) mean less than the perception by officials that the way the issue is being received either domestically or internationally has changed. If it shifts, a whole new set of implications may arise—what once seemed an unpopular domestic option, and so provided no support for those in the state who were its advocates, might now be perceived very differently. This dynamic process goes on all the time, with the shifting configuration of issues yielding new dangers and opportunities, allowing previously dormant alternatives to become feasible.

It is at this intersection that the skill of the individuals themselves, their personal beliefs, and the advantages their particular office confers, comes into play. They are making real judgements, puzzling out the appropriate response, and working to secure it, based upon this complex of skill, belief, and opportunity. Officials do not simply ebb and flow with changes in contexts. They have the power to resist, manipulate, or even to try to oppose, the circumstances lined up against them. They may seek to manipulate the context by leaking sensitive information, fostering the activities of opposed groups, or by simply making the internal division public, thereby stirring hitherto silent support.

It is also important to note that the resolution of an issue with a policy decision, while properly viewed as the end of one skirmish within an ongoing process, does confer advantages on the victorious. Thus, the state officials who prevail may well have succeeded in establishing their interpretation as predominant, defining the issue in terms which favour their arguments in the future and therefore enhancing the impact supportive societal groups can make. Opponents will work to undermine and weaken this consensus but it may take time to achieve. Institutionalizing a particular policy option becomes a key part of securing structural advantages within the state itself. Defining the implications of an issue, and the appropriate forum for dealing with it, both at the time and, as importantly, in the future, becomes a vital element in this longer-term struggle.

Using the idea of *contexts* has certain advantages. It enables one to concentrate not just on those actors specifically involved in lobbying for policy choices on a particular issue, but also to see 'the big picture' as well. Specific constituencies are, of course, a vital part of the story, but the activities of other groups on other issues (i.e. trade, nuclear weapons), also matters crucially. Contexts thus counteract the tendency to focus solely on those groups closely associated with a specific policy area. These particularistic claims are only part of the raw material for policy-makers. They have other concerns in mind as well, running the territorial state as a whole. Contexts enable one to envisage the melting-pot of complex and often contradictory issues with which these officials are faced.

A further advantage of the 'context' idea is that it captures international pressures and domestic pressures alike. Just as the make-up of the domestic political context presents constraints and opportunities, so do the activities of other governments and international institutions. A whole new set of issues may be present here—arms control, international wealth redistribution, alliance politics—and these too may strengthen and weaken forces within the state. This is compounded by the domestic–international overlap as illustrated in the activities of the international media or transnational environmental groups.

In 1972, for example, the stigma of Vietnam *strengthened* the activists' position by allowing them to argue that an 'apolitical' issue like the international environment would be good publicity for the administration. In 1992, by contrast, during the last year of the Bush administration, the storm of protest environmental groups stirred up against the president actually strengthened the hand of sceptics who argued that environmentalists would not support a Republican president. The fierceness of the criticism weakened pro-environmental forces within the state. In addition, it is important to note that both 1972 and 1992 were election years for an incumbent Republican which heightened sensitivity to the electoral dimension of the political context.

State officials operated within these domestic and international political contexts and they interpreted and used them to better pursue their own preferences within the state itself. These officials represented neither embodiments, nor conduits, of societal interests, but independent actors able to process information and turn it to their own advantage. It is in this way that the political scene, both at home and abroad, can be envisaged as the 'terrain of battle'. This terrain is composed of the various coalitions of interests, the proliferation of information, the extent of media and public interest, the interests of other states, the activities of international institutions, and the structure of the international system. State officials use this terrain to their own advantage, making arguments and pursuing strategies designed to promote their own preferences. Their opponents, of course, are also using the same terrain as best they can. Through the idea of context, one can see that officials are always conscious of and affected by political developments outside the state.

High-profile environmental campaigns matter, therefore, not because they force 'the administration' to adopt a more pro-environment policy but because they give extra leverage to activists within the state who can argue that a more enlightened policy would be a good idea for a number of reasons like, for example, improving the president's electoral prospects or developing better relations with a key ally. A range of reasons is given in argument by officials even though in essence they *already* want to take the proposed action themselves. Other factors compete, however, and the sceptics, as in 1992, may also derive strength from the ferocity of protests against the administration.

Similarly, in the mid-1980s the business community shifted its stance on CFC elimination, favouring more universal regulation, but sceptics continued to work for a non-regulatory approach. They *still believed* regulation ought to be resisted, whatever the views of the business community, and they continued to manœuvre to try to achieve that end. They lost ground because a key piece of 'ammunition', that business was in support of non-regulation, changed. The activists—who had been arguing for regulation all along—suddenly found themselves with a strengthened hand and they used it accordingly. The preferences of state officials *had not changed*. It was their ability to realize them that had altered; the activists were up, the sceptics down.

The dynamism of the 'contextual' approach captures change over time and over issue. As policy contexts are transformed, so the coalition of forces within the state may be changed. As more is known about an issue, so the strength of one faction may be increased. Officials who have been urging preventive action on ozone depletion may, for example, receive a sudden boost as scientific evidence confirms the depletion hypothesis. It is not the case that the pressure on the state to act becomes unbearable, but that this group on the inside gains more capital with which to make its case. This interactive process means that the enhancement of the pro-environmental faction within the state may in turn boost societal support and further strengthen the position of sympathetic state officials. It will also, of course, incite opposed groups within state and society to redouble their efforts, and it may also weaken public protest as the perception develops that the government is acting.[97] This struggle over policy is not boundless, however. There are limits to the search for options and we now briefly consider the idea of an 'envelope' of consensus comprised by certain fundamentals about the process of foreign-policy formation.

THE 'ENVELOPE'

Preceding sections have established a basic theory of state–society

[97] See Anthony Downs, 'Up and Down with Ecology: The Issue-Attention Cycle', *The Public Interest*, 26–9/28 (1972), and Riley E. Dunlap, 'Public Opinion and

interaction. There is one factor absent from this picture, however, and that is the extent to which officials share certain beliefs which conflict with none of the options they advance. This consensus provides the 'envelope' within which policy is formed; it does not *motivate* choice, it *constrains* it, ruling certain options out of account. Without this consensus, the struggle would become even more acute because there would be few extra-state limits to policy choice. Thus one could argue:

It is at least often plausible to think of 'the national interest' as a policy defined through a power struggle among competing bureaucracies and termed 'the national interest' as a mark of the winner's success in the competition.[98]

On such an understanding, the national interest would be defined anew each time, in stark contrast to the realist understanding of 'national interest' which does not reflect the outcome of an internal (either within state or society) process, for then it could vary with time and place. Thus we have two, distinct pictures. If policy were the result of processes within the state, for example, logically almost any policy could emerge providing there was a strong intrastate constituency for it. Although the input of societal groups matters, as we have seen, it only serves to strengthen or weaken one or other faction within the state, not to create an intrinsic limit on policy competition. It is these limits on competition—the 'envelope'—which bound policy choice, structuring the intrastate process.

These boundaries can be conceived of as an 'envelope' for policy choice, delimiting the discussion of alternatives, setting the ground rules, ensuring that the policy which is finally chosen honours certain fundamentals. This interest is not in fact dissimilar to that adopted by the realists but the mistake is to see it as a *motivation*, rather than as a *constraint*, or a filter, on the choice of foreign policy. It stands guard over the definition of alternatives. Realists are also mistaken when they see this interest as best explained by the international system. It is, in fact, the social and political experiences of the participants in the process which enshrines this

Environmental Policy', in James P. Lester (ed.), *Environmental Politics and Policy: Theories and Evidence* (Durham, NC: Duke University Press, 1989).

[98] Hollis and Smith, *Explaining and Understanding*, 151. They are describing, rather than subscribing to, this argument.

'national interest' and ensures that whatever specific route the state takes, it continues to travel in a broadly 'progressive' direction.

The 'envelope' is essentially *a shared commitment to maintaining the integrity of existing institutions and core values*. Senior state officials hold an attachment to the fundamental social values they perceive their society to be based on, and to prosper with. This claim seems simple but its implication is powerful; that the selection and pursuit of policies by any intrastate faction will remain consistent with the norm that no decision should be detrimental to the long-term interests of the United States *as understood by the officials concerned.*[99]

Thus, state officials do not consider options which have potentially severe adverse effects, even though under some scenarios the problem may be of such potential seriousness that no other choice will do. They do this not because they are concerned about their electoral chances, or because they fear congressional disapprobation, but because, even without thinking, they take it for granted that a good choice is one which fits within the envelope. The political system enjoys high legitimacy and its most senior officials do not consider options which go against core social values, values which they share. In some states there may not be a sufficient internal consensus to create an 'envelope', but in the United States there is. To emphasize again, the limits to policy are best understood as constraints, not as motivations.[100]

Nevertheless, state officials do want their country to benefit from international negotiations as much as anyone else's (*should* they

---

[99] My colleague John Sidel has pointed out that the complexity of post cold war foreign-policy making may be glimpsed in the relative uncertainty with which—as we shall see—senior officials in 1992 understood the confines of this envelope. For some, for example, exercising leadership—to steer international negotiations towards the 'American' position even if this was to take no action—was a *sine qua non* of cold war foreign policy and *remained* a given. Others, however, sceptics about environmental politics, were happy to isolate the United States internationally and abdicate involvement let alone leadership, something unthinkable even ten years earlier.

[100] The idea of an 'envelope' bears upon the argument between neoliberals and neorealists over absolute versus relative gains; see Grieco, *Cooperation Among Nations*, 40, and on the related idea of 'loss aversion', Janice Gross Stein, 'International Cooperation and Loss Avoidance: Framing the Problem', in Janice Gross Stein and Louis W. Pauly (eds.), *Choosing to Cooperate: How States Avoid Loss* (Baltimore: Johns Hopkins University Press, 1993), 13–15.

want it to be otherwise?).[101] This is then compounded through time by the process of socialization. The route to success within the American political system—perhaps within most systems—weeds out radicals.[102] Those promoted to, or selected for, high office, share an essential belief in the preservation of societal integrity. This is reinforced through the process of climbing the state hierarchy. As Morton Halperin argues:

> ... it is rare for the images shared within the government to diverge radically from those within the society as a whole, and the appointment of individuals who cannot accept the broader images shared within the bureaucracy is probably equally rare. Moreover, the socialization process within the government is such that individuals who come in with doubts about, or in ignorance of, particular aspects of the set of shared images prevalent in the bureaucracy frequently find themselves quickly coming to support them.[103]

Why, then, is this national interest better conceived of as emerging out of social experience (from the bottom up), rather than as a response to an anarchic international system? After all, in isolation the realist might well find something to sympathize with in the ideas outlined above.

There are three arguments for a societal origin. First, even though some state officials do use the threat of relative losses to other states, many officials do not. Yet, all still accept the limits on policy the envelope provides. They may not see the deliberations on foreign environmental policy as a competition for national ad-

---

[101] John Vincent made the following claim in describing the bureaucratic wrangle over human rights within the Carter administration: 'It is not necessarily the heavies of the State Department pushing the good guys around for the hell of it. The State Department is charged with guarding the national interest, not the human interest. It sees it as no part of its duty to place at risk the safety or well-being of American citizens in the service of some supposed obligation to humanity' (R. J. Vincent, *Human Rights and International Relations* (Cambridge: Cambridge University Press, RIIA, 1986), 135.

[102] The exception in the American case might be 'burrowers', originally political appointees who manage to outlive an administration and worm their way into the permanent civil service hierarchy. In 1993, a General Accounting Office investigation found that Interior—bastion of anti-regulation in the 1980s—had more burrowers than any other department (see James Conaway, 'Babbitt in the Woods', *Harper's Magazine* (Dec. 1993), 54).

[103] Morton H. Halperin, with Priscilla Clapp and Arnold Kanter, *Bureaucratic Politics and Foreign Policy* (Washington, DC: The Brookings Institution, 1974), 14.

vantage, but they do feel constrained to ensure that boundaries are respected.

Second, state officials from both the activist and sceptical factions demonstrated a firm belief in the efficacy of the American approach, arguing in often quite similar terms about the importance of technological developments, investment in monitoring and information gathering, and against any changes in consumption or lifestyle which, for other countries, formed an important dimension of the environmental issue. This evidence of a shared consensus about the limits of policy, and about the appropriate and restricted sphere in which environmental relations were to be considered, arises directly out of the nature of the American political and social system. These issues were not seen by US officials as legitimate matters for discussion within the forum of international environmental negotiations, but as properly the province of the domestic-policy sphere. In addition, these officials also demonstrated a shared faith in the superiority of American procedures, experience, and technical capacity.

Third, a realist analysis would have to maintain that the pursuit of even relative national advantage functioned as a motive and thus dictated the adoption of certain policies. Yet opportunities to pursue this advantage were not taken. At no point did the desire to gain at the expense of other states adequately explain the thrust of policy. To stipulate a concern with national advantage as the key determinant of policy not only ignores the evidence from the intrastate process, it also fails to explain why the United States did not even act *as if* it was pursuing this interest. The concern with American integrity is much better understood as a constraint rather than a motivation.

This final part of the argument serves two purposes. First of all, it explains the limits to policy choice in a way independent of direct societal factors. It does, of course, also highlight just how deeply national officials are products of their societies. As argued, however, the institutional and 'mission' responsibilities they possess within the state provide insulation from immediate pressure and enable them to lobby for the policy choices they prefer. Thus, to be in the state does change the nature of the relationship one has with one's society.

Secondly, it shows how something not unlike a 'realist' national interest, which has been the subject of intense criticism is, in fact, discernible, even on an issue that appears so clearly transnational. State officials do acknowledge and operate within a shared notion of 'American' interests. This is properly understood as a constraint rather than a motivation. Whether or not this may once, in some way, have been derived from the competitive international system, it is now part of the political culture of the United States and so affects policy in a way irreducible to the idea of a simple response to an anarchic world 'outside'.

The United States may not be 'exceptional' in this regard, but the core support for social institutions and values is certainly strong.[104] The system of socialization—which has a personal dimension (peer-group pressure) and an institutional one (the duties of office)—serves to reinforce this. One is unlikely to opt for, or attain, high office in the United States—as a bureaucrat or as a politician—without sharing the consensus to a large degree. Even further, the life histories of these officials are often very similar, usually including previous government experience, a business, legal, or academic background, and an Ivy League education.[105] The system functions well for these people—their status is proof of that.

CONCLUSION

The argument presented in this initial chapter forms a theoretical framework for the empirical material which follows. It has three core elements.

First, the central and continuing importance of the state as the key to framing national choices. Envisaged in institutional terms, this state is conceived of as an actor linking domestic and foreign policies. Nevertheless, these are dealt with very differently, with the nature of foreign issues empowering the core state to the detriment of peripheral state actors and societal and international pressures. Thus a more institutional view of the state also serves to render the burgeoning literature on 'postinternational politics' problematic.

[104] See, however, Seymour Martin Lipset, 'American Exceptionalism Reaffirmed', in Byron E. Shafer (ed.), *Is American Different? A New Look at American Exceptionalism* (Oxford: Clarendon Press, 1991).
[105] Kegley and Wittkopf, *American Foreign Policy*, 256–7.

Second, ideas are not simply the currency in which state officials advance their interests as both realists and Marxists would have us believe. Ideas matter, and once 'inside' the state apparatus officials can indulge them. These ideational struggles are limited, however, by consensual boundaries drawn from the social experience these officials have enjoyed within a particular national culture, socialization within the state, and the abiding requirements of office.

Third, societal and international factors are crucial to a convincing explanation for why certain courses of action are pursued. Not only does the positioning of officials within the state depend crucially on these factors, once in office the ammunition and resources these officials have to 'spend' are drawn from these forces. State officials work to restructure the domestic and international context in their favour at the same time as supporters outside the state give them the firepower they need to try to secure preferred policy choices within.

The evidence from Stockholm in 1972 and Rio in 1992 shows a world where domestic and foreign policy were still formed in very different ways, and where access to the state for plural influences, whether at home or abroad, was strictly limited. Neither pluralists nor realists can adequately explain policy on this issue even though there are points of similarity between a 'state-centric' argument and those that critics from either tradition would advance. The empirical material which follows will show the predominance of the state in the process of policy formation. It will confirm the division between the domestic and the foreign spheres, and will show how the high visibility of interest groups belies their lack of impact. The story of policy development for both conferences—separated by twenty years of domestic and international environmentalism—is the task to which we now turn.

2

American Preparations for the Stockholm Conference

This chapter deals with American preparations for the United Nations Conference on the Human Environment (UNCHE), held in Stockholm in June 1972. At the time, it was one of the largest United Nations gatherings ever to have been held, securing, in the process, the permanent arrival of environmental issues on the international agenda. It took place during an era of substantial readjustment in global affairs. The hostility between East and West had dimmed as the United States, under the leadership of Richard Nixon and Henry Kissinger, sought to remake the international balance of power. A key element in this strategy was the readmittance of the People's Republic of China to the realm of multilateral diplomacy.

In a parallel development, the pace and scope of decolonization had introduced a large number of poor former colonies to a newly independent role in the international system. These countries of the 'South' had tried, during the 1960s and into the 1970s, to effect changes in both the distribution of wealth and the structure of the world's economy. Their numerical superiority had now assured them of a solid and permanent majority in the General Assembly of the United Nations, if not in the main locus of power, the Security Council itself.

Within the United States, the years between 1968 and 1972 were among the most traumatic in the nation's history. Caught in a deeply unpopular and unwinnable war in Vietnam, the world's most powerful state was also facing economic crisis in the form of rising inflation and a looming trade deficit. The affluence of the postwar years was at last beginning to fade, just as a whole raft of 'new' issues burst onto the domestic political scene, including the environment. Many disaffected young Americans joined these movements, marching to protest about race discrimination, the treatment of women, the war in

Vietnam, and the destruction of the natural world around them.

The first section of this chapter tells the story of the conference's origins, and the second gives an account of the domestic situation in the United States in 1968. Once this background is established, the story of American preparations unfolds in the third and fourth sections: 'Initial Responses' and 'Policy Development'. This is followed by a brief section on the make-up of the US delegation, and a short conclusion. The conference itself then forms the first part of Chapter 3.

CONVENING THE CONFERENCE

The resolution to hold a United Nations conference on the human environment was initiated and inspired by Sweden's ambassador to the UN, Sverker Astrom.[1] Astrom had raised the issue during a debate in December 1967 on the peaceful uses of atomic energy, calling on the General Assembly to 'examine the advisability of convening such a conference devoted to the human environment question'.[2] A year later the General Assembly was adopting resolution 2398 decreeing that the first United Nations environmental conference be held in 1972. This conference was to 'provide a framework for a comprehensive consideration of all the problems of human environment within the United Nations'.[3] It was also to 'identify those aspects of [the human environment] that can only or best be solved through international cooperation and agreement'.[4] This preparatory process produced a conference agenda and supporting documentation, a 'Declaration on the Human Environment', and an 'Action Plan'.

In 1969, a Norwegian proposal (submitted on behalf of Sweden) established a conference secretariat and a preparatory committee (eventually composed of twenty-seven nations chosen on a

---

[1] David E. Luchins, 'The United Nations Conference on the Human Environment: A Case-Study of Emerging Political Alignments, 1968–1972', Ph.D. diss., City University of New York, (1977), 52–3. See also Lynton K. Caldwell, *International Environmental Policy: Emergence and Dimensions*, 2nd edn. (Durham, NC: Duke University Press, 1990), 41–54.

[2] Luchins, 'The United Nations Conference', 52–3.

[3] UNGA XXIII, A/PV.1732, p. 5.

[4] UNGA XXIII, resolution 2398, E/4667, p. 23.

regional basis). These preparatory committee (prepcom) meetings, of which four were held, provided the main focus for the pre-Stockholm process.[5] They decided quickly that 'the Conference's main efforts would be devoted to the formulation of specific proposals for concerted national and international action'.[6]

Sweden's desire for an environmental conference was largely inspired by the problem of acid rain although this emphasis on environmental problems as the side-effects of development made Southern nations wary about what industrialized countries intended.[7] As Marion David Tunstall argues: 'The nations of the less-developed South were not enthusiastic in their support of the initial phases of the planning for the Stockholm Conference. The constant references to mistakes which must be avoided alarmed them.'[8] Although tension between the industrialized and industrializing nations placed the future of the conference in jeopardy, an uneasy truce was eventually brokered by the conference secretary-general, Maurice Strong.[9] Rather than just a pollution conference, the South succeeded in reorienting the agenda for Stockholm towards the more contentious question of development.

The preparatory committee for the UNCHE had divided itself into subcommittees and working groups in order to better handle the wealth of material.[10] It was the draft declaration, however,

[5] They were held in New York (10–20 Mar. 1970), Geneva (8–19 Feb. 1971), New York (13–24 Sept. 1971), and New York (6–17 Mar. 1972). Unfortunately, in accordance with General Assembly resolution 2358 (XXIV), no summary records were kept of these committee meetings; A/CONF.48/PC/6.

[6] Luchins, 'The United Nations Conference', 116.

[7] According to John McCormick: 'If there was any single issue that spawned Stockholm, it was acid pollution. Swedish research during the late 1960s had revealed a disturbing increase in the acidity of rain falling in the region... prompting Swedish scientists to demand preventive action' (*The Global Environmental Movement*, 91).

[8] Marion David Tunstall, 'The Influence of International Politics on the Procedures of Multilateral Conferences: The Examples of Conferences on Human Environment and the Law of the Sea', Ph.D. diss., University of Virginia (May 1979), 150.

[9] The appointment of an aid and development expert like Strong was, argues Luchins, an important concession to the South; Luchins 'The United Nations Conference', 117 (see also Tunstall, 'The Influence of International Politics', 139). On the uneasy truce see Luchins, 'The United Nations Conference', 191, 192; McCormick, *The Global Environmental Movement*, 92; and Robin Clarke and Lloyd Timberlake, *Stockholm Plus Ten: Promises, Promises?* (Earthscan/IIED: London, 1982), 7.

[10] One panel, for example, led to the publication—at Maurice Strong's instigation—of Barbara Ward's and Rene Dubos's, *Only One Earth: The Care and Main-*

which exercised the committee and its working groups most. The second prepcom had called for a 'statement of understanding mutually agreed by all countries' which 'could carry moral strength'.[11] Although an initial draft of this declaration was completed by June 1971, the South sought, during the next two preparatory meetings, to insert language about additional funding for environmental projects, a practice the North steadfastly resisted.

As a result, the declaration failed to secure pre-Stockholm agreement and was simply forwarded to the conference for final resolution, together with an Action Plan of substantive initiatives. This brought to an end a preparatory process which had stimulated a new environmental awareness in many countries throughout the world.

THE AMERICAN ENVIRONMENT, 1968–1972

Although international environmentalism on the scale of the Stockholm Conference was placed on the American political agenda by the United Nations, opportunities existed to reformulate and redefine parts of the issue in ways the USA found more conducive. Nevertheless, within the state, both activists and sceptics were partially limited in the extent to which they could define the initial terms of debate. This external agenda-setting function constituted the central avenue of impact for other nations, especially the South, on US foreign environmental policy, able as they were to use the UN successfully to alter the conference's focus.

The growth in domestic American environmentalism by this time had far outstripped that in any other country. A burgeoning protest movement had raised the profile of environmental politics substantially, which helped, in turn, to fuel the development of international expertise, especially through non-state organizations like the International Council of Scientific Unions (ICSU) and IUCN, both bodies in which US scientists were prominent. In addition, the state itself had become involved in more limited

tenance of a Small Planet (London: Penguin/André Deutsch, 1972) which, according to Clive Archer, was an important text in the 'globalist' tradition of thinking about international organizations (see C. Archer, _International Organizations_, 2nd edn. (London: Routledge, 1992), 125–6).

[11] Tunstall, 'The Influence of International Politics', 182.

international co-ordination efforts in arenas where the United States received a favourable hearing, most significantly NATO and the OECD.

As the Stockholm process unfolded, policy-making in the USA became dominated by core state actors, with the State Department in pole position. The opportunities for input by societal groups were carefully controlled. The policy context mattered in several ways: electoral imperatives enhanced the role of activists to whom others looked for positive media coverage on the environment, while the poor publicity created by Vietnam further enabled those who were pro-environmental to argue that a significant effort would be a public relations boon. In the opposite direction, however, concern over trade and aid gave grist to the mill of the conservatives.

Domestic Environmentalism

Awareness of human impact on the natural environment in the United States dates back to the nineteenth century when, in contrast to Europe, and its wholly appropriated territory, significant parts of western North America remained open for settlement.[12] It was only after World War II that previously unwanted land in the West was taken up and, as a result, land prices started to rise.[13] Despite this abundance of territory, Congress passed an act as early as 1864 transferring Yosemite Valley and the Mariposa Grove of Big Trees to California to be preserved for public recreation and resort. Then, in 1872, the world's first national park—Yellowstone—was created in Wyoming.[14]

By the mid-1950s, however, a shift away from traditional conservation towards preservation—or environmentalism—was beginning to take shape, as demographic changes and the spread, ironically, of car ownership opened up 'the great outdoors'.[15] These newly mobile Americans became attuned to 'the aesthetic qualities of nature and wildlands', quickly demonstrating a keen interest in

[12] McCormick, *The Global Environmental Movement*, 10.

[13] Samuel P. Hays, *Beauty, Health and Permanence: Environmental Politics in the United States, 1955–1985* (New York: Cambridge University Press, 1987), 137–8.

[14] McCormick, *The Global Environmental Movement*, 11–12.

[15] On conservation and environmentalism see Henry P. Caulfield, 'The Conservation and Environmental Movements: An Historical Analysis', in Lester (ed.), *Environmental Politics and Policy*, 20–2.

the natural world as a resource to be enjoyed for leisure, rather than cultivated for growth.[16] In 1962, reflecting this concern, President Kennedy established a Bureau of Outdoor Recreation, appointing as its head the environmentalist Stuart Udall (who later became Secretary of the Interior under both Kennedy and Johnson).[17]

This fledgeling environmental movement began to surge with the publication in 1962 of Rachel Carson's enormously influential book on pesticides (especially DDT), *Silent Spring*, described as 'the morning star of modern environmentalism'.[18] According to John McCormick, Carson's book, which sold half a million hardback copies, was one of several factors behind the rise, in the 1960s, of what he terms 'new environmentalism'.[19] This upsurge is traced by Samuel Hays to postwar affluence and the shift to a consumption-based society.[20] This was, in turn, reinforced by demographic changes, with more people moving from the North to the South and West of the United States, and within counties away from resource-poor neighbourhoods to those with better natural amenities.[21]

Public-opinion polls first asked about the environment as an 'issue' in 1965 and, in the same year, White House conferences were held on natural beauty (organized by the President's wife, Lady Bird Johnson) and, more importantly, on international co-operation (at which one topic was 'conserving the world's resources'). This latter gathering, held between 29 November and 1 December, included a proposal for a 'World Heritage Trust' to preserve 'unique and irreplaceable' resources such as the Serengeti

---

[16] Hays, *Beauty, Health, and Permanence*, 53.

[17] Stuart Udall published a best-selling book on the environment: *The Quiet Crisis* (New York: Holt, Rinehart, and Winston, 1963). See also McCormick, *The Global Environmental Movement*, 67.

[18] Rachel Carson, *Silent Spring* (London: Hamish Hamilton, 1962); Neville Brown, 'Planetary Geopolitics', *Millenium: Journal of International Studies*, 19 (1990), 449 (for quotation).

[19] Other social movements, for example, contributed activists who moved into environmentalism as civil rights and the anti-war movement lost momentum; see McCormick, *The Global Environmental Movement*, 47–9, 64.

[20] Samuel P. Hays, 'Three Decades of Environmental Politics: The Historical Context', in Michael J. Lacey (ed.), *Government and Environmental Politics* (Washington DC: Woodrow Wilson Center Press, and Baltimore: The Johns Hopkins University Press, 1991), 22.

[21] Ibid. 26–7. See also Marc K. Landy, Marc J. Roberts, and Stephen R. Thomas, *The Environmental Protection Agency: Asking the Wrong Questions* (New York: Oxford University Press, 1990), 22.

Plains, Angel Falls, and the Grand Canyon.[22] It not only drew together US activists working in the environmental field who would later team up within the state, it also highlighted proposals which would be developed for Stockholm by the Nixon administration, especially the heritage trust (and a convention on trade in endangered species which was signed in 1973).

Finally, in 1969, the National Environmental Policy Act (NEPA) was passed. This landmark piece of legislation established a Council on Environmental Quality (CEQ) within the White House itself. The CEQ was empowered to demand 'environmental impact statements' from other government agencies and departments on major federal projects. In addition, under the terms of the act, President Nixon set up the Environmental Protection Agency (EPA) in 1970. The EPA was designed to regulate and administer the large amount of domestic environmental legislation being produced by Congress.

The growth in environmental awareness was reflected in other ways as well. In April 1970, an 'Earth Day', sponsored by Senator Gaylord Nelson, was marked by a nationwide series of events so extensive that New York's Fifth Avenue was closed to traffic and Congress recessed.[23] Interest-group membership was also increasing rapidly, and new organizations began to emerge to transform this pro-environmental sentiment into federal action. Some existing groups, the Sierra Club (formed in 1892), the National Audubon Society (1896), and the National Wildlife Federation (1936), all had distinguished histories dating back—in the former's case—to the origins of the conservation movement. All grew into large pressure groups from the 1960s onwards. They were then joined by new bodies like the Environmental Defense Fund, Friends of the Earth, the Natural Resources Defense Council, Environmental Action, and Greenpeace. Membership in the traditional groups increased spectacularly—from 124,000 in 1960, to 819,000 in 1969. Augmented by the newer groups, and inspired by Earth Day in 1970, membership rose a further 300,000 between 1969 and 1972 before levelling off until the 1980s.[24]

---

[22] Richard N. Gardner (ed.), *Blueprint for Peace (Being the Proposals of Prominent Americans to the White House Conference on International Cooperation)* (New York: McGraw-Hill, 1966), 142.

[23] McCormick, *The Global Environmental Movement*, 66–7.

[24] Robert Cameron Mitchell, 'From Conservation to Environmental Movement: The Development of Modern Environmental Lobbies', in Lacey (ed.), *Government and Environmental Politics*, 97.

International Environmentalism

Although the UN-sponsored process would come to dominate international environmental politics, the USA was already active on environmental issues in two other international forums. In the North Atlantic Treaty Organization (NATO), the USA had been instrumental in setting up the Committee on the Challenges of Modern Society (CCMS) in December 1969, which was partly to study and promote national research on environmental problems.[25] In addition, the international environment was addressed by an environmental committee of the Organization for Economic Cooperation and Development (OECD), where the trading implications posed by remedial actions were discussed.[26]

Compared with the UN General Assembly, the USA enjoyed a more prominent and powerful role in both the OECD and NATO, composed as they were of industrialized Western and Northern countries already sympathetic to the general objectives of American foreign policy and to environmental agreements which stressed the benefits of industrialization and growth. Most member countries suffered similar pollution-related problems which enabled issues to be more narrowly defined.[27]

The Committee on the Challenges of Modern Society was criticized by some as a public-relations exercise for NATO's non-military functions and as 'blatantly cosmetic in purpose'.[28] For example, it adhered to the American-pioneered principle of single-country pilot projects to try out environmental initiatives. The result was that projects already being pursued by member countries could be regarded as contributions towards international

[25] Brian Johnson, 'The United Nations' Institutional Response to Stockholm: A Case-Study in the International Politics of Institutional Change', *International Organization*, 26/2 (1972), 262.

[26] Gordon J. MacDonald, 'International Institutions for Environmental Management', *International Organization*, 26/2 (1972), 383. MacDonald was vice-chairman of the first CEQ and he represented the United States at OECD environmental meetings.

[27] The architect of America's postwar policy of containment, George Kennan, proposed an International Environmental Agency composed of the ten or so wealthiest countries from both West and East. This body should be staffed, he urged, with 'disinterested' scientists who would gather information and give, presumably, 'neutral' advice (G. Kennan, 'To Prevent a World Wasteland: A Proposal', *Foreign Affairs*, 48/3 (1970).

[28] Johnson, 'The United Nations' Institutional Response to Stockholm', 262; also Wayland Kennet, 'The Stockholm Conference on the Human Environment', *International Affairs*, 48/1 (1972), 35.

cooperation. The CCMS was established as the result of an initiative from President Nixon who hoped to consolidate and deepen the Western alliance in areas outside national security concerns.[29]

Within the OECD, the USA pursued international regulations which were broadly in line with the effects of domestic environmental regulation. This was especially true in the case of the 'polluter-pays' principle.[30] This was a rejection of uniform international regulatory standards which some White House officials believed other countries would abuse by merely subsidizing their industries. American firms would then suffer because of their greater production costs. Others, Gordon MacDonald, for example, appreciated that national standards could be used just as successfully to protect domestic industries (by imposing environmental conditions which one's own firms could more easily meet).[31]

By 1972, therefore, the United States was active in three different arenas. Despite the obvious benefits of pursuing environmental agreements in NATO and the OECD, the global interest in environmental problems ensured that most attention would eventually centre on the United Nations where the USA enjoyed a far less sympathetic hearing.

INITIAL ADMINISTRATION RESPONSES

The two sections which follow demonstrate the dominance of state officials in the policy-making process. These key figures, from the CEQ and State, were almost entirely responsible for the develop-

[29] Letter from Richard Nixon to Russell Train, 14 Jan. 1971, *Nixon Presidential Materials Staff*, US National Archives and Records Administration, White House Central Files (WHCF), Federal Government (Organizations), Box 1. Train was the first chairman of the CEQ.

[30] Despite the polluter-pays principle, the setting of uniform *national* standards provided the rationale, from 1965 onwards, for the large-scale involvement of Congress in environmental affairs. According to Joseph Zimmerman: 'Individual States failed to solve environmental problems, particularly air and water pollution, which had adverse spill-over effects on other States. Television must be credited with generating public pressure upon the Congress to enact preemption statues as news and documentary programs often highlighted the degradation of the environment' (*Contemporary American Federalism* (Leicester: Leicester University Press, 1992), 58). For a classic account of how local-citizen activism stimulated national action see Charles O. Jones, *Clean Air: The Policies and Politics of Pollution Control* (Pittsburgh: University of Pittsburgh Press, 1975).

[31] MacDonald, 'International Institutions', 385.

ment of initiatives for Stockholm. They made little attempt to include societal groups, and Congress, in the process, and the principal battles they fought were internal. Those at State had strategic advantages which gave them an edge in directing policy-making, whereas CEQ, which was well prepared with existing initiatives, was responsible for originating the most substantive proposals. The publicity attending domestic environmental issues at this time failed to open these internal workings to public scrutiny and the policies the USA took to Stockholm owe their development to a few key officials within the state.

Although the United States had not launched the Stockholm process, the State Department began preparing an offer to both pay for and host the conference. This attempt was led by John W. McDonald, a career foreign-service officer who had specialized since 1967 on ECOSOC, and Christian A. Herter, Jnr., the Secretary of State's special assistant for environmental affairs. Both recall the freedom they had to decide on their own initiative what the United States response ought to be to the Stockholm decision. Herter had the environmental portfolio and was left to his own devices in the absence of any interest from his superiors. The UN wasn't a high-profile area within State either and McDonald remembers: 'All of the attention in the State Department was directed towards the political side, so there was very little interest in the subjects I was involved in. And that was just fine with me because it allowed me to do things that I thought were useful.'[32]

One drawback with this lack of senior interest was the absence of either new or budgeted funds. McDonald and Herter wanted Washington, DC as the venue and sought $3 million for this from one of Congress's most high-profile environmental supporters at the time, Senator Edmund Muskie.[33]

I finally went to Senator Muskie, who was very interested in the whole environmental issue, and asked him if he would put forward a bill which would allocate $3 million to the State Department so we could tell the United Nations the United States would like to host the conference. The very day Senator Muskie agreed to do this, the Swedish Government sent

---

[32] Interview with author, 14 April 1993.
[33] On Muskie's somewhat inconsistent brand of environmentalism see Landy *et al.*, *The Environmental Protection Agency*, 26–30.

a formal letter to the Secretary General of the United Nations, saying they would like to host the conference.[34]

The Swedish offer came on 17 February 1969 and was immediately accepted. For the next year, however, uncertainty existed as to precisely what the conference would discuss and how it would be organized. In the United States, as in the UN itself, no institutionalized preparatory process really got underway before 1970 by which time US involvement in three different arenas was causing problems within the Nixon administration as various individuals and agencies jockeyed for priority. This was perhaps unsurprising: the issue was new (thus 'turf wars' were more likely), and the multi-institutional approach meant different parts of the state were active in bodies with varied objectives and rationales. The President's own representative at CCMS, Daniel Patrick Moynihan, came into conflict with the State Department's environmental head, Christian Herter, and with CEQ's Russell Train and Gordon MacDonald, whose brief led them into bilateral negotiations and into discussions at the OECD in Paris.[35]

In an August 1970 memo to President Nixon, national security advisor Henry Kissinger proposed a 'peace treaty' to prevent the three central individuals in international environmental policy (Moynihan, Train, and Herter) from feuding with each other. Kissinger described the situation to President Nixon:

There are three major prongs to the US attempt to generate effective international action to deal with environmental problems. Each prong is under the direction of a separate individual. This has raised some problems and confusion as to which, if any, of our several efforts in the field has priority. Messrs. Moynihan, Train and Herter seem to have reached an

---

[34] John W. McDonald, 'Global Environmental Negotiations: The 1972 Stockholm Conference and Lessons for the Future', working paper WP-2, American Academy of Diplomacy/Paul H. Nitze School of Advanced International Studies, Johns Hopkins University (Jan. 1990), 3.

[35] The split between domestic and foreign environmental policy is demonstrated here by the virtual absence of the Environmental Protection Agency (now one of the largest US government agencies). Despite a wide-ranging remit, its involvement in the early 1970s was limited to implementation in the domestic sphere. The CEQ retained the policy role within the White House and Russell Train recalls that he and the EPA's first administrator, William Ruckelshaus, had an explicit understanding that, despite the rising profile of EPA, the CEQ would continue to lead in international environmental politics. A year after Stockholm Train had become head of the EPA himself.

agreement, but seem also to believe that some sort of language blest by you is desirable in view of the past confusion.[36]

Accompanying this memo was a detailed State Department outline of US policy towards the three major international environmental institutions. It concluded that CCMS was the most appropriate forum for substantive environmental action.[37] The State Department memo did acknowledge, however, that involvement would therefore be limited to Western industrialized countries and that Stockholm did have the advantage of including developing countries.[38]

The concentration on NATO allowed McDonald and Herter room to manœuvre on UN matters and, as a result, State eventually came to play a larger role in the Stockholm Conference than the early emphasis on CCMS would suggest. The White House focus was on NATO and the OECD, especially after Russell Train took over from Moynihan and brought both under the auspices of the CEQ. The shadow of the State Department affected this decision too. In an intra-White House memo of 7 January 1971, John Whitaker, deputy to Nixon's chief domestic-policy advisor, John Ehrlichman, recommended Russell Train for the job at CCMS by arguing that an alternative choice would 'reduce Train's ability to outmaneuver Herter at State on the UN Conference for '72 where we already have a bad situation with Herter running the form and protocol and nobody in State understanding the environment. Train is helping, but if he doesn't get CCMS, he will get pushed out by State.'[39]

In 1970, therefore, as the administration established a formal policy-making process for Stockholm, fears about the ascendancy of State were already evident. This formal process was comprised by a State-hosted task force named the Committee on International Environmental Affairs. It was in the Office of

[36] Memo, Kissinger to Nixon, 24 Aug. 1970, *Nixon Presidential Materials Staff*, WHCF, Welfare, Box 6. The memo is signed 'Haig for HAK for Pres' by Kissinger's deputy Alexander Haig.

[37] Memo, 'Summary description and appraisal of the major international organizations dealing with the environment', U. Alexis Johnson to Nixon, 24 Aug. 1970, *Nixon Presidential Materials Staff*, WHCF, Welfare, Box 6.

[38] The President had publicly pledged American support for the Stockholm Conference in a speech to the United Nations General Assembly in Sept. 1969.

[39] Memo, Whitaker to Cole, 7 Jan. 1971, *Nixon Presidential Materials Staff*, WHCF, Federal Government (Organizations), Box 1.

Environmental Affairs—within the Bureau of International Scientific and Technological Affairs—and Herter was its chairman.[40] This gave Herter and McDonald (who was secretary) a pivotal position as 'honest broker' between several competing agencies and departments.[41]

Whereas other arms of government had specific interests to advance, the broad nature of the State Department's brief gave it the opportunity to establish an overall framework for discussions. No other group became involved in *all* aspects of the process in this way. Each was active in subcommittees on discrete issues but only the State Department participated on every dimension. This gave State an agenda-setting function described as follows: 'We did not have the expertise to make some of those things happen. But the State Department is the senior agency in our government . . . and so when there is a strong leadership role there then other people fall in behind. By having a focal point with knowledge and ability and asking people to do different things they got done.'[42]

McDonald describes the attitude both he and Herter brought to this task in the following terms: 'Chris and I were a good team. We worked well together and we wanted to make something happen as he is an activist too and I believe a lot in the power of individuals to make a difference.'[43] The lack of detailed knowledge generally about environmental problems, coupled with McDonald's knowledge of the UN and Herter's attendance as US representative at the four UN preparatory meetings held before Stockholm, gave the State Department a further advantage.

The *political* role of the State Department also mattered. Briefing papers on all the political questions were drawn up by State. Other agencies, according to McDonald, were just not interested. In addition, the State Department was responsible for the overall policy outlook contained in a *scope* paper. Thus it fell to the State Department to set the overall tone of the delegation and to integrate the various fragmented strands in this one document, described as follows:

---

[40] The formation of a task force like this was Nixon's standard practice.

[41] For a list of involved agencies and departments, see Secretary of State's Advisory Committee, *Safeguarding Our World Environment*, Department of State publication 8630, Mar. 1972, 29.

[42] John McDonald, interview with author, 14 Apr. 1993.

[43] Ibid.

It is designed for the information of all the delegation to put the whole conference in perspective—why is it important for the United States to support the conference? And this allows the people who are working on one small segment of the process to understand how it fits in with the whole. A scope paper is very difficult to develop and very difficult to clear because you have to have everything in there that we want as a US initiative, we're talking about the style, the approach, the stance of the United States and so on. And we try to get those out maybe three months before the conference starts as what you have to do always is educate the delegation, and educate the people the delegation is interacting with. So that's why that is an important vehicle.[44]

In addition, many participants cared little about the environment and were only involved, according to Christian Herter, because they knew President Nixon and his closest aides were interested for electoral reasons.[45]

The Institutional Process

The task force established in 1970 was the focal point for policy initiation and the machinery through which State and the CEQ dominated the process. At the first meeting, the need for co-ordination became clear:

We invited 45 different government agencies to attend and some 60 people gathered around the table. We explained why we were there, what our plans were, and how we wanted to involve them. I then went around the table and asked each agency to define the one word 'environment'. You would think it was a very simple thing to do. We got forty-five different definitions—and nobody was going to change their definition. We went on to the next agenda item.[46]

Although the agencies on this task force were all from the core

---

[44] Ibid.

[45] Interview with author, 8 Apr. 1993. Nixon read and heavily annotated quite lengthy articles on the relationship between environmental politics and broader industrial processes by writers such as Peter Drucker and Abram Chayes, see *Nixon Presidential Materials Staff*, White House Subject Files, Confidential Files, Federal Government (Organizations), Box 17. In a memo to chief-of-staff Bob Haldeman, however, John Ehrlichman makes it clear the President was not naturally sympathetic to environmentalists, describing him as having 'an instinctive distrust of this issue' (memo, Ehrlichman to Haldeman, 'Re Reelection campaign', 6 Nov. 1971, Haldeman, Box 117, *Nixon Presidential Materials Staff*, p. 6).

[46] McDonald, 'Global Environmental Negotiations', 3–4.

state itself, the influence of State and CEQ was still pronounced, especially in the formulation of the USA's two most prominent initiatives at Stockholm; a $100 million voluntary fund for the environment and a new UN institution to co-ordinate environmental actions. In addition, the CEQ also promoted several developments of which the World Heritage Trust and a moratorium on whaling were the most ambitious. The only pressure external to this came from a Secretary of State's Advisory Committee, established early in 1971 under the chairmanship of Senator Howard Baker, and from hearings held in Congress early in 1972.

The Secretary of State's Advisory Committee was the only organized attempt made by national officials to solicit the views of the public. The committee first held open hearings in Miami and Washington in 1971 before visiting Chicago, New York, Ohio, Houston, Washington, and San Francisco in 1972. Its membership (just under thirty) was dominated by the business community although prominent national figures included future President Jimmy Carter and Lady Bird Johnson.

Despite being a State Department creation, the advisory committee enjoyed less than full co-operation. By December 1971, seven months after its inception, the committee still had no administrative support and only a visit by its chairman to Secretary of State William P. Rogers led to a staff being hired in January 1972. The advisory committee issued two reports a few months later but its recommendations went unadopted by the administration. In fact United States policy was all but decided by January 1972.

One member of the committee, Dennis Hayes, of pressure group Environmental Action, told the *New York Times*: 'There was no real interchange between the advisory committee and its staff and Mr Herter and his.' The *Times* continued: 'There was "utter disregard", Mr Hayes said, by the State department and the intergovernmental committee of the advisory committee's recommendations on key issues.'[47]

On several important questions the advisory committee offered alternative recommendations to those adopted by the US government. For example, the committee recommended in favour of the General Assembly not ECOSOC having overall responsibility for

[47] *New York Times*, 22 May 1972, 23.

UN environmental policy.[48] It also argued that the US ought to be more receptive to demands for East Germany to be allowed to take part in the conference in order to ensure 'universal participation'.[49] Finally, it suggested that a voluntary fund of $100 million each year was required, not $100 million every five years as the USA actually proposed.[50] This lack of input for the advisory committee was noted by Senator Claiborne Pell who claimed the USA had filed a national report with the UN long before there had been any input from these societal sources.[51]

The advisory committee's two reports were a thirty-page brief entitled *Safeguarding our World Environment* and a final report called *Stockholm and Beyond*. Although the later, more detailed, report did not diverge markedly from US interests as perceived by the State Department, the differences of opinion were, none the less, significant. For example, the advisory committee's recommendation for $100 million a year as a suggested fund target included a formula for assessing contribution which would have made any US offer more of a requirement than an act of largesse.[52]

The committee had originally been seen in part as a way to promote interest-group involvement, albeit with a strong business element. Russell Train, chairman of the board at the World Wildlife Fund in 1993, saw the absence of interest-group pressure at the time in the following light: 'I can make two points on it. One, I don't think that most of the mainstream environmental organizations in the United States at that time had much of an international dimension to their thinking. And secondly, the connection between

[48] 'U.N. Conference on Human Environment: Preparations and Prospects', Subcommittee on Oceans and International Environment of the Committee on Foreign Relations, the Senate of the United States Congress, 3, 4, 5 May 1972, CIS NO:72-S381–22, p. 107.

[49] Ibid.

[50] Secretary of State's Advisory Committee, *Stockholm and Beyond* (Department of State pub. no. 8657, International Organization and Conference Series 101 (Apr. 1972)), p. 132.

[51] Senate Subcommittee on Oceans and International Environment, 3, 4, 5 May 1972, pp. 5–7. The State Department's 'national report' to the UN was submitted to the conference secretariat in Apr. 1971. The more substantive proposals on international action were finalized later although on funding, for instance, the task force recommendation was sent to President Nixon via the Secretary of State in Jan. 1972.

[52] *Stockholm and Beyond*, p. 3. Principal differences apart, however, the report was in no way a critique of broader policy direction. Indeed, Senator Baker was a member of the US delegation to Stockholm.

domestic policy and international policy really just hadn't been made that much at that time.'[53] Christian Herter, alternatively, recalls some pressure from interest groups but makes the point that their inexperience in pressuring government, especially the insulated State Department, rendered their efforts ineffective. He remembers:

There were interest groups; they weren't nearly as influential as they've become since. I can remember very well, all over the place we had environmental groups that sprang up. All of them were besieging me and others in the State Department . . . they had a whole bunch of demands and I can remember saying that if you people get yourselves together we can deal with you, we'll talk with you about this thing, we'll put on a show, we'll go over the whole thing but we can't endlessly keep answering questions. They refused to in the beginning. Everybody thought they were the most important environmental organization known to Man . . . and the result was a certain amount of chaos.[54]

The inexperience of these groups, many of which had only just been formed, coupled with the expertise within the State Department and the almost total control the state had over policy formation, left the advisory committee as the only body, bar a few editorials and witnesses before congressional committees, to make any societal impact on the policy process.

Nevertheless, congressional hearings did provide the most detailed account of the thinking behind the administration's policy positions for Stockholm. Witnesses, especially Christian Herter and Russell Train, were questioned comprehensively about all aspects of American involvement. Of the final official delegation of thirty-five, twelve were congressmen or senators, including Claiborne Pell and Clifford Case.

Although representatives held a hearing into the conference as early as November 1969, urging the USA to adopt a leadership role at Stockholm,[55] the main House hearings, before the subcommittee on international organizations, weren't conducted until 15 and 16 March 1972. The main Senate hearings were held by the subcom-

[53] Interview with author, 5 May 1993.
[54] Interview with author, 8 Apr. 1993.
[55] 'U.S. participation in 1972 United Nations Conference on Human Environment', Subcommittee on International Organizations and Movements, Committee on Foreign Affairs, House of Representatives, 13 Nov. 1969; CIS NO:70-H381-5.

mittee on oceans and international environment in early May 1972. The House discussions were the most comprehensive on Stockholm and revolved around the question of trading implications which might arise from environmental initiatives. The tone was set by Seymour Halpern (New York) who proposed a national commission be set up on international trade and the environment. He told subcommittee members:

Now that we are all threatened by a common menace, it becomes clear that the most bothersome obstacle to effective world consensus on environmental protection has been each individual nation's fear that strict pollution measures at home will ultimately result in undeserved trade and balance-of-payments disadvantages abroad.[56]

Halpern proposed neither a 'lazy social policy' of de-escalating domestic environmental legislation, nor tariffs and subsidies, but a commission to gather information in order to better estimate US 'ability to pay', as well as urging a commitment to international agreement. The principal State Department official at the hearings, Christian Herter, argued that such a commission was unnecessary and that the fears of many congressmen about trading disadvantages were misplaced. He told committee members:

... other developed countries are raising their environmental standards and our own observations are that as time goes on, the rest of the world, in fact our major trading partners, will be forced to continue to move in this direction in response to growing public pressures and concern about the environment.[57]

These congressional hearings provided a forum for the discussion of US policy and its underlying motivations. Despite claims to the contrary at the time, administration policy was set by this stage and they served more as opportunities for administration justification. Although a considerable amount of congressional legislation was being passed on the domestic environment, the international side remained a matter on which the Nixon administration was expected to initiate.

---

[56] Subcommittee on International Organizations and Movements, 15, 16 Mar., p. 4.
[57] Ibid., p. 29.

POLICY DEVELOPMENT FOR STOCKHOLM

Although the motivations of key officials involved with conference preparations differed, they shared the hope that the USA would be prominent in efforts to protect the international environment. Within the CEQ, both MacDonald and Train tried at times to use this aspect of the political context in their favour. In a memo to Henry Kissinger, for example, Train explained that: 'It is our belief that the U.S. currently has a strong position of leadership in environmental matters that should be built on. Specifically we need to develop sharp and substantive proposals that will be of interest not only to the industrialized countries but also to the developing world.'[58] Referring to a report compiled by Gordon MacDonald, who toured five Asian countries in October 1970, Train claimed:

The most important observation was that President Nixon's leadership in the environment was widely recognized and acclaimed by government leaders, academics and press. The strong substantive actions taken by this Administration are recognized as putting the U.S. in a position of world leadership with respect to the environment. This positive image of the U.S. is to be contrasted with a large number of divisive issues in which we are involved abroad.[59]

Others, especially within the White House, saw in the environment an issue which might prove a vote winner for the president. The scale of environmental politics on a domestic level gave the issue high saliency and, in 1971, John Whitaker was entrusted with developing an overall strategy. He told the president that the 'liberal-dominated press' were 'enthralled by the vocal minority of environmental activists' and saw the administration's pro-environmental acts as the work of a few 'white hats', namely Russell Train and EPA administrator William Ruckelshaus. In addition, Whitaker argued that Nixon's stance of 'reason and moderation' on the trade-off between the environment and development was perceived as negative, largely because of the aforementioned 'conspiracy theory' perpetuated by the media.[60]

[58] Memo, Train to Kissinger, 3 Dec. 1970, WHCF, International Organizations, Box 16, *Nixon Presidential Materials Staff*.
[59] Ibid., pp. 1–2.
[60] Memo, Whitaker to Nixon via Ehrlichman, 3 Dec. 1971, White House Central Files, Welfare, Box 9, *Nixon Presidential Materials Staff.*

Whitaker later wrote a book about environmental policy during these years in which he defended the value of actions taken by Richard Nixon. In one passage, Whitaker demonstrates the deep difference between domestic and foreign policy at this time, illustrating in the process the suspicion Republican sceptics have generally shared of the environmental movement. Whitaker records:

On the last day of 1970, Richard Nixon signed the Clean Air Amendments into law. Curiously, in retrospect, there was little debate within the administration about the wisdom of signing the bill. Besides, given the nearly hysterical support for the environmental movement, a veto would have been futile: Congress would have promptly overriden it.[61]

In his memo to Nixon, Whitaker recorded his concern that the issue was being grabbed by one of the Democratic front-runners for president in 1972, Senator Edmund Muskie. He told the President:

While it is not your style generally to demagogue an issue like this, I presently see no other way out of this dilemma. Muskie has launched a major campaign against you based on the difference between your rhetoric and actions in the environment. He is hitting us both for attempting to bring sanity to the water bill and for tying Ruckelshaus' hands on enforcement of the Clean Air Act. I don't think you can afford to let him style himself as Mr. Clean while painting you as the protector of the polluters.[62]

Whitaker proposed Nixon make 'a strong signal of your personal involvement and commitment'. In addition, in March 1972, he wrote to Russell Train telling him:

There is no one within the Administration who can take your place as the leading advocate on the environment issue. In terms of background, ability and scope of responsibility your are in the unique situation to present and advocate the President's complete environmental program. Because his time to become personally involved in publicizing his domestic program is so limited, and because each event he will do will become increasingly characterized as cynically partisan, we must capitalize on your position as his chief environmental advisor to be his public surrogate on the issue.[63]

[61] John C. Whitaker, *Striking a Balance: Environment and Natural Resources Policy in the Nixon–Ford Years* (Washington, DC: American Enterprise Institute, 1976), 93.

[62] Memo, Whitaker to Nixon, 3 Dec. 1971, p. 3.

[63] Memo, Whitaker to Train, 3 Mar. 1972, White House Central Files, Federal Government (Organizations), Box 1, *Nixon Presidential Materials Staff*.

Whitaker stressed media exposure and told Train: 'You might be thinking about which forthcoming events, such as Earth Week, the Stockholm Conference, and your Annual Report, might be appropriate to use as an entre for national television exposure.'[64] Whitaker recommended that Train hire a full-time staff member to schedule publicity trips and media exposure.

It is also clear from a further memo, sent by Train to Ehrlichman in December 1971, that Nixon's advisors were already pressuring him to enhance the President's environmental profile. The first paragraph of Train's memo reads:

In our discussion earlier this week of an environmental strategy designed to insure a strong position for the President on this major issue in the coming year, I emphasized that a positive environmental legislative program should be a keystone of such a strategy.[65]

In this memo, Train used the domestic political context to argue that 'the press and the public and our political opponents will be quick in this political year to seize upon any evidence of backing off or slackening up in interest'.[66] He argued for 'a wide-ranging, hard-hitting set of new proposals' and concluded by warning that failure to produce it 'could add to the impression left by the press that the Administration's commitment to the environment is waning'.[67]

It is clear that the Nixon administration was well aware of the need to cultivate environmental votes. This demonstrates not only that the administration was sensitive to its public image on environmental issues, but also that it was actively seeking positive environmental publicity.[68] Thus, the high profile enjoyed by Russell Train

[64] Memo, Whitaker to Train, 3 Mar. 1971, p. 2.
[65] Memo, Train to Ehrlichman, 3 Dec. 1971, White House Central Files, Federal Government (Organizations), Box 1, *Nixon Presidential Materials Staff*.
[66] Ibid., p. 1.
[67] Ibid., p. 2.
[68] In a memo written for Nixon's chief of staff H. R. Haldeman in 1972, pollster Robert Teeter argued the environment would remain important because 'it is an easy and attractive issue for the media to cover and an even more attractive one for politicians because it has virtually no negative side'. He claimed the Republicans might get young middle-class voters on the environment but on no other issue, concluding: 'I do not think the environment will be one of the primary issues in the campaign, but I do think it will be an important secondary issue and that a small but significant number of people may vote on [*sic*]. Even if this group is only 2 or 3% they could be critical to us in close states and I see no risk in appealing to them. While I realize that the President must act responsibly, there is no risk in terms of losing votes with strong environmental position [*sic*]' (memo, Teeter to Haldeman,

was partly a result of domestic environmentalism which in turn allowed him to become heavily involved in international environmental politics.

Despite this concurrence of aims, there were clearly differences over the degree and form which US involvement should take. Most officials wanted the USA to 'lead' but this meant different things to different people. To some, it entailed an exemplary effort based on a significant commitment, to others it meant co-ordinating or *steering* the process to suit what they perceived as American interests. What is noticeable, however, is the extent to which officials shared an acceptance of the limited scope of policy-making on the international environment. Even those stressing leadership by example had a restricted view of the international sphere, reducing its importance at the same time as accentuating the much greater value of domestic legislation which, if universally adopted, would solve certain collective action problems. It is in this way that the achievements of environmentalism at home, which they all viewed as considerable, established the benchmark or status quo which international activities had to respect.

The task force generated broad policies and specific proposals centred around money, institutional reorganization, future monitoring, conventions on whaling and ocean dumping, and a World Heritage Trust. Common to these proposals was a stress on the split between national and international policy. In official statements, the USA maintained that most environmental actions were more properly undertaken at the domestic level. This circumscribed the scope of international actions, forestalling arguments about the responsibility of the developed world for its poorer neighbours.

In this way, the Stockholm agenda's reorientation towards development was partly neutralized. Christian Herter made this domestic:international distinction explicit, for example, in a speech to the second session of the UNCHE preparatory committee in

---

Committee for the Re-election of the President, 6 Jan. 1972, *Nixon Presidential Materials Staff*, Haldeman Papers, Box 338). Teeter's arguments appear to have been 'commissioned' as a response to an earlier Ehrlichman memo advocating more environmentalism (to garner votes in what Ehrlichman calls a 'cold, calculating, and thoroughly political' way) (see memo, Ehrlichman to Haldeman, 'Re Reelection campaign', 6 Nov. 1971, Haldeman, Box 117, p. 6, and memo, Higby to Strachan, 'Ehrlichman's memo on campaign', 14 Dec. 1971, Haldeman, Box 338, both *Nixon Presidential Materials Staff*).

Geneva in February 1971. He argued that 'the agenda divides pretty distinctly into two categories, primarily global or regional action items and primarily national action items'.[69] Actions requiring global efforts included the need for monitoring and co-ordination but reflected little of the South's concerns for equitable development.

One of the task force's first publications was the US 'national report', as requested of every country by the UNCHE secretary-general. Written in the State Department, and submitted in April 1971, it was strong on domestic detail but unrevealing on foreign policy and generally vague about substantive American initiatives. A more detailed set of documents was in preparation within the task force and was transmitted to Strong, Secretary of State William P. Rogers, and Senator Baker's advisory committee in August 1971.[70] These documents contained detailed analyses of problems ranging from the loss of genetic pools, soil conservation, research and monitoring, growth and the environment, and a World Heritage Trust. Extensive suggestions were also made about steps the USA felt the conference ought to consider.

One of the tasks of the conference secretariat was to prepare an 'Action Plan' for Stockholm and the State Department was keen to have as much input into this agenda as possible. This meant the submission of extra reports as well as spending time in discussion with Strong and his staff. This process worked in the following way: 'We would often sit down informally, exchange ideas with them, and even send up position papers to try to help them develop what we called a "plan of action". The plan of action was going to be the document that the World Conference was going to focus on. We tried subtly, and sometimes not so subtly, to get our ideas into that plan, believing that if we got them there first, there would be more opportunity for a favorable discussion than if we had to do it at the conference itself.'[71]

The documents sent to Strong in August 1971 did not represent

[69] Christian A. Herter, Jnr., speech to second preparatory committee meeting, Geneva, 9 Feb. 1971; *Department of State Bulletin* (15 Mar. 1971), 335–6.

[70] 'Suggestions Developed Within the US Government for Consideration by the Secretary-General of the 1972 UNCHE', Department of State Publication 8608 (Aug. 1971), International Conference and Organization series 97.

[71] McDonald, 'Global Environmental Negotiations', 6.

definitive US policy, merely 'suggestions for discussion', but in a covering letter to the Secretary of State, Christian Herter noted: 'We are now turning our attention and efforts to the study of these papers to determine this Government's priority interest among the many proposals.'[72] Priorities which emerged included marine pollution and global environmental monitoring. For example, the report included a draft convention on marine pollution which Russell Train had been pursuing for some time. It was considered at Stockholm and, after being endorsed by the conference, was finally settled in London later in 1972. Russell Train recalls that 'we had already passed domestic ocean dumping legislation in the US and this was an international extension of it which made a great deal of sense and was on our home agenda to get done'.[73]

Before the Senate in May 1972, Train narrowed US aims to four: establishing a new institution, endorsing the World Heritage Trust, signing a convention on ocean dumping, and securing a co-ordinated monitoring framework.[74] A ten-year moratorium on whaling was also promoted. The World Heritage Trust was to ensure the preservation of 'certain areas of such unique worldwide value that they should be treated as part of the heritage of all mankind and accorded special recognition as part of a World Heritage Trust'.[75] Train claimed this Trust would 'help to preserve on a worldwide basis the unique scientific and cultural areas that can be considered of significance to all mankind, rather than simply of importance to individual nations'.[76]

This Trust was born out of a paper presented to Lyndon Johnson's White House Conference on Cooperation in 1965. Russell Train was one of its co-authors and he recalls proposing the Trust and, as CEQ chairman, getting it into Richard Nixon's environmental message to Congress in 1971.[77] The other authors were

[72] Covering letter, Christian A. Herter, Jnr. to William P. Rogers, 10 Aug. 1971, accompanying 'Suggestions Developed Within the US Government'.
[73] Interview with author, 5 May 1993.
[74] Senate Subcommittee on Oceans and the International Environment, 3, 4, 5 May 1972, p. 8.
[75] 'Suggestions Developed Within the US Government', 94.
[76] House Subcommittee on International Organizations and Movements, 15, 16 Mar. 1972, p. 50.
[77] Interview with author, 5 May 1993. Before entering government service (he became Under-Secretary of the Interior in 1969), Train had been one of the found-

Harold Coolidge and Joe Fisher. The CEQ's chief scientist in the early 1970s, Lee Talbot, remembers the Trust as Coolidge's idea (and describes him as the unacknowledged 'father of international conservation').[78] This Trust was adopted by IUCN (of which Talbot was a board member) in 1966 and worked up into a legal convention. Thus, when Talbot joined CEQ he recalls informing Train of his forthright intentions:

I told him I had an agenda that I wanted to see the council deal with—this included what became CITES, the World Heritage Trust, and a series of other things involving both national and international, and he said go to it.[79]

The two most important prongs of US policy, however, revolved around the financing of future international environmental co-ordination.

THE VOLUNTARY FUND AND
THE ADMINISTRATOR

The most important specific proposals the United States made concerned the funding of international environmental initiatives, and the type of institutional mechanism to be established in the United Nations after Stockholm. The initial proposals for US policy entered the task force through CEQ which was already well prepared for such an interagency process. Lee Talbot remembers: 'Some of us were planning really in advance of that and laying out what we thought out to be some of the component parts. Among them what became UNEP, and the fund, and a series of actions like the endangered species convention, World Heritage Trust. When we got this formal inter-agency committee going we really had a head start, we already had our agenda.'[80]

Talbot recalls that battles over jurisdiction formed a large part of these task force meetings. CEQ had, he records:

ing trustees of the World Wildlife Fund in 1961, and president of the Conservation Foundation in 1965.

[78] Interview with author, 14 Apr. 1994. Talbot was also director of international affairs. He joined the CEQ from the Smithsonian on a one-year loan which extended to eight years.

[79] Interview with author, 14 Apr. 1994. CITES—the Convention on International Trade in Endangered Species—was signed in Washington in 1973.

[80] Interview with author, 14 Apr. 1994.

well fleshed-out proposals at the time of the first meeting and there was no argument of business versus environment at all, on any of these issues, the arguments had nothing to do with that but rather questions of how do you do it, what mechanisms will work, and rather bureaucratic kinds of things . . . there was a great deal of inter-agency competition for turf, territoriality, they were the kind of issues we had rather than is this a good idea or is it not a good idea.[81]

The State Department's UN specialist, John McDonald, remembers working on these proposals in the interagency process. He claims:

We decided it was up to the United States, since we were taking a major leadership role in preparation for the conference, to develop a workable model which would restructure the United Nations and enable it to cope with the problems of the global environment. This turned out to be my task. A great deal of time and effort was spent on this issue. We knew that money would be important. Initially we talked about a $2 million fund for the environment. I realized we weren't going to get very far with that kind of money, so I came in to a task force meeting one day and proposed a $100 million United States contribution to the fund. The task force finally agreed and we made a presentation to the White House using that figure.[82]

The figure of $100 million as a US contribution was transmitted to the White House unofficially in autumn of 1971 and was rejected by the Office of Management and Budget (OMB) as too high. The task force stuck to its proposal, however, and in January 1972 the Secretary of State officially recommended that President Nixon approve such a fund and announce it in his February environmental message to Congress. Secretary Rogers urged: 'I recommend that you propose the establishment of a United Nations Fund on the Environment and pledge substantial United States support over three years beginning in FY 1974. Internal staff work has been prepared on the basis of a total United States commitment of $100 million.'[83]

This fund, to be voluntary, would be co-ordinated by an administrator and, in its scope and operation, would 'be the source for

[81] Ibid.
[82] McDonald, 'Global Environmental Negotiations', 4–5.
[83] Memo, 'United States International Environmental Initiative', Rogers to Nixon, 12 Jan. 1972, *Nixon Presidential Materials Staff*, White House Central Files, International Organizations, Box 37.

financing programs and projects of global or regional significance, the benefits of which would be reaped by the industrial as well as the developing nations'.[84] In order to assuage fears about prosperity, the memo argued: 'Providing a large share of U.S. support in equipment and services would assist in employing greater numbers of U.S. scientists and technicians and providing increased opportunities for U.S. manufacturers to capture markets for monitoring, research, and eventually control equipment.'[85] In the memo, the State Department made clear that the fund would not be 'merely another channel for technical assistance to developing nations'.[86]

Russell Train and Henry Kissinger reviewed the Secretary of State's memo and concluded that the adoption of its proposals was domestically and internationally desirable. They argued, however, that the USA ought only to commit $50 million over five years starting in Financial Year 1974 (while proposing that the total fund be $100 million).[87] This total figure of $100 million was seen by Train and Kissinger as enough for 'psychological impetus'. They also argued that making the US contribution dependent on matching funds, up to a total of $50 million, would encourage donations from other countries, would make the package more saleable in Congress and more consistent with the President's 'burden-sharing' philosophy.

The only 'issue' was over the initial level of US commitment. OMB director George Shultz wanted a 40 per cent commitment (up to a total of $40 million). Train and Kissinger argued that 50–50 was better on the grounds that it dramatized US leadership, sounded less 'permanent' than 40–60, and was more likely to provide the kind of programme the USA wanted. In their memo to the President they concluded:

The initiative would provide a focus for international activity in the environmental field. This would be useful in protecting the environment, and good for the UN. It would also be consistent with your position that the UN should address the new tasks for diplomacy.[88]

[84] Memo, Rogers to Nixon, 12 Jan. 1972, annex 6, p. 2.
[85] Ibid., annex 5, p. 4.
[86] Ibid., annex 6, p. 1.
[87] Memo, Kissinger and Train to Nixon, 25 Jan. 1972, *Nixon Presidential Materials Staff*, White House Central Files, International Organizations, Box 37, 'Economic and Social Council, 1969–1974'.
[88] Ibid.

This proposal was approved by the President and submitted to Congress as part of his environmental message in February 1972, the level of funding having been settled at OMB's figure of 40 rather than 50 per cent.

As far as the new institutional set-up was concerned, the task force decided that a high-level official with a small permanent staff in the office of the secretary-general was appropriate. The concept of a single administrator had been tied intricately (within the 12 January State Department memo) to the question of spending decisions associated with the voluntary fund proposal. In other words, the fund came first. The administrator and secretariat were to administer the fund. It had three dimensions: an administrator at a senior level within the UN, an intergovernmental group to guide the secretariat, and an interagency group to co-ordinate the activities of the various UN bodies concerned with environmental problems. This proposal required some 'selling' by the State Department, but eventually a new if circumscribed institution was proposed by the United States at the fourth prepcom, held in New York in March 1972. It was also outlined by Russell Train to the House hearings during the same month.[89]

The USA's two main initiatives reflected a limited commitment towards the solution of existing environmental problems and the early recognition of future ones. The voluntary fund was a significant step in terms of international commitment, but was to be established at a relatively low level of funding and was certainly not a device for reinvigorated aid to the developing world or for technology transfer. The climate of fiscal conservatism at the time reinforced this, with aid-spending a programme high on Congress's hit-list.[90]

Thus, even if some had wanted to make an argument for greater

[89] McDonald argues that the 'State Department model' included 'the creation of a new UN agency (UNEP), with a permanent secretariat staff to carry out the recommendations coming out of Stockholm' ('Global Environmental Negotiations', 5). The USA actually pursued something less ambitious and certainly less 'autonomous' than UNEP.

[90] In addition, aid gave Congress an opportunity to pressure Nixon on Vietnam. Senate anger at its impotence fuelled this fire. Willard Thorp argues that 'since foreign policy does not often come up for congressional action, the foreign aid legislation offered a symbolic opportunity to react to the existing foreign policy posture by expressing a desire for the United States to reduce its international responsibilities' (Willard L. Thorp, *The Reality of Foreign Aid* (New York: Council on Foreign Relations/Praeger Publishers, 1971), 11).

aid, there was simply no sizeable strand of popular support upon which they could draw. Any official making this case would be without 'resources' and so could not prevail. Time and again, therefore, US officials resisted what they saw as development aid masquerading as environmental support.[91]

Congressional concern about the US economy spilled over into trade as well. In relation to environmental protection, congressional concerns embraced three strands: that national pollution-control measures would hit US firms, or that international standards would, or that other nations' domestic standards would constitute non-tariff barriers. At Senate hearings, Senator Harrison A. Williams, Jnr. (New Jersey) urged US delegates to Stockholm to 'advocate and support enforceable multilateral accords to achieve standards and regulations to promote environmental protection'.[92] Meanwhile, Seymour Halpern argued that the USA had 'far excelled all other nations of the world in its efforts to curb pollution'.[93]

This all gave strength to the sceptics. In the White House, Secretary of Commerce Maurice Stans had already fought to limit some domestic environmental initiatives which Train's CEQ was proposing. Stans claimed jobs were being lost and, although backed by Nixon for electoral reasons, Train's intra-White House memos reflect his concern to stress how the international trading and commercial implications of US proposals were always uppermost in the mind of environmental officials. For example, in listing why the USA had a 'significant self-interest in international environmental improvement', Train told John Ehrlichman that:

... it is in the U.S. competitive interest to have other nations raise environmental standards (and thus their production costs) and strengthen their enforcement of those standards.[94]

and that:

... international concern over environment provides a major potential market for the export of U.S. pollution abatement technology—estimated

[91] See, for example, Department of State Bulletins: 11 Jan. 1971, p. 69; and 10 Apr. 1972, p. 562.

[92] Senate Subcommittee on Oceans and International Environment, 3, 4, 5 May 1972, p. 50.

[93] House Subcommittee on International Organizations and Movements, 15, 16 Mar. 1972, p. 5.

[94] Memo, Train to Ehrlichman, 20 Sept. 1971, Nixon Presidential Materials Staff, White House Central Files, Federal Government (Organizations), Box 1.

by industrial sources to be somewhere in the range of $250–$400 million annually. (A trade show entirely centred on U.S. pollution cleanup technology opens in Tokyo December 6).[95]

Thus, officials in the State Department and CEQ used strategic and contextual advantages as best they could to advance their causes, including an environment fund and a new if limited institution.

What of other key elements in the international political context? There were two elements of *détente* which affected Stockholm. First, the US decision to recognize communist China made Stockholm the first major UN conference attended by a full Chinese delegation. Secondly, the Nixon Doctrine entailed a qualified withdrawal by the USA from the unilateral leadership of Western international institutions and more partnership in what the President called 'new dimensions of diplomacy', one of which was the environment. In the third annual foreign policy report to Congress in 1972, Nixon attributed these 'new dimensions' to the 'rise of modern science and the technological revolution' which had raised new issues as the by-product of dealing with old ones.

American involvement in Vietnam also allowed activists to argue for the value of a pro-environment stance in offsetting the poor publicity the war was creating for the administration. Indeed, criticism of the war was pressed very publicly at the conference proper with allegations of 'ecocide' and superpower imperialism.

The story told thus far reveals the key role of state officials—and their interaction with the political contexts within which they worked—in explaining American foreign environmental policy for the 1972 conference. Both industry and environmental groups played a peripheral role in the formation of policy for Stockholm. This failure to exert direct influence has two explanations; first, the State Department and the CEQ proved well insulated from direct domestic societal pressure; and secondly, interest groups formed in the domestic arena were too poorly organized in the first years of the 1970s to effectively campaign for *foreign* policy choices.

The State Department's most significant advantage over other domestic actors was its non-accountability to a specific American constituency. Although subject to the will of the prevailing administration, the State Department had space to pursue its own

[95] Ibid.

agenda. The very way it was organized made it difficult for societal groups on the 'outside' to make an impression, and it had no need to court popularity with the public at large because to the extent that 'popularity' mattered at all, this was dependent on the administration.

This insulation from outside domestic interests led the State Department to establish the citizens advisory committee which, as we have seen, had little or no impact on policy at all. One member (who was also on the US Stockholm delegation), J. Ross Vincent, was highly critical of the co-operation State had provided to the committee.[96] In a post-Stockholm congressional hearing, Vincent quoted the submission of one prominent environmentalist, Dr Roger Hansen, to the advisory committee.[97] In it, Hansen lambasted the American government (and the UN secretariat) for purposely excluding environmentalists. Hansen claimed: 'Information about, let alone involvement with, the Conference, has been almost impossible to obtain.'[98] Vincent extended this criticism:

Mr Hansen's sentiments have been echoed time and time again by people at all levels in virtually every meeting in which I have participated since getting involved in the preparations for Stockholm. Virtually all, including eminent scientists and environmentalists like Roger Hansen—people who are accustomed to being consulted as experts in areas such as this—were systematically excluded from active or even passive participation in U.S. preparations. More American scientists were involved as consultants to the conference Secretariat in Geneva than as advisers to our own government.[99]

While environmental interest groups were unable to gain much access, industrial lobbyists had a route into the White House through the National Industrial Pollution Control Council (NIPCC), an *ad hoc* advisory body set up by President Nixon. Russell Train periodically met with this committee as well as with the environment committee of a Secretary of State's business advi-

[96] Vincent was vice-president and director of research at the Ecology Centre of Louisiana in New Orleans.
[97] Hansen was executive-director of the Rocky Mountain Centre on Environment and on the legal advisory committee for the CEQ.
[98] House of Representatives, Subcommittee on International Organizations and Movements, 'Participation by the United States in the United Nations Environment Program', 5, 10 Apr. 1973; CIS NO: 73-H381-13, p. 39.
[99] House Subcommittee on International Organizations and Movements, 5, 10 Apr. 1973, p. 40.

sory group chaired by Carl Gerstacker (of Dow Chemical). There was also business membership on Senator Baker's advisory committee, something criticized by Vincent who described industry as 'grossly over-represented' compared with scientists and the environmental community, (something not really borne out by the list of participants).[100]

There is, however, no evidence of the NIPCC having any real influence on the policy process. Policy was made in the task force where business could have its say only through a state agency or department as conduit. This 'representative' for business interests was then forced to engage in the struggle for policy along with other parts of the state. President Nixon was already committed to deregulation, and to the idea that the polluter should pay, and thus it was in the interests of business to have the same principle applied to its competitors abroad. It would be wrong, however, to see this initiative as emerging out of sustained pressure from the business community on the administration. The policy outcomes reflected a much more complex process.

The second reason for interest-group failure was the speed with which international environmental politics had arisen. At a time when, through uncertainty and the lack of established policy positions, their influence might, potentially, have been most pronounced, they had no machinery for it. The preparations for Stockholm did much, in fact, to alter this.

One reason was the essentially local base upon which the majority of environmental groups drew. Although mass membership organizations were on the increase, as we have seen, most people still became involved in some aspect of the environmental movement because of their individual circumstances. Samuel Hays argues:

For the general public the crucial aspects of the debate were not the broad concepts and ideologies, but the persistent changes in circumstance within which people made daily choices. As they faced the rising cost of raising children and buying energy, or the destruction of air, water, and land resources they prized, or pollution that brought sickness and adversely affected their physical and mental capabilities as well as their living conditions, they made choices that more eloquently addressed the limits of growth than did the arguments of high-level debate.[101]

[100] Ibid., p. 43.
[101] Hays, *Environmental Politics in the United States*, 213.

White House pollster Robert Teeter drew exactly the same conclusion from his studies, telling chief-of-staff H. R. Haldeman that
the environment was a 'quality of life' issue:

Almost all of the individual environment and consumer issues have the
common characteristic of dealing with the individual's problems of living
in a complex urban society in which he is dependent on a multitude of
institutions of which he has little or no knowledge and virtually no control.
This means that the individual doesn't know whether or not there is
mercury in his fish, whether his vegetables have been sprayed with a
harmful pesticide or whether the air he breathes is killing him, and even if
he did, he's powerless to do anything about it.[102]

This lack of popular interest in international environmental
questions is highlighted by the post-Stockholm congressional testimony of two senior environmentalists. Dr Elvis Stahr, who was
president of the National Audobon Society, and a member of the
US delegation, told congressmen in April 1973 that the NAS was
just in the process of establishing an Office of International Environmental Activities with one official and one secretary.[103] At the
same hearing Patricia Rambach, international officer of the Sierra
Club, said that only in 1971 had the Club's board of directors
decided to extend its interest beyond US borders. Thus, in April
1972, an Office of International Environmental Affairs was established in New York opposite the United Nations, with Rambach in
charge.[104] The Stockholm Conference did more to stimulate than to
reflect this interest.

Realists are equally poorly served by the evidence from 1972.
First, factors in operation at the domestic level are part of a satisfactory explanation for the approach the USA took at Stockholm.
The role of popular interest in environmentalism, especially
electorally, was essential to give intrastate activists the power necessary to push through the environment fund and administrator,
together with the World Heritage Trust. Despite concerns about

---

[102] Memo, Teeter to Haldeman, Committee for the Re-election of the President,
Nixon Presidential Materials Staff, Haldeman Papers, Box 338. This is, of course,
one of the strongest arguments used by the state for the expansion of national
regulation.
[103] 'Participation by the United States in the United Nations Environment Program', House Subcommittee on International Organizations and Movements, 5, 10
Apr. 1973, CIS NO:73-H381-13, p. 27.
[104] Ibid., p. 53.

the USA's economic position, the electoral advantages of a positive environmental stance blunted the sceptics' concerns. In addition, factors internal to the state, especially State's strategically advantageous position and the expertise at CEQ, gave activists an edge.

The intrastate deliberations suggest that few officials were at all concerned with the relative gains their state might make. In the White House, Richard Nixon's closest aides worried about getting environmental votes for the President while CEQ head Russell Train and his science advisor Lee Talbot advanced quite far-reaching pro-environmental measures. The State Department, the official repository of the 'national interest', left the two most involved officials, Herter and McDonald, with plenty of room to manœuvre and their desire to host the conference and to have input into its agenda was motivated by the expansion of State's (and their own) role in the process and the wish to make a mark in international environmental politics.

The strongest realist case can be made from memos concerned with the USA's relative trading position.[105] Train acknowledged in a memo to Ehrlichman, for example, that there was a possibility of environmental subsidies harming the USA's competitive position.[106] But this is better understood, especially coming from a lifelong activist like Train, as an acknowledgement of part of the political context rather than as a motivation for policy. If trading fears, for example, had motivated policy then state officials would have used environmental protection as a non-tariff barrier in order to retaliate for other countries' import restrictions. In fact, the successful completion of the Kennedy GATT round in 1967 led to the whole question of non-tariff barriers becoming more acute, with environmental regulation a key problem area.

There were no deliberations about using the environmental issue to make gains for the United States or about avoiding concessions in some areas because they would adversely affect the USA's power position internationally. This holds for the more abstract, 'as if', argument concerning state actions. The United States had the most advanced domestic position at the time and the preparations

---

[105] Which is, of course, a weakened starting-point for the realists anyway as economic factors have usually been perceived as of secondary importance.

[106] Letter from Train to Ehrlichman, 5 Oct. 1971, *Nixon Presidential Materials Staff*, WHCF, Federal Government (Organizations), Box 1.

for the conference entailed its immersion in the politics of development, Vietnam, and superpower imperialism. Even so the USA made ambitious proposals, by the standards of the time, for a new UN set-up, conventions in key areas, monitoring and co-ordination, and money. This in the face of constant and, at the conference, virulent attacks on its foreign policy.

What can explain this degree of involvement? Why didn't the state seek to persuade others to pay, to frustrate any new institution which might gain some independent power to 'tax' and spend, or to tie environmental aid, for example, to security concessions? The environment fund proposal, and the spare institutional dimensions of any new UN body, *might* have been intended to entrench American dominance over the process thereby enabling the USA to steer environmental developments along lines conducive to foreign policy more broadly, such as consolidating anti-Soviet alliances. None of these accounts is adequate, however, according to the evidence.

A better explanation for American international prominence is one drawn from the motivation of the state officials involved and the institutional opportunities they possessed. The perception that the USA was out in front in environmental terms certainly existed within the White House. The United States could provide analysis and leadership through the institutions created partly in response to domestic environmental pressures. The CEQ had three original members already active in the environmental field. Russell Train had been a founding member of the World Wildlife Fund, Dr Gordon MacDonald was an environmental scientist and a member of the Environmental Studies Board of the National Academy of Sciences, and Robert Cahn had won the Pulitzer Prize in 1969 for his writings on national parks in the *Christian Science Monitor*. Their staff included the Smithsonian's Lee Talbot, and the future administrator of the Environmental Protection Agency and president of the Conservation Foundation, William K. Reilly.

Although their contact with the President was infrequent, they were all highly involved in environmental matters and thus gave the USA expert knowledge where it counted most. The Environmental Protection Agency, also established in 1970, provided an even greater institutional device for pursuing the environmental legislation which Congress was passing with frequency, the most important part of which was the 1970 Clean Air Act which set basic air quality standards across the United States. No other country had anything like this degree of interest or institutional set-up, all of which was in process by 1969 well before Stockholm gave these officials a major foreign policy question to consider.

CONCLUSION: CHOOSING A DELEGATION

The thirty-five-strong US delegation to Stockholm was chosen by Nixon administration officials who presented the President with an annotated list for his consideration. It contained high-profile figures like John Ehrlichman and interior secretary Rogers Morton as well as Senators Howard Baker, Claiborne Pell, and Clifford Case, the National Audobon Society's Elvis J. Stahr and 3M's chairman Bert Cross. Comments on the list about Stahr, for example, said: '(Stahr is President of the National Audobon Society, a leading conservationist, not an extremist. He is presumably a Democrat, having been Secretary of the Army under Kennedy (?), but is supportive of the Administration and helpful)'.[107] While some delegates were genuinely part of the negotiating team, others were being rewarded for their support of Nixon.[108] In addition, Ehrlichman's presence on the delegation was viewed with suspicion. He was seen, by Claiborne Pell for example, as a White House 'spy' concerned to limit the damage caused by US policy in Vietnam.[109]

Russell Train chaired the delegation with Herter as deputy. Although an obvious choice, Train felt the need to head off any attempt to appoint someone else. He sent the following memo to John Whitaker:

While it would be entirely appropriate for the Secretary of State to head the delegation, for any official of the government other than myself to do so (assuming neither the President nor the Vice-President expect to do so) would thoroughly undermine my relationships with these key people

[107] *Nixon Presidential Materials Staff*, White House Special Files, HRH (Haldeman), Box 93, 'John Ehrlichman 1972 March' (question mark in original).

[108] Christian Herter remembers John Ehrlichman saying 'we don't give one good God damn about this conference as far as the environment is concerned. I'm interested in making sure that supporters of the president get a chance to go to Sweden' (interview with author, 8 Apr. 1993).

[109] Interview with author, 6 May 1993.

[foreign environmental officials] and permanently prejudice my ability to represent the U.S. in international matters effectively. It would indeed be personally embarrassing to the point that I would necessarily have to consider whether I should go to Stockholm at all.[110]

Train continued: 'More importantly, from the White House standpoint, such a move would throw into complete disarray the effort we have made (with great success) to provide within the Executive Branch a focal point for international environmental policy-making that is fully coordinated with domestic policy and responsive to the President's interests.'[111]

This paragraph reflects Train's concern that the State Department would be able, were a cabinet member appointed, to assume an even larger role in policy-making thereby depriving the President of influence in this area. He warned of 'a full State Department take-over with results we have seen in the past' and added: 'We work closely with State on all of this, and I think have developed a good relationship. The suggestion to which this memorandum has been addressed would throw that relationship into a cocked hat.'[112] Train argues today that as a relatively non-political figure he was a better choice than someone like Henry Kissinger. He maintains:

My feeling was that to have a top political officer as opposed to a top environmental officer of our government chairing the delegation would tend to politicize the conference, or could, in a way which was undesirable from our standpoint . . . and if we wanted to keep the conference on an environmental track it made a lot more sense to send me as head of the delegation. I think that last argument was probably persuasive in the White House.[113]

Thus Train explicitly used the international political context to consolidate his position as the administration's senior environmental official and, in the process, he succeeded in maintaining CEQ pre-eminence over the State Department. Both were equally concerned, however, to keep the delegation united behind administration policy. On Wednesday 17 May 1972, delegates were called to

---

[110] Memo from Train to Whitaker, 20 Mar. 1972, *Nixon Presidential Materials Staff*, White House Central Files, Federal Government (Organizations), Box 1.
[111] Ibid.
[112] Ibid.
[113] Interview with author, 5 May 1993.

an all-day meeting with Train and Herter. They gave members a paper setting out 'five critical issues on which the delegation must firmly oppose recommendations contrary to the specific United States position'.[114]

These five 'critical issues' were:

(1) To oppose efforts to turn the voluntary environmental fund into a broader development fund.

(2) To oppose a new specialized agency, and to support ECOSOC as an oversight body.

(3) To oppose attempts to increase the UN target for aid donations by developed to developing countries, established at one per cent of gross national product.

(4) To oppose efforts to seek new funds for environmental clean-ups through other specialized agencies.

(5) To oppose any attempt to alter the language of a vague preparatory committee recommendation on nuclear testing (this last paper was marked 'secret' and was only to be given to delegates on arrival in Stockholm).

The *New York Times* recorded that several delegates, especially senators, were unhappy with some of the USA's positions and with the tone of the meeting as a whole.[115] The *Times* claimed:

According to one participant in Wednesday's meeting, Mr Train told the delegates 'to read the position papers, study them and not argue with them'.

The *Times* further reported:

It is expected that some Senators on the delegation—possibly Clifford P. Case, a Republican, and Harrison A. Williams, Jr., a Democrat, of New Jersey, and Gaylord Nelson, Democrat of Wisconsin, who are environmentalists, and Frank E. Moss, Democrat of Utah, sponsor of freedom of information legislation—may balk at not being able to speak their minds even if they have to vote as instructed.[116]

Such a rebellion failed to materialize, however, and US publicly stated policy remained consistently that which had been decided upon during the two years of preparations.

The evidence presented so far suggests a key role for the US

---

[114] *New York Times*, 22 May 1972, 23.
[115] Ibid.
[116] Ibid. Gaylord Nelson was, in the event, unable to go to Stockholm.

state on this relatively new issue. Indeed, its very *newness* played a part. Few people knew a great deal about the subject but state officials like Lee Talbot, Gordon MacDonald, and Russell Train certainly did. This was accentuated by the concept of 'human environment' which made foreign environmentalism even more alien to the pollution-based understanding most Northern populations shared and gave state officials further freedom.

Newness also entailed an initial (though short-lived) absence of established positions—precedents—which meant some flexibility in policy choice, a position enhanced by the *uncertainty* associated with environmental issues. Because concrete information was hard to obtain, calculations about costs and benefits were difficult to make. Those with some knowledge and some experience were therefore privileged. They could use their advantage to overcome the arguments of the less well-versed or to mould the agenda and discussion so as to preclude certain options and advance others. Experience of international environmental politics and of international organizations was an added advantage.

The *complexity* of environmental politics also gave State Department officials the chance to co-ordinate the process of policy-making. Not only did environmental politics involve issues which were inherently transnational, thereby giving State an edge, they also cut across the domestic constituencies of many of the other state actors involved with the policy process. As a result, the one department without a domestic constituency, State, was able to broker between these interests. This gave it a significant agenda-setting opportunity. The fact that the State Department hosted, chaired, and staffed, the main policy-making task force simply reinforced its strategic advantages.

Policy contexts filtered into this process by raising environmental preparedness in the USA, by elevating environmentalists to key positions, and by giving them an opportunity to develop policy which would enhance the President's profile. The international context provided a plus—in that Stockholm was seen as a 'good news' story to counteract Vietnam—and a minus, that is, economic fears (especially over trade). Even so, the nature of the issue at this time gave activists an added advantage (its newness and their greater access to information) and the result was a commitment to Stockholm significant enough to secure for the United States the mantle of leadership in international environmental affairs. The voluntary fund, the administrator, the World Heritage Trust, and CITES (which emerged out of the pre-Stockholm process) were all significant achievements pioneered by key state officials for whom these issues were important in their own right and who took their chance in the early 1970s to make an impact.

3

The Stockholm Conference
and its Aftermath

Stockholm reflected, for the first time, the emergence of the idea of the 'collective responsibility of nations for the quality and protection of the earth as a whole'.[1] It was attended by more than 1,200 delegates from 113 nations who met under the slogan 'Only One Earth'. As well as the intergovernmental gathering there were several alternative events, the most important of which was the 'official' NGO meeting called *Environment Forum*. There were other, increasingly radical, gatherings as well, such as the *People's Forum*, organized by Scandanavian environmental groups, and the *Life Forum*, organized by an American 'counter-culture' group.[2]

Of the hundreds of pressure groups which attended the *Environment Forum*—much the most consequential NGO gathering—the most from one country were from the United States.[3] Although many were given observer status by Maurice Strong—who had raised money to help NGOs attend—they were not seen as integral to the process of policy-making itself. Indeed, according to Anne Thompson Feraru, they were welcomed mainly because they provided information and helped to communicate conference decisions to the general public. Strong and other UN officials did not see the 'pressure group' aspect of NGO activities as particularly important at all.[4]

[1] Caldwell, *International Environmental Policy*, 55.

[2] Peter Thacher, a former US official and an aide to Maurice Strong, recalls one of the main differences between 1972 and 1992 as the number of campaigners at Stockholm who were essentially hippies, as opposed to members of highly organized environmental pressure groups (interview with author, 13 Apr. 1993).

[3] More than 300 organizations—industry and environmental—were granted observer status of which seventy-three were listed as based in the United States. Some organizations sent several delegates—the Sierra Club is listed as sending eleven, the Natural Resources Defense Council, and the World Wildlife Fund, four each, and Friends of the Earth, seven (A/conf.48/inf.6/rev. 1, 10/11/1972).

[4] Anne Thompson Feraru, 'Transnational Political Interests and the Global Environment', *International Organization*, 28/1 (1974), 42–3. Feraru recognizes a difference between international and domestic NGOs. Although the latter are

At the *Environment Forum* highly critical speeches and presentations were made about all aspects of the conference from poverty to defoliation in Vietnam. A senior American anthropologist, Dr Margaret Mead, became a spokeswoman for the *Forum* and made a speech to the main conference itself outlining the principal complaints of the NGOs marooned outside.[5] The co-author of *Only One Earth*, Barbara Ward, also helped to organize daily NGO briefings, recruit speakers, and arrange tickets for main conference sessions.[6] These parallel deliberations were, however, only a forum for alternative discussion. They were unable to make any impact on the conference. Indeed, John McDonald recalls having to advise Margaret Mead about more effective lobbying.

She was angered at the fact that she couldn't impact on the policies of the government during the conference itself. So I had to sit down with her and spend several hours on several occasions telling her how the government worked and telling her what the role of NGOs was and how to impact on policy which meant she had to start a year earlier. You couldn't do it at the time. I showed her a copy of the position papers. She had never seen a position paper, she didn't know what we were talking about. She had no concept of how policy was formed in preparation for a world conference. I don't blame her. No one had bothered to even think about the role of NGOs.[7]

Despite the presence of many American NGOs at Stockholm their influence on US policy was negligible. They created publicity and provided a conduit for conference deliberations to be transmitted to a global audience. But their substantive contribution was highly restricted both before and at the conference. When EPA administrator and delegation member William Ruckelshaus reluctantly appeared at the *Environment Forum* he was castigated about US policies in Vietnam and was reduced to saying that 'his job was the environment, not foreign policy' and that 'there wasn't much he could say that would affect U.S. policy in Asia, nor to change

nominally absent from her analysis, this division proves hard to maintain in practice and her conclusions apply equally well to both domestic and international varieties.

[5] The limited amount of coherence at the *Environment Forum*, which did eventually result in an agreed statement, is attributed by Peter Bennet Stone to the energies of Mead and Barbara Ward (*Did We Save the Earth at Stockholm?* (London: Earth Island, 1973), 134).

[6] Mead and Ward were seen as a 'bridge' between the two conferences; Feraru, 'Transnational Political Interests', 49.

[7] Interview with author, 14 Apr. 1993.

anybody's mind in the audience'. He concluded by telling the gathering he would tell Richard Nixon: 'I was invited to a very interesting meeting where there were a lot of people who seemed to regard the issues of war and the environment as one and the same.'[8]

The chairman of the Sierra Club in 1993, Michael McCloskey—a member for more than thirty years—recalls the foreign-policy inexperience of domestic groups in relation to Stockholm:

We didn't even have any idea that a lot of the federal decisions are made in advance at preparatory conferences. Our whole thought was that we would go there and mix it up and look for opportunities to influence things but we quickly discovered that it was a big, bewildering show, a many-ringed circus, and that it was not easy to find ways to get involved in the governmental process. I do remember our chief international person hanging around the governmental sessions and talking, trying to figure out what were the critical issues being debated.[9]

As Peter Bennet Stone concluded: '. . . all those organizations which went to Stockholm can be expected to be more enthusiastic, more understanding, and more creative in the international communications effort now required'.[10] In other words, Stockholm can be seen as the dawn for international environmental NGOs. As the 1970s and 1980s unfolded, this interest was to result in high-profile international environmental campaigns and the presence of much more organized NGOs as part of the policy process. Stockholm was a spur to this development, not a symptom of it.

THE CONFERENCE PROPER

The Stockholm Conference had four main goals: to agree a Declaration on the Human Environment, and an Action Plan, to discuss the formation of an environmental fund, and to consider creating a new environmental institution. As soon as the conference began, however, the United States was confronted with a barrage of criticism. The catalyst for this assault was the war in Vietnam compounded by demands for a ban on the testing of nuclear weapons.

---

[8] Frances Gendlin, 'Voices from the Gallery', *Bulletin of Atomic Scientists* (Sept. 1972), 28.
[9] Interview with author, 7 Apr. 1994.
[10] Stone, *Did We Save the Earth?*, 136.

The Nixon administration had not been unaware of this danger, as we have seen, and it was the hope of officials like Russell Train that the UNCHE might provide a form of rehabilitation for the United States.[11]

Implied criticism of US foreign policy began with the opening address of UN Secretary-General Kurt Waldheim when he called for the cessation of nuclear testing above and below ground. This attack was compounded by Swedish Prime Minister Olaf Palme, a man whose existing anti-Vietnam stance had already incurred the wrath of Richard Nixon, when he launched a broadside against US foreign policy (without naming the United States directly). In presenting the Swedish position on the draft declaration, Palme claimed:

The immense destruction brought about by indiscriminate bombing, by large-scale use of bulldozers and herbicides is an outrage sometimes described as ecocide, which requires urgent international attention.[12]

This provoked a furious reaction from the US delegation which was reportedly close to walking out.[13] The tension was heightened still further when several delegations announced their determination to secure an outright international ban on the testing of nuclear weapons.

In his initial speech to the conference, Train pledged the USA to broad support for most of the tabled initiatives while emphasizing the necessarily limited potential for international co-operation.[14] He told delegates: 'The fact of national sovereignty entails frank recognition that many or even most of the crucial environmental actions have to be taken freely by governments and by citizens in their own interest as they see it.'[15] As far as actions in the international sphere were concerned, Train committed the USA to a high-level

[11] Anti-Vietnam war protests reached such an intensity that the US embassy was stoned and the Swedish government put a bodyguard on Russell Train.

[12] New York Times, 7 June 1972, 3 (see also, somewhat more pejoratively, The Economist, 19 June 1972, 32). This 'outburst' was, according to some, largely for domestic consumption; The Times (London), 7 June 1972, 1.

[13] American delegates were told by the White House to threaten a walk-out if criticism didn't subside; The Times (London), 8 June 1972, 7. See also New York Times, 7 June 1972, 3, and 8 June 1972, 13, and Edward P. Morgan, 'Stockholm: The Clean (But Impossible) Dream', Foreign Policy, 8 (Fall 1973), 151.

[14] Train's speech was written by William K. Reilly, then a young member of the CEQ, who headed the US delegation to the Rio Conference in 1992.

[15] Russell Train, 6 June 1972, Department of State Bulletin (24 July 1972), p. 109.

secretariat under the aegis of ECOSOC, to paying 40 per cent of a $100 million environmental fund, to a co-ordinated information and monitoring network, and to agreements on whaling, a World Heritage Trust, and the prevention of ocean dumping.

No sooner had the more detailed committee work begun, how-ever, than the United States was embroiled in another highly public confrontation over Vietnam, this time with the Chinese delega-tion.[16] At the first day-long meeting of the working party on the reopened draft Declaration on 9 June, the Chinese launched a vitriolic attack on 'US aggression in Indochina'. American repre-sentatives were left to counter that Vietnam was not a proper subject for discussion at an environmental conference.[17] The Chinese sought the insertion of language on Vietnam, the explicit recognition that capitalism caused environmental degradation, an acknowledgement that imperialistic superpowers had contributed greatly to environmental damage, and the transfer of scientific and technological skills free to the developing world. In response, the United States stated its intention to take the argument into that autumn's UN General Assembly meeting if necessary in order to avoid acceptance of such a Declaration.[18]

The Chinese then attacked the United States in open session the following morning for what they described as 'barbarous atrocities' in Vietnam. Chinese spokesman Tang Ke told delegates that capi-talism and imperialism were largely responsible for damage to the human environment and urged them to propose amendments to the Declaration (twenty-seven were forthcoming that day, but most were later dropped).[19] In responding to this attack, maintaining good relations with China, which Nixon had so historically visited just months earlier, was the central White House aim. As a result, Russell Train called Henry Kissinger's deputy, Alexander Haig, to

[16] Although this was China's first UN conference, Maurice Strong, and his adviser Peter Thacher, used an Austrian student acquaintance of premier Chou En Lai's to pass conference documents to Chou in 1971 in anticipation of Chinese admittance to the United Nations; Christian A. Herter, Jnr. and Jill E. Binder, *The Role of the Secretariat in Multilateral Negotiation: The Case of Maurice Strong and the 1972 UN Conference on the Human Environment* (Washington, DC: Johns Hopkins Foreign Policy Institute, 1993), 41.

[17] *New York Times*, 10 June 1972, 4.

[18] *Washington Post*, 10 June 1972, A7.

[19] *Washington Post*, 11 June 1972, A9. Developing countries were by no means united on this issue and despite the large number of amendments, many wanted to see the declaration agreed for which US acceptance was more or less essential.

discuss the appropriate US reaction. It was correspondingly muted.[20]

As well as this public criticism, the United States was also trying to deal with opposition to its particular concept of an environmental fund. Erstwhile supporters like Canada, the United Kingdom, and Japan, all accepted the need for an increase in aid for developing countries to help with environmental problems. Despite the US proposal for a $40 million five-year contribution, this was paralleled by a freeze in increments for funding environmental projects within UN specialized agencies.[21] The debate came to a head early in the conference over the question of 'additionality', the principle that additional funds should be made available for environmental projects. This would, in practice, have meant an increase in aid flows from the North to the South.

As we have seen, US delegates were under instruction to resist such demands. During one of the first sessions of the conference on 7 June, the United States proposed amendments to each of four draft proposals on additional funding. These were defeated each time by a majority of at least thirty-five which included pro-aid developed countries as well as developing ones. These Action Plan proposals were merely recommendations and as such unenforceable. In committee consideration of Action Plan Recommendation 103, the United States recorded its opposition, 'as a matter of principle, to compensating nations for declines in their export earnings regardless of cause'.[22] As the *Washington Post* recorded: 'Under the highly precise instructions contained in its position paper . . . the U.S. delegation has come here rigidly bound not only to reject the additionality principle, but to "firmly oppose recommendations contrary to the specific U.S. position".' The *Post* further recorded the anger of other developed nations at American 'pigheadedness', describing the US delegation as 'harried and weary'.[23]

The US negotiator on the committee which considered the question of compensation was Gordon MacDonald, the only

---

[20] Interview with author, 5 May 1993. Comparisons are startling between the response to Palme and to China; see *Bulletin of the Atomic Scientists* (Sept. 1972), 45, 55.

[21] *Washington Post*, 7 June 1972, A16.

[22] *Report of the United Nations Conference on the Human Environment: Stockholm, 5–16 June, 1972*, A/conf.48/14/Rev.1 (NewYork: United Nations, 1973), 59.

[23] *Washington Post*, 8 June 1972, 29.

environmental scientist on the delegation and vice-chairman of the CEQ. Details of the negotiations in which he was involved were contained in a post-Stockholm report to the House of Representatives.[24] The report outlined US support for recommendations to prevent environmental standards being used as non-tariff barriers, to use GATT (and, as a concession to the South, UNCTAD), to monitor environmentally related trade practices, and to eschew uniform environmental standards. The USA opposed, however, advanced consultation on planned environmental actions affecting trade and, most importantly, the call for compensation for countries where environmental actions hampered exports.

Although the issue of atomic weapons testing provided additional discomfort for the USA, France and China bore the main burden of demands for a nuclear test ban. There were also some US successes in this first week, most notably on the establishment of a World Heritage Trust and on the US-sponsored moratorium on whaling.[25] As the conference continued into its second week the central issues became funding and institutional set-up. Added to this was the continuing question of the Declaration (the Action Plan had proved relatively non-controversial).[26] The centrepiece of American policy was the environmental fund proposal which entailed a limited US commitment. The proposed institutional framework was to be comprised by a small secretariat, not a new UN agency, and was therefore also modest in scope. In both of these endeavours, the US delegation was largely successful. On funding, it had in effect promised $40 million on a matching basis and it was therefore irrelevant how large the whole fund was: if it reached $80 million the USA would pay its offer in full and be committed to no more.

The fact that the conference secretariat had recommended a fund as high as $164 million made no difference to this US commit-

[24] 'Report on the United Nations Conference on the Human Environment'. House of Representatives Committee on Public Works, Sept. 1972, p. 12; CIS-NO: 72-H642-10.

[25] Whaling appeared on the agenda courtesy of a chat between Strong and Lee Talbot, the latter wanting to push the issue but finding resistance within his own government due to the possibility of a diplomatic clash with Japan (interview with author, 14 Apr. 1994).

[26] Many of the 109 recommendations had involved small skirmishes but they centred in the main on the creation of monitoring, management, and implementation procedures such as Earthwatch (to generate environmental information) and Infoterra (to centrally co-ordinate the resulting data).

ment (which it would have done if the USA had pledged 40 per cent of an unspecified total). In this sense the arguments over additional aid and compensation were more material because the fund proposal exposed the USA to limited liability. In addition, the fund was to provide support for monitoring and information collection, not to finance programmes which the USA saw as properly the work of other environmentally connected UN agencies. The servicing costs of the governing council and the secretariat were to be borne by the regular UN budget.[27] As it was, the total fund was set at $100 million.

The institutional question proved more troublesome and the USA, while succeeding by and large in avoiding a major new agency or an extended financial commitment, was unable to prevent a more ambitious organization being established. Negotiations had taken place pre-Stockholm between countries with draft organizational proposals—the USA, Brazil, Kenya, and Sweden—and three others, Canada, Egypt, and India. John McDonald recalls the last meeting:

It was decided that we should meet, those countries who had put forward plans, four days before Stockholm started, in Stockholm, to see if we could come up with at least a single text with brackets to start the negotiations. So we did that. But my experience over the decades has been first up with an idea, first up with a proposal, then people amend your proposal and theirs drops by the wayside. So we went in to the conference as far as I was concerned with about 98 per cent of what we had put forward.[28]

On the positive side for the USA, this '98 per cent' was comprised by a governing council and a small secretariat headed by an 'executive director' (there were even disagreements about the title by which this administrative co-ordinator should be known).[29] This council was to be answerable to ECOSOC, as the USA had hoped,

[27] $40 million still represented one of the lowest absolute contributions the USA had made to a new enterprise in which it had a stake 'Participation by the United States in the United Nations Environment Program', (House Subcommittee on International Organizations and Movements, 5, 10 Apr. 1973, pp. 5–7, CIS-NO: 73-H381-13).

[28] Interview with author, 14 Apr. 1993. It was, however, Sweden which presented the agreed draft at the conference itself.

[29] The USA wanted 'administrator' to emphasize the post's procedural element, the Swedes and Brazilians wanted 'executive director' to highlight the policy-oriented body they favoured (Tunstall, 'The Influence of International Politics', 196).

and the secretariat was specifically labelled as 'small'.[30] On the negative side, the governing council, which the USA had hoped to restrict to twenty-seven members, was eventually expanded to fifty-eight members.[31] The perception at the time was that this new body—UNEP—represented a success for the USA, with the *Washington Post* claiming the US delegation 'fought hard to see the resolution through two weeks of negotiation, renegotiation and re-renegotiation'.[32] The USA had wanted something less independent than the agency which emerged, however, and siting UNEP soon became a *cause célèbre* as well, with the South determined it should be the first UN body outside the developed world.

The final outstanding issue was the question of the draft Declaration. The issue of nuclear testing was eventually agreed through semantic inventiveness, although a disagreement over a principle on information exchange was eventually referred to the UN General Assembly (where it was rejected). After this, the conference accepted the Declaration as a whole by acclamation, subject to the various observations and qualifications of nations like the United States. China was alone in not actually approving the final Declaration.[33]

POST-STOCKHOLM DEVELOPMENTS

Overall the USA professed itself satisfied with the outcome. In a post-conference analysis the delegation identified forty recommendations it had particularly wanted, and John Whitaker was quick to report back to President Nixon in the following terms:

Despite the efforts of a number of demonstrators, both those representing particular countries and private groups, the U.N. Conference on the Hu-

---

[30] *Report of the UNCHE*, p. 30.

[31] Asian nations demanded expansion in an attempt to alter the UN formula for seat distribution which dated back to 1963 (since when decolonization had increased Asian and African membership). This effort was successful at 1972's UN General Assembly when Thailand secured an amendment increasing the governing council to fifty-eight members which, for the first time, created an Afro-Asian majority on a UN representative body (Luchins, 'The United Nations Conference', 351).

[32] *Washington Post*, 16 June 1972, 1, A21.

[33] A delicate compromise with Tang Ke, head of the Chinese delegation, who neither cast a vote nor walked out, enabled the illusion of consensus to be maintained (Herter and Binder, *The Role of the Secretariat*, 41).

man Environment, which was held in Stockholm from June 5 through 16, was in my opinion successful from our point of view. The attempts to gain headlines by embarrassing the United States delegation with charges of 'ecocide' in Vietnam and militant disarmament requests by some of the peripheral attending nations tended to overshadow the following concrete accomplishments which I believe will long outlive the demonstrations.[34]

Whitaker went on to list the $100 million fund, the environmental secretariat, the proposed whaling moratorium, support for an ocean convention, the World Heritage Trust, and the establishment of a monitoring network. On this memo, Nixon wrote: 'To Whitaker, Train et al.—Excellent job under very difficult circumstances.'[35] Russell Train's report, attached to Whitaker's memo, was even more detailed about US achievements at the conference and requested of Nixon 'your personal identification with the Stockholm Conference at the earliest practicable date'.[36] To this end he attached a draft presidential statement on US successes which was released through the White House press office the following day.[37]

The most substantive matter which arose out of the conference itself was to settle the location of UNEP. During committee discussions at Stockholm, sites in both the North and South had been proposed. The United States strongly preferred New York or, failing that, Geneva. It was John McDonald's responsibility to represent the USA at the United Nations during October and November 1972's General Assembly discussions on Stockholm, and he recalls making two 'political misjudgements'.[38] First, to underestimate Austrian determination to site UNEP in Vienna (which fragmented Northern unity). Secondly, overlooking Kenyan strength of purpose. Jomo Kenyatta and Indira Gandhi were both determined to have a UN body situated outside the North but it was the Kenyans who carried the day, something McDonald attributes to their playing 'hardball' at the United Nations. He claims:

[34] Memo, Whitaker (via Ehrlichman) to Nixon, 19 June 1972, *Nixon Presidential Materials Staff*, White House Central Files, President's Office Files, Box 17.

[35] Ibid. (Nixon's underlining).

[36] Memo, Train to Nixon, 19 June 1972, *Nixon Presidential Materials Staff*, White House Central Files, President's Office Files, Box 17.

[37] Text in *Department of State Bulletin*, 24 July 1972, p. 107.

[38] The subject was discussed in the UNGA's second committee seventeen times between 19 Oct. and 10 Nov. (Luchins, 'The United Nations Conference', 329).

The Kenyans let the Indians know, through their ambassador in New York, that unless Mrs Gandhi withdrew the Indian offer, Mr Kenyatta was going to expel all Indians from Kenya! Since Idi Amin had just done that a few years before, it was taken seriously. Mrs Gandhi did withdraw. The issue went to a vote and we lost because the West was split and didn't have the votes anyway, and Kenya won in a landslide.[39]

On an initial vote to place UNEP in a developing country, and specifically in Kenya, the USA cast the only negative vote. As for an executive director, Maurice Strong was unanimously elected by the general assembly for a four-year term. In preparation for this, however, Strong had, Christian Herter recalls, lobbied the United States for its support in his pursuit of the new post.[40]

Further assessment of American achievements at Stockholm was provided by Senators Claiborne Pell and Clifford Case, who told congressional colleagues in October 1972 that the USA's image had suffered because of strict administration instructions to 'vote against any proposals that would increase aid levels to the developing nations'.[41] In addition, Christian Herter met with Congress to persuade it to vote the fund money, and told representatives the USA bore a particular burden as a major polluter. (He also argued that the transboundary character of environmental problems made a global improvement in the long-term interests of the United States.)[42]

In these hearings, Herter, was asked what provision existed for public input into future international environmental policy-making and he revealed that the State Department was actively soliciting views by writing to forty or fifty organizations to ask: 'At this stage of the game, are you interested in continuing this kind of liaison? What sort of an arrangement would you like to see the State Department set up—a day's conference, for example, to go over what has happened since Stockholm—what initiatives have been undertaken? What should our position be with respect to the pro-

---

[39] McDonald, 'Global Environmental Negotiations', 9.

[40] Interview with author, 8 Apr. 1993.

[41] 'United Nations Conference on the Human Environment', report to the Senate by Senator Claiborne Pell and Senator Clifford Case, Oct. 1972, CIS NO: 72-S382-22, p. 9. They accused the USA of weakening an Action Plan proposal on the measurement of climate change because they believed the administration was working on weather modification weapons.

[42] House Subcommittee on International Organizations and Movements, 5, 10 Apr. 1973, p. 6.

gram submitted by the Executive Secretary? et cetera. We are in the position of getting replies.'[43]

In other words, nearly a year after Stockholm the State Department was still in the position of soliciting views from societal groups. The conference had undoubtedly stimulated awareness of international environmental problems in the United States but the insulation of the executive so prevalent before 1972 remained. The contrast persisted between domestic policy, where the EPA and Congress were increasingly involved in a battle with interest groups for influence, and foreign policy.

The evidence from the conference itself supports the argument for state autonomy, and the importance of policy contexts, in several ways. First, the extent to which the White House chose delegates demonstrates on a very minimal level the role of the core state. Secondly, meaningful interest-group pressure was absent during the conference in the same way that it had been during the pre-Stockholm process. Despite the appearance of many American interest groups in Sweden, they struggled, as we have seen, to make any substantive impression at all. Indeed, the resort to public criticism was an option equally available to non-American groups illustrating the ordinariness of their position relative to their own government. The Nixon administration's pursuit of good environmental coverage was, noted more than one observer, quite blatantly cynical.[44]

The dominance of the core state is also in evidence if one looks at the internationally related congressional legislation passed in the years after 1968. For example, Harvey R. Sherman lists the many developments which Congress made into law. These measures, some of which pre-dated Stockholm by years, included protection for marine mammals, and for migratory and threatened species (the Endangered Species Conservation Act, 1969, for example). However, at the end of his report, he concludes:

The foregoing account of action by the United States in large measure represents initiatives on the part of the Executive Department, since the division of Federal powers grants the President great responsibility in

---

[43] Ibid., p. 18. Herter showed an awareness of 'new dimensions' emerging in international politics such as population, drugs, and conservation which ought, he believed, to be under a single policy heading because they were 'all part of the same thing' (p. 21).

[44] Morgan, 'Stockholm: The Clean (But Impossible) Dream', 153.

international affairs, subject to concurrence by the Senate. Nevertheless, the peculiar and extranational dimensions of environmental concern and problems of themselves bring the whole Congress into fuller play in the formation and implementation of the Nation's international environmental commitments than is the case with many other foreign policy issues.[45]

Thirdly, the importance of the international political context can be seen in the degree of White House involvement during Stockholm which threatened to eclipse the advantage Train had secured for himself through arguing for the environment as a 'non-political' issue. The raising of the stakes in terms of Vietnam, aid transfers, and arms control, all led the executive to take a closer interest in the conference. From the very beginning this proved divisive, isolating the USA and ensuring that Train's flexibility at Stockholm was curtailed by the oversight of Ehrlichman and the administration's concern about broader political questions.

Nevertheless, the US delegation did make a significant contribution to Stockholm based upon its preparatory work and the *de facto* predominance it enjoyed in environmental politics generally. Indeed, Russell Train maintains that Maurice Strong looked to the United States to exercise international leadership at Stockholm and that, indeed, it did: 'We exercised leadership, I don't think in any domineering way, but we sort of were out front from the beginning. I think Strong tended to look to us as extremely important in putting together the agenda of the conference, and looked to us for support and leadership at the conference itself. I think he hoped for some of the same in Rio, but of course he was disappointed in that.'[46]

THE AMERICAN ENVIRONMENT AFTER 1972

Even though the Stockholm Conference came slightly after the peak of the first phase of modern environmentalism in the United States, the issue itself was now not only firmly established on the political agenda, it was also institutionalized in numerous statutes and entrenched in a developing struggle between interest and busi-

---

[45] H. R. Sherman, 'The Role of the United States Congress in International Environmental Conservation', *Environmental Policy and Law*, 2 (1976), 38.

[46] Interview with author, 5 May 1993.

ness groups. We have already seen the extent of the first rise in the membership of American environmental groups, reaching well over a million by 1972. This figure remained stable and may even have declined slightly in the 1970s before being boosted again by the perceived anti-environmentalism of the first Reagan administration.

Throughout this period, however, widespread public support for environmental action remained. Indeed, Robert Cameron Mitchell argues that not once during the 1970s did the number in public opinion polls who thought 'too little' was being spent on the environment drop below 46 per cent.[47] In addition, regardless of their static membership figures at this time, the environmental groups—both traditional and new—were being transformed into a highly organized professional lobby increasingly prepared to use litigation as well as political pressure to try to secure preferred options in Congress and speedy implementation by the EPA.

Early Congressional Activism

The surge in environmentalism had already led Congress to take a bigger role in the environmental affairs of states, thereby expanding its power in relation to sub-national government and tipping the federal balance towards the centre. The occasion for increasing congressional involvement in environmental politics came with the development, from the mid-1960s onwards, of what Joseph Zimmerman describes as 'preemption powers'.[48] In essence, the demand for uniform air and water quality standards—for both commercial and public health reasons—led Congress to become more and more deeply involved in the area of national pollution control. From 1965, and the Water Quality Act, onwards, Congress exercised its power increasingly readily to establish minimum standards. Although New Deal related grants-in-aid meant this development was in train before 1965, claims Zimmerman, the burgeoning of environmental interest groups pressuring Congress

---

[47] Robert Cameron Mitchell, 'Public Opinion and Environmental Politics in the 1970s and 1980s', in Norman J. Vig and Michael E. Kraft (eds.), *Environmental Policy in the 1980s: Reagan's New Agenda* (Washington, DC: Congressional Quarterly Press, 1984), 53.

[48] Zimmerman, *Contemporary American Federalism*, 11. See also Caulfield, 'The Conservation and Environmental Movements', in Lester (ed.) *Environmental Politics and Policy*, 35–8.

added a further impetus to 'the growth of national power'. He maintains:

Coinciding with the post-1965 enactment of preemption statutes has been the establishment of numerous public interest groups seeking enactment of preemption statutes which protect the environment. Television in particular has generated broad public support for environmental preemption statutes by highlighting environmental disasters such as the Exxon Valdez oil spill in Alaska. The proliferation of federal mandates and restraints . . . has led associations of state and local governments to become more active in lobbying the Congress to prevent the enactment of preemption bills and to seek congressional relief from existing preemption statutes and court decisions.[49]

Clean air also drew Congress into the environmental fray. By the early 1960s, it was providing research support for pollution measurement and engaging in more and more congressional oversight. As Charles O. Jones maintains:

History shows that once the federal government establishes regulatory authority, it tends to move rather swiftly to preemptive authority, or at least dominant control.[50]

Increasing public interest in improving air quality enhanced the role of the federal government and weakened the power of industry to block pollution controls. Before 1965 the lack of public awareness corresponded with an absence of political attention.[51] After this time, the incentives for politicians changed as more and more voters expressed concern about the environment and eventually, in 1970, the landmark Clean Air Act amendments were passed which included ground-breaking reductions in car emissions. This legislation, still regularly amended today, sits with the National Environmental Policy Act of 1969 as the peak of early domestic environmentalism in the United States. Recall John Whitaker's remark to the effect that there was 'nearly hysterical support for the environmental movement' at this time, and that any presidential veto would have been promptly overridden by Congress.[52]

The growth of congressional involvement continued into the 1970s with federal legislation on the environment covering air and

---

[49] *Contemporary American Federalism*, 195.
[50] Jones, *Clean Air*, 62.
[51] Ibid. 141.
[52] Whitaker, *Striking a Balance*, 93.

water quality, toxic substances and the disposal of hazardous waste, fishing, the use of land, forest policy, pesticide regulation, and many other areas.[53] This impetus was maintained for several reasons. First, a number of prominent congressmen were keen supporters of environmental legislation. Powerful senators like Edmund Muskie (D-Maine) and Henry Jackson (D-Wash.) were joined by representatives Morris Udall (D-Arizona) and Paul Rodgers (D-Fla.) to form 'an extraordinary group of policy entrepreneurs who provided the leadership essential to enactment of the landmark policies of the 1960s and 1970s'.[54]

Although it took a change in political context to raise the profile of these representatives, individual congressmen had been trying for much longer to make an impression. As early as 1958, representative Paul Schenk (R-Ohio) had proposed emissions standards for cars but his idea, according to Jones, '. . . was simply ahead of its time. Lacking public and administration support, this particular effort to set standards beyond existing capabilities could not be enacted into law.'[55]

A second reason was the edge that the Democrats traditionally enjoyed amongst environmentalists which made Congress a focus for policy development. As Michael Kraft and Norman Vig explain:

Congress traditionally had played a more dominant role than the president in initiating environmental policies, and that pattern continued in the 1970s, particularly because the Democratic party controlled Congress during the Nixon and Ford presidencies. Although support for environmental protection was bi-partisan, Democrats provided more leadership on the issue in Congress and were more likely to vote for strong environmental policy provisions than were Republicans.[56]

Finally, the profile of environmental issues meant that many

[53] For a survey of major pieces of legislation in the 1970s see Norman J. Vig and Michael E. Kraft (eds.), *Environmental Policy in the 1990s* (Washington, DC: Congressional Quarterly Press, 1990), app. 1, and Dallas Burtraw and Paul R. Portney, 'Environmental Policy in the United States', in Dieter Helm (ed.), *Economic Policy Toward the Environment* (Oxford: Blackwell, 1991), 291–302.

[54] Michael E. Kraft, 'Environmental Gridlock: Searching for Consensus in Congress', in Vig and Kraft (eds.), *Environmental Policy in the 1990s*, 107.

[55] Jones, *Clean Air*, 33–4.

[56] Michael E. Kraft and Norman J. Vig, 'Environmental Policy from the Seventies to the Nineties: Continuity and Change', in Vig and Kraft (eds.), *Environmental Policy in the 1990s*, 13.

congressmen adopted a positive stance. This was compounded by changes in the institutional organization of the legislature which opened up its workings to more public scrutiny and allowed younger members, who were often more sensitive to environmental issues, to ascend quite rapidly. Even though the depth of congressional interest in the environment may not have been particularly deep among members, it was an issue for which the public expressed consistent support and thus a good environmental image constituted an essential requirement for some legislators.

The role of Congress was also enhanced by the emergence of the Environmental Protection Agency. The EPA was charged with implementing congressionally mandated national standards. For example, efforts to get catalytic converters fitted on all new cars required, as a first step, the elimination of lead from gasoline with which the EPA, now under administrator Russell Train, was tasked.[57] The EPA's first chief legal officer, John Quarles, recalls how interest groups used Congress to try to ensure that the agency zealously pursued this mission:

During the fall of 1971 they [environmentalists] began to fear that compromises by EPA would jeopardize achievement of the clean air objectives, and they transmitted these fears to their friends and supporters in Congress. In December we heard reports that the Senate Public Works Subcommittee on Air and Pollution, the 'Muskie Committee', which had championed the act through to passage, would soon be holding oversight hearings. The subcommittee's purpose would be to explore charges that EPA was improperly softening the stringent requirements of the act.[58]

Quarles records EPA's confrontations with Muskie over the Clean Air Act which saw the agency caught in a difficult position between the Senator and the White House. His account is instructive because it shows the pressure the legislature was able to wield against a recalcitrant president through his 'own' executive agency. These changes in Congress were compounded by the developments taking place within the environmental movement.

Interest Groups

After startling initial successes in the late 1960s, interest groups

---

[57] John Quarles, *Cleaning Up America: An Insider's View of the Environmental Protection Agency* (Boston: Houghton Mifflin Company, 1976), 191.
[58] Ibid. 77.

faced several new challenges: maintaining the saliency of environmental issues, resisting the growth of business associations which sought to exert countervailing pressure in a more organized way than previously, and dealing with the fact of 'institutionalization', that is, regular access and consultation, combined with the powerful weapon of legislative precedent. The first and most important development has been in the growth of group membership.[59]

Although figures vary about the membership of major environmental groups, with some experiencing a much larger increase since 1972 than others, the combined totals show that considerably more Americans now belong to or participate in these pro-environment organizations.[60] As we have seen, membership in the traditional groups—like the Sierra Club and the National Audobon Society—increased spectacularly in the 1960s from 124,000 to 819,000. These early groups had often been narrowly based on a specific geographical location or among sportsmen and so were not in any sense national, mass-membership organizations. As the 1960s ended, however, both these characteristics began to change. The number of groups doubled as the movement began to put down roots in the wider public and, after Earth Day in 1970, membership rose a further 300,000.[61]

Robert Cameron Mitchell has been prominent in detailing this

[59] Of course the tactics, strategies, and general orientation of these groups differs. Some are more radical than others, some emphasize the courts over Congress, or research over public protest, but all are part of the societal universe of organizations seeking to change either public policy or popular conceptions. Thus the division of groups into categories such as 'direct action, 'education', and 'policy reform' better approximates the differences in approach while disguising the fact that they are all engaged in broadly the same activity: securing pro-environmental change. Indeed, the idea of 'contexts' allows different forms of activity—from picketing to scientific research—to figure equally as important parts of the political landscape within which policy is made. See Robert Cameron Mitchell, Angela G. Mertig, and Riley E. Dunlap, 'Twenty Years of Environmental Mobilization: Trends Among National Environmental Groups', in Dunlap and Mertig (eds.), American Environmentalism: The U.S. Environmental Movement, 1970–1990 (Philadelphia: Taylor and Francis, 1992), 19.

[60] Between 1987 and 1990, according to one survey, the percentage of people who said 'Yes' when asked whether they or someone in their household had donated to, or been active in, an organization working to protect the environment went up from 15% to 40% (Riley E. Dunlap 'Trends in Public Opinion Toward Environmental Issues: 1965–1990', in Dunlap and Mertig (eds.), American Environmentalism, 113).

[61] Robert Cameron Mitchell, 'From Conservation to Environmental Movement: The Development of Modern Environmental Lobbies', in Lacey (ed.), Government and Environmental Politics, 97.

development.[62] While he accepts that environmental groups did experience stasis in the mid-1970s, leading, for example, to staff cutbacks, he amply demonstrates that the perceived anti-environmentalism of the Reagan administration reinvigorated the movement as a whole. In 1972, the Sierra Club's membership stood at 136,000 but by 1983 this was up to 346,000. The National Audobon Society went from 232,000 to 498,000 in the same period. Some groups did experience a fall, such as the Izaak Walton League (from 56,000 to 47,000, although it disavowed the pursuit of a mass membership), but other groups like the National Wildlife Federation (NWF) increased spectacularly from 525,000 to 758,000. Other, newer, groups like Friends of the Earth and the Environmental Defense Fund (EDF) also grew. Overall this growth gave the movement nearly two million members (although some members belonged to more than one group lowering the real figure).

This growth continued in the 1980s. One of the newest groups, Greenpeace USA, which had begun a direct-mailing campaign in the United States in 1979 had, by 1989, a remarkable 1.35 million members. Other organizations also continued to grow throughout the decade. The EDF had increased its membership to 100,000 by 1989 and the Sierra Club's was up to 496,000. The Natural Resources Defense Council (NRDC) had 117,000 members (up from 42,000 in 1980), while Audobon was at 575,000 and the Wilderness Society at 317,000 from just 45,000 in 1980.

Indeed, the improvement in the fortunes of the Wilderness Society is instructive. Formed in 1935, the group experienced tremendous growth in the 1980s. From 1982's figure of 62,000 it rose to 150,000 in 1985, 190,000 in 1987, and 350,000 by 1989. Its high point was 354,000 members in 1991.[63] The Society's revenues in 1980 were $1.76 million which, by 1992, had risen to $16.8 million. As its 1989 annual report explains:

By the end of the decade there were 135 full-time employees at work on our issues—economists, foresters, environmental lawyers, resource man-

---

[62] The following paragraphs are based on two already cited articles by Mitchell, 'From Conservation to Environmental Movement', 95–8, and 'Public Opinion and Environmental Politics in the 1970s and 1980s', 90–5.

[63] Although membership has declined since this point, with the figure in 1994 standing at 275,000 (313,000 in 1992), during preparations for Rio (1990, 1991) the Society enjoyed its highest ever figure.

agers, ecologists, writers, and media specialists—together with a highly trained network of support people and perhaps the most sophisticated computer and communications infrastructure in the conservation community.[64]

The figures for 1995 also confirm a general upward trend.[65] The NRDC now has 170,000 members (a figure which has been steady for about three years) while the Sierra Club claims about 600,000 members. Although groups like Audobon have experienced a slight fall (to 544,000) the Environmental Defense Fund gives its membership as 350,000. The size of the World Wildlife Fund (WWF) in the United States alone is put by the organization at 1.2 million—a rise in membership from just 85,000 in 1982. Indeed, the WWF's revenue has increased from just over $12 million in 1984 to just under $80 million in 1994.[66] The National Wildlife Federation (NWF) had a revenue in 1994 of $101.4 million.[67] Although all these figures show a remarkable increase in the numbers of Americans now involved in some way with environmental groups, it is the NWF which has experienced the most spectacular change.

The NWF has been a special case. In 1962, it launched a direct-mail programme which offered members a magazine in return for a small subscription fee. This proved very successful, bringing nearly half-a-million members into the group by 1969. Since that time many new categories of membership have been introduced. This multi-level approach has reaped rich dividends, enabling the organization to claim an awe-inspiring membership of 4.3 million in 1997.[68] Many of these people do no more than pay a modest subscription for the NWF's magazine which is deliberately produced to

[64] The Wilderness Society, *1989 Annual Report* (Washington, DC: Wilderness Society, 1989), 5.

[65] These figures are based on telephone conversations the author undertook with membership officials in the various groups, and on their annual reports.

[66] World Wildlife Fund, *Annual Reports 1992* and *1994* (Washington, DC: World Wildlife Fund, 1992 and 1994). According to the WWF's chairman, Russell Train, who helped found the organization in the United States in 1961, when he became president in 1978 the membership was 25,000 and the budget just $2 million (see 'Chairman's message', *Annual Report 1994*, 2).

[67] National Wildlife Federation, *1994 Annual Report* (Washington, DC: NWF, 1994), 20–1.

[68] In 1985 the NWF was reported as having only 850,000 members which confirms that interest in the environment, although high in the mid-1980s, continued to rise at an astonishing rate (see Helen M. Ingram and Dean E. Mann, 'Interest Groups and Environmental Policy', in Lester (ed.), *Environmental Politics and Policy*, 140).

a very high standard. They are given the option to make a voluntary donation on top of this but it is not a condition of membership. This may mean that many members feel they get value for money just receiving the magazine, (thus they are first and foremost consumers rather than environmentalists), but it still means a huge number of Americans retain a long-term involvement with a recognized environmental group.

This active support for environmental groups is also confirmed by survey evidence of the population at large. Paul Wapner records that in 1981, 45 per cent of those polled in a US survey supported environmental protection regardless of cost, a figure that had risen to 74 per cent in 1990.[69] In a 1986 survey of opinion-poll results dating back to the 1970s, Gillroy and Shapiro found 'a consistently high level of public support for environmental protection' and—even in the face of the Reagan agenda—continuing support for national regulation of many environmental issues.[70] They claim that 'the evidence shows a consistently high level of public support for environmental protection'.[71]

Or, in the words of Riley Dunlap, '. . . environmental quality appears to have become an enduring concern in our society, reflecting the fact that it has achieved the status of an important value among Americans'.[72] Dunlap quotes a Harris poll from 1989 in which 97 per cent responded 'more' when asked if the USA should be doing more or less than at present to protect the environment and curb pollution.[73]

Although environmental issues are rarely the deciding factor for voters, they do enjoy a consistent level of support and have become a 'consensual issue'.[74] At certain moments, high-profile events can increase public concern—the 1988 drought, the ozone hole, the *Exxon Valdez* oil spill—such that the salience of environmental issues is greatly enhanced, making them pivotal for more voters. By and large, therefore, they remain an important if not determining

---

[69] Wapner, 'Politics Beyond the State', 323–4. He also points out that the 1992 budgets of Greenpeace International ($100 million) and the World Wildlife Fund ($200 million) exceeded UNEP's budget of only $75 million (p. 315 n. 12).

[70] John M. Gillroy and Robert Y. Shapiro, 'The Polls: Environmental Protection', *Public Opinion Quarterly*, 50 (1986), 270–1.

[71] Ibid.

[72] Dunlap, 'Public Opinion and Environmental Policy', 133.

[73] Dunlap, 'Trends in Public Opinion', 105–6.

[74] Ibid. 105.

element in the voting calculus. What matters, however, is that there is very little anti-environmental feeling; few people are in favour of a 'worse' environment. The influence that interest groups can exert is, of course, directly affected by the amount of popular sympathy their cause enjoys. Static public support in the late 1970s was reflected in Congress which had, until this time, been a global standard-bearer. As we have seen, public concern levelled off and thus 'environmental lobby groups lost the political clout provided by strong electoral support'.[75]

Environmental groups have usually used quite orthodox methods to try to turn this popular support into influence, and to secure their preferred policy options. This includes lobbying of Congress, either as a whole or of individual congressmen, public campaigns to raise environmental awareness, consumer boycotts of selected goods and firms, and financial donations. This transformation into a well-established Washington lobby—which some have since blamed the movement's problems on—was facilitated by the new opportunities for impact offered by Congress. For example, legislation opened up a legal window for interest groups.

The spate of environmental laws passed by Congress during the 1970s shifted responsibility for pollution control from the states to the central government, thus enabling the groups' overworked lawyers to gain their objectives by filing a single suit in the federal courts instead of fighting legal battles on a state-by-state basis.[76]

Any form of concerted lobbying like this was a change from their traditional role, however, and it soon caused splits within the movement. The Sierra Club, for example, lost its non-profit status through the aggressive tactics of its executive-director, David Brower. Brower then formed Friends of the Earth, a more direct action group which adopted a more activist posture.[77] Another

[75] Lennart J. Lundqvist, *The Hare and the Tortoise: Clean Air Policies in the United States and Sweden* (Ann Arbor, Mich.: University of Michigan Press, 1980), 155. He also quotes Quarles, *Cleaning up America*, 213 n, to the effect that: 'The meetings and the mail fell off; every Congressman could feel the difference.'

[76] Mitchell, 'From Conservation to Environmental Movement', 100–1. Under the Clean Air Act of 1970, citizens were given the explicit power to sue the EPA administrator to ensure implementation. Thus the opportunity for individuals to 'trigger the enforcement mechanism' was institutionalized (see Lundqvist, *The Hare and the Tortoise*, 92, 98).

[77] Mitchell, 'From Conservation to Environmental Movement', 85. Brower is proud of this achievement because it lifted constraints on the scope of lobbying (see *The Progressive* (May 1994), 37).

example is the group Environmental Action, formed directly out of student protests during the Earth Day in April 1970. As Samuel Hays records, this group targeted Congress from the start, determined to pressure representatives into cleaning-up their environmental images.

Each year it singled out twelve legislators in both the House and Senate who had extremely poor environmental voting records and then set out to aid in defeating them. Hence was born the bi-annual compilation of the 'Dirty Dozen' list, which aroused considerable attention in congressional political campaigns.[78]

Not only did the environmentalists organize, however, but businesses, too, sought the benefits of more aggressive collective action. David Vogel has shown that from the early 1970s the environmental and consumer movements scored many notable successes against the business lobby in the United States. He argues convincingly that the corporate lobby found it almost impossible to mobilize against negative public-policy decisions, making little impact, for instance, with the threat of capital disinvestment. Slowly, however, these commercial interests reorganized themselves and, in effect, pursued political strategies copied from the activities of newly 'professionalized' groups like the environmental lobby.

Almost without exception, they represent a mirror image of those pioneered earlier by the public-interest movement. Increasing the physical presence of corporate officials in Washington, using lawsuits as a device to influence the implementation of government regulatory policy, grooming chief executives to be comfortable when dealing with the public, organizing citizens at the grass roots, making more extensive use of coalitions and *ad hoc* alliances, enhancing the awareness of common interests among diverse organizations and constituencies, using the press as a forum for influencing public opinion, seeking allies in the universities, and even becoming less partisan, each of these strategies was in large measure consciously modelled on those successfully employed against business by the public interest movement.[79]

Both sets of interests were reorganizing in these years and it is probably more accurate to portray this process as an interactive one where both lobbies campaigned, litigated, and learned simulta-

---

[78] Hays, *Beauty, Health, and Permanence*, 463.
[79] David Vogel, 'The Power of Business in America: A Reappraisal', *British Journal of Political Science*, 13 (1983), 30.

neously. In one prominent instance, for example, coalitions representing industry and the environment clashed head-to-head over
the building of an Alaskan pipeline. For five years, the American
Petroleum Institute (including Mobil, Exxon, Arco, and Union Oil)
was frustrated in and out of court by the Alaska Public Interest
Coalition (which counted Sierra Club, National Wildlife Federation, Wilderness Society, Environmental Defense Fund, and
Common Cause amongst its members).[80] Although the coalition
lost its battle in 1973, it fought hard to pressure Congress—directly
and through public protest—to try to counteract a massive ad-
vertising campaign staged by the pipeline's oil and gas supporters.
This learning experience stood the groups in good stead for the
future as Hrebenar and Scott record:

Following their defeat these conservation-minded groups vowed to use the
courts, the regulatory agencies, and congressional lobbying to counter the
power of oil. The leadership of the Sierra Club directed environmental
lawyers to press their case before federal agencies and to 'use all available
means to persuade, embarrass, prod and force those agencies to do the job
they should be doing anyway'. Relying on these three avenues of attack,
these groups have become a substantial force in public policy. After a
five-year effort to get federal regulation of the strip-mining of coal over
the opposition of the coal-mining industry, such a bill was signed into law
in August 1977. The coal lobbyists were unable to thwart further the
environmentalists.[81]

As they go on to say, the environmentalists swapped 'their earth
clothes for three-piece suits' and developed legislative and legal
expertise, becoming a widely respected Washington lobby with
good contacts, increasingly well-developed skills in writing and
pressing for legislation, and using a variety of tactics from direct
action to court proceedings. If this was becoming true in the 1970s,
it is firmly the case now. The environmental movement has become
a permanent player on the national scene, with most major groups
maintaining Washington offices, attending briefings and committee
hearings, and seeking to exert pressure in a highly traditional manner. Through comprehensive records, for example, the NWF is
aware not just of where members live but also the kinds of issues

[80] Ronald J. Hrebenar and Ruth K. Scott, *Interest Group Politics in America*
(New Jersey: Prentice-Hall, 1982), 252.
[81] Ibid.

they are most concerned about. They can then be mobilized with great selectivity. In the case of Congress, for example, NWF vice-president Lynn Greenwalt argues that one may only need to pressure a few congressmen who hold the balance of power in a committee:

> If you have a congressman on a committee dealing with the endangered species act and you know that he is wavering, let's say, you can get a few hundred letters, sometimes a dozen letters, at the right time, and his staff will flip through and look at the zip codes and think, 'oh boy, here are three hundred people in my district who are all of a sudden willing to express a concern about the endangered species act', and then run in and tell the boss 'hey, we'd better think twice about this'.[82]

It was this strategy which was first adopted in the 1970s when groups like Environmental Action, Friends of the Earth, the Environmental Defense Fund, and the Natural Resources Defense Council, sought to exert pressure on Congress and the EPA. Resorting to direct mailing of the public, write-in campaigns to Congress, and to the judicial process, through which NRDC, especially, sought to force EPA to meet its legislative obligations, and to the high-profile stigmatizing of congressmen, these groups have endeavoured to maintain constant pressure on legislators.

One issue which emerged in the 1970s and pitted the environmentalists against business was that of ozone depletion. As part of the hearings into new Clean Air Act amendments, Congress heard its first testimony on the problems posed by chlorofluorocarbons (CFCs) in December 1974. Shortly afterwards, the White House set up a task force to examine conflicting scientific evidence and this body concluded in June 1975 that there was 'legitimate cause for concern'.[83] For the next year, environmentalists and industry clashed over ambiguous scientific opinion while Congress and several executive agencies and departments waited for the result of National Academy of Sciences (NAS) deliberations. When they came, in September 1976, they showed enough concern that the EPA, the Food and Drug Administration, and the Consumer Product Safety Commission, all supported a ban on non-essential uses which came into effect in late 1978. By this time, consumer sales of

---

[82] Interview with author, 15 Apr. 1994.
[83] Sharon L. Roan, *Ozone Crisis: The 15-Year Evolution of a Sudden Global Emergency* (New York: John Wiley, 1989), 41.

CFC aerosols had fallen significantly and industry took almost no time at all to market alternatives.[84]

The increase in environmental concern and the substantial involvement of Congress worked very much in harmony. Congressional interest enabled groups to concentrate their activities in one place—Washington—and to press for country-wide legislation. This focus was then enhanced by new problems like ozone depletion which could best be dealt with adequately at the national level. In addition, the establishment of the NEPA and the new prominence of environmental issues made them a subject for executive attention. As the decade closed, environmentalists in the Carter administration sponsored three important developments.

In issuing Executive Order 12114 in January 1979, President Carter extended the application of environmental impact statements (established by the NEPA of 1969) to apply to the activities of the US government abroad. Then, in January 1981, Carter signed Executive Order 12264 which banned the export of toxic waste to other countries. In addition, he also commissioned a hugely detailed study of environmental problems in May 1977. Called *Global 2000 Report to the President*, this study was released in 1980 in the middle of the presidential campaign and, being pessimistic in tone, was attacked by Reagan supporters and quietly ignored by Democrats. Once elected, the new President set about having *Global 2000*'s findings rebutted and overturning his predecessor's executive order banning toxic waste exports.[85]

The Reagan Agenda

The flavour of the Reagan administration's approach to environmental politics is captured by the following observation:

Virtually all environmental protection and resource policies enacted during the 1970s were reevaluated as part of the president's intent to reduce the scope of government regulation, shift responsibilities to the states, and rely more on the private sector.[86]

---

[84] Ibid. 83–5.
[85] Lynton K. Caldwell, 'The World Environment: Reversing US Policy Commitments', in Vig and Kraft (eds.), *Environmental Policy in the 1980s*, 324–5.
[86] Kraft and Vig, 'Environmental Policy from the Seventies to the Nineties', in Vig and Kraft (eds.), *Environmental Policy in the 1990s*, 15.

The central pillars of the Reagan ideology had the effect of overturning and revising numerous pieces of environmental legislation passed during the preceding two decades. Following the advice of a task force on regulatory relief chaired by Vice-President George Bush,[87] the Reagan 'mandate' for economic recovery—as interpreted by the CEQ (composed of screened Reagan nominees)—led to an emphasis on government withdrawal and the efficiency of the free market. To this end the administration stressed the costs, as opposed to the 'value', of environmental programmes, and operated environmental federalism, devolving as much responsibility as possible to state and local levels.

This approach to environmental politics was reflected in senior appointments. To head the EPA Reagan selected Anne Burford (née Gorsuch), a combative figure who visited UNEP headquarters in Nairobi in 1982 (to celebrate the tenth anniversary of Stockholm) and dismayed the assembled gathering by arguing that the free market was the appropriate way to solve environmental problems.[88] At Interior, Reagan appointed an even more controversial figure, James Watt, who had also served in the same department (in a less senior position) under Richard Nixon.[89]

Both Burford and Watt were relatively inexperienced in the field of environmental politics and their dismissive treatment of the environmental movement created much negative publicity.[90] Secretary Watt, for example, tried to open up parts of the National Parks for commercial exploration, as well as restricting government access for major environmental groups. In addition, environmental agencies suffered budget cuts and staff restrictions designed to reverse the process of institutionalization which had taken place during the previous decades.

These actions were, however, politically counter-productive. The restricted access to the executive for environmental groups drove them into Congress and the courts. The former was, as we have already seen, more open to lobby pressure while the latter, charged with interpreting the extensive legislation passed during the 1970s,

---

[87] In which C. Boyden Gray, later counsel to Bush in the White House, was a prominent member.

[88] Caldwell, 'The World Environment', 321.

[89] For a good account of Burford's and Watt's origins, see Philip Shabecoff, *A Fierce Green Fire* (New York: Hill & Wang, 1993), ch. 10.

[90] See McCormick, *The Global Environmental Movement*, 136.

provided environmental groups with a powerful forum to maintain the momentum for change. Congress, for example, resisted one of the new administration's most aggressive decisions—to end US contributions to UNEP—by restoring a (reduced) level of funding. In addition, the relaxation of regulations at local levels simply created or exacerbated environmental problems and led more people to join or at least support interest groups because they perceived their individual circumstances to be deteriorating. In 1982, environmental groups spent a staggering $42 million organizing volunteers in more than seventy congressional election campaigns.[91]

After 1983, when both Burford and Watt resigned, the administration's public profile began to improve. The President tried to reverse anti-Republican feeling on environmental issues by reappointing William Ruckelshaus, the first EPA director, and by moving his national security advisor, Judge William P. Clark, into Interior.

Although the basic clash between Reagan's pro-industry stance and the interests of environmentalists continued into his second term, it did so with less venom. The environment had not been an issue in the 1984 election, when Reagan's challenger, Walter Mondale, who was much preferred by environmentalists, was badly defeated. At the EPA, where the change was most noticeable, the new administrator, Lee Thomas, continued Ruckelshaus's work of rebuilding the agency's capacity and enforcement actions against polluters reached record levels.[92]

For example, the total of administrative actions and criminal and civil referrals to the justice department by the EPA rose from 1,225 in the financial year 1981 to 4,560 in FY 1989.[93] There was still controversy, however, especially over amendments to the Clean Water and Clean Air Acts. Changes to the former were eventually passed by Congress despite a presidential veto. The Clean Air Act amendments proved impossible to legislate, however, and it wasn't until 1990 and a new president that they

[91] David Vogel, *Fluctuating Fortunes: The Political Power of Business in America* (New York: Basic Books, 1989), 262.

[92] Vig, 'Presidential Leadership and the Environment', 42.

[93] Kathleen Segerson and Tom Tietenberg 'Defining Efficient Solutions' in T. Tietenberg (ed.), *Innovation in Environmental Policy* (Brookfield, Vt.: Edward Elgar, 1992), 68.

were passed. In addition, the Interior Department, although more open under its new secretary, Donald Hodel, still pursued a pro-development agenda which resembled that of Reagan's early years.

As well as some small successes on the domestic level, there were also achievements in the international sphere despite the Reagan administration's aversion to most forms of multilateralism. Not only had Reagan tried to eliminate funding for UNEP, he had also refused to sign the Law of the Sea Treaty (which was finally ready in 1981 after seven years of hard bargaining). In addition the USA had stopped funding for population projects and had withdrawn from UNESCO. Despite this retrenchment, American NGOs succeeded in persuading the USA to pressure the World Bank into applying environmental criteria when assessing development projects. This was feasible because it was Congress, not the executive, which held the purse-strings for US contributions to the Bank. A coalition of key American NGOs explicitly targeted Congress from 1983 onwards. They knew how important bank-lending policies were for the environment, and they also knew that through Congress they had an avenue for influence. Congressional control of the largest national contribution to the Bank gave it real leverage which the groups tried to tap into. As Barbara Bramble and Gareth Porter claim:

The potential influence that the US Congress could exert was central to the environmental NGOs' strategy for reshaping the policies of the World Bank and other MDBs [multilateral development banks].[94]

The area of international environmental politics which figured most highly in US calculations during the 1980s was, however, ozone depletion. From a position of some scepticism—especially as the USA was domestically more advanced than any other country having phased out aerosol CFCs in 1978—the Reagan administration, particularly in its second term, pushed hard for an agreement to limit CFC consumption.[95] A variety of factors explain this effort. The improved domestic political context, for instance, gave envi-

---

[94] Barbara J. Bramble and Gareth Porter, 'Non-Governmental Organizations and the Making of US International Environmental Policy', in Hurrell and Kingsbury (eds.), *The International Politics of the Environment*, 328.

[95] Richard Elliot Benedick, *Ozone Diplomacy: New Directions in Safeguarding the Planet* (Cambridge, Mass.: Harvard University Press, 1991), 53.

ronmentalists within the state the chance to pursue a stringent agreement. According to Bramble and Porter:

Most governments were convinced of the need for at least minimal action, and the argument was over speed and funding. The NGO role was thus to support the voices for stricter controls inside the governments—to prove that decisive action would be good politics.[96]

In the EPA, for example, the removal of Anne Burford had reinvigorated the Stratospheric Ozone Program which received new resources and commitment.[97]

Part of this contextual change was the adoption of a new strategy by the principal business association opposing regulation. The Alliance for Responsible CFC Policy, established in 1980, had always had as its primary goal the prevention of unilateral domestic legislation (which only hampered American firms). By 1986, however, what Daniel McInnis calls 'a rising tide of bad public relations, hostile legislation, and continued uncertainty' had persuaded the Alliance to actively support international regulation in preference to either domestic congressional action or a continued loss of market share, especially to the European Community.[98]

Thus societal factors were supportive of international regulation, giving activists within the state a strengthened hand. Indeed, once the administration decided to push for increasingly tight controls on CFCs, activist state officials enlisted NGOs to put pressure on other governments.[99]

In addition to these points, the nature of the issue was also important in explaining the quick and committed effort made by the United States. The costs of abatement were significant but also finite—it was possible to estimate how much phasing out CFCs would cost. This kind of calculation is impossible to make with even minimal certainty about climate change. Relatively cheap and efficient substitutes were thought to be feasible and the incentives

---

[96] Bramble and Porter, 'Non-Governmental Organizations', 347.

[97] Daniel F. McInnis, 'Ozone Layers and Oligopoly Profits', in Michael S. Greve and Fred L. Smith (eds.), *Environmental Politics: Public Costs, Private Rewards* (New York: Praeger, 1992), 143.

[98] McInnis, 'Ozone Layers', 144–5.

[99] Benedick, *Ozone Diplomacy*, 28. As suggested earlier, the intrastate battle continued throughout these years with many senior figures in the second Reagan administration and the first Bush term struggling to try to blunt US CFC policy (see for example, Benedick, *Ozone Diplomacy*, 58, 159).

provided by increased international regulation would, it was thought, speed this process along. The dominance of Dupont in the world CFC market, accounting at one stage for half global CFC production, also meant that there was good informational exchange about the progress of research into substitutes, and about the likely spin-offs in terms of clean technology. Furthermore, the science of ozone depletion was much more certain, and, in 1987, the discovery of an 'ozone hole' over Antarctica graphically illustrated the damage which CFCs were alleged to cause.

Overall, therefore, the outgoing Ronald Reagan bequeathed his successor a mixed legacy. Domestic environmental politics were still combative but the hard edge of the early 1980s had disappeared. Indeed, some commentators accused environmental groups of having contracted 'Potomac fever', eschewing aggressive litigation, mass protests, and consumer boycotts for 'the legislative fix' which saw the major mainstream organizations lose the momentum of the previous decade.[100]

The heads of the ten most prominent environmental groups (the Group of Ten or G10) had met in early 1981 to plan their strategy to counter the deregulatory approach being espoused by the Reaganites.[101] The Ten differed initially on the extent to which confrontation was appropriate but, according to Robert Gottlieb, by the mid-1980s the various members were seeking to establish and institutionalize contacts with the business community.[102] This Group—which accounted for the vast majority of paid-up environmentalists—had, by the time of its demise at the end of the 1980s, recast mainstream environmentalism as what Gottlieb calls 'an adjunct to the policy process'.[103]

The outstanding domestic environmental issue still to be settled was that of the Clean Air Act amendments which had become

[100] Mark Dowie, 'American Environmentalism: A Movement Courting Irrelevance', *World Policy Journal* (Winter 1991–2). See Chapter 5 for an expansion of these criticisms.

[101] See Michael McCloskey, 'Twenty Years of Change in the Environmental Movement: An Insider's View', in Dunlap and Mertig (eds.), *American Environmentalism*, 84.

[102] Robert Gottlieb, *Forcing the Spring: The Transformation of the American Environmental Movement* (Washington, DC: Island Press, 1993), 123. Interestingly, the head of the Conservation Foundation, William K. Reilly, declined to join the Group because of his wariness about some of the staff-based adversarial groups involved like the EDF and NRDC.

[103] Ibid. 124.

stalemated in Congress during the Reagan years. On the international scene the United States had a rather better profile, with substantial efforts having been made to establish the USA as the leader on ozone depletion. This issue would reach its climax within the first two years of the Bush presidency at about the moment when preparations for the Rio Summit began to significantly tax the administration.

The Bush Presidency to 1990

Although George Bush had been intimately involved with the project of regulatory relief, he set about during his campaign, while still Vice-President, to distance himself from the anti-environmentalism of the early 1980s. One difference he immediately faced was the resurgence of the environment as an election issue, a problem with which Ronald Reagan had not had to contend in 1984. Bush styled himself 'The Environment President' and, much to the discredit of Democratic strategists, succeeded in stealing a march on the traditional party of environmentalists by highlighting the pollution in Boston harbour in Massachusetts, the state in which his challenger Michael Dukakis was governor.

Once elected, George Bush succeeded in impressing some with his appointments to key positions, especially his new head of the EPA, William K. Reilly, a former president of the Conservation Foundation. In addition, Bush tried to elevate the EPA—now one of the USA's largest government agencies—to cabinet status and volunteered to host an international meeting to consider drafting a treaty on global warming.[104] Finally, he supported a strengthened Clean Air Act which was eventually passed through Congress in 1990. The amendments to this Act—unveiled by the President in June 1989—followed considerable wrangling within the White House between the environmentalists, now led from the front by Reilly, and the sceptics, a powerful combination of chief-of-staff John Sununu, and budget director Richard Darman. As Norman Vig records:

The proposals followed a long and heated struggle among the factions within the White House that was largely resolved by the president in favor of EPA's arguments for a strong environmental bill. In retrospect, this was

---

[104] Shabecoff, *A Fierce Green Fire*, 252.

to be one of Reilly's few clear-cut victories over the more conservative forces within the administration.[105]

The passage of these amendments still involved a struggle with Congress and the act which emerged was weaker than that which the President had originally proposed. Yet, by the administration's own admission, the bill threatened to cost industry $20 billion to implement and therefore, according to Vig:

Bush felt he had fulfilled his most important environmental pledge and that it was now necessary to hold the line on any further regulation opposed by business and industry.[106]

Thus the initial enthusiasm which the administration displayed for environmental issues waned. The domestic political context changed as a global recession began to bite and employment creation became an increasingly important issue for the President. As one would expect, the voices of the environmentalists were drowned out by those within the Bush administration who promised economic success. This pro-growth stance was often accompanied by a healthy dose of anti-environmentalism from those who saw the green movement as inimical to the best interests of the United States. Thus, by September 1992, George Bush was telling his electorate: 'It's time to put people ahead of owls.'[107]

The Clean Air amendments were undoubtedly the high-point of domestic environmental politics during the Bush years, representing, as they did, the culmination of ten years' effort. On the international scene before 1990, the two international issues which dominated were the final stages of a treaty to ban CFCs and the issue of climate change. As already noted, administration sceptics had tried, until the very last minute, to derail the process of ozone negotiations in which the USA had been such a major player. They failed, and a protocol to the 1985 Vienna Convention (on substances that depleted the ozone layer) to ban CFCs by the year 2000 was agreed in London in 1990.[108] The reasons for the vociferous objections of, principally, Sununu and Darman, are, however, instructive. They had two concerns: the principle of providing *addi-*

---

[105] Vig, 'Presidential Leadership and the Environment', 82.
[106] Ibid. 83.
[107] Ibid. 71.
[108] Thomas, *The Environment in International Relations*, 233.

tional funds for environmental agreements, and the *precedent* that would be established in forthcoming negotiations about global warming (climate change). As Richard Benedick recalls:

Several European and other governments had already endorsed a global climate fund in principle, and the U.S. administration was uneasy about the possibility of unpredictably large future demands to aid developing countries in reducing greenhouse gas emissions and adapting to the consequences of climate change. At least one commentator noted a philosophical consistency between the new U.S. policy and a speech by Darman a week earlier at Harvard University, in which the budget director had been critical of a type of 'anti-growth, command-and-control, centralistic environmentalism' that was aiming at 'global management'.[109]

The sceptics lost on the issue of ozone and the United States agreed, at the last minute, and on a strictly non-precedential basis, to provide some extra funds to help in the elimination of CFCs. It was clear, however, that climate change would be a much more complex and difficult issue with which to deal.

CONVENING THE RIO CONFERENCE

This section deals with American preparations for the United Nations Conference on Environment and Development (the UNCED or Earth Summit), held in Rio de Janeiro in the first two weeks of June 1992, exactly twenty years after Stockholm. With the attendance of more than one hundred heads of state and government (compared with just two at Stockholm), it was to be the most high-profile international gathering held on any issue.

Preparations by the United States started from a much more advanced position than in 1970, with a large amount of domestic and international environmental legislation already in place and important institutional and political actors now long established. The picture of policy-making which emerges is more complicated than that for Stockholm, as one would expect, but it still supports the argument for the importance of the state. The role played by state officials is even more striking in 1992, in fact, because of the development of highly professional interest groups and extensive environmental legislation, together with the international

[109] Benedick, *Ozone Diplomacy*, 159.

institutional advocacy of both UNEP and the scientific community.

The principal international cleavage at Stockholm—that between North and South—re-emerged both before and at Rio in similar form. In addition, a new divide opened up between the EC and the United States. Although on many issues they remained united, on climate change a rift developed which left the USA with Saudi Arabia and Kuwait as its only allies.

The United Nations resolution to hold a second major conference on environment and development was passed by the General Assembly in December 1989.[110] From the beginning the arguments which attended this decision reflected very closely those which had marked Stockholm two decades earlier.[111] Initially, for example, there were two alternative calls for a second conference, a G77 resolution calling for a development-oriented gathering versus a Northern proposal that the environment form the principal focus. A compromise settled on Brazil as host country and Geneva as the base for the conference secretariat (the South had favoured New York to better utilize its UN missions).[112] An organizational meeting was held in April 1990 and two working groups established along with four five-week preparatory (prepcom) meetings.[113]

Prepcoms and Conventions

As with Stockholm, these four meetings were largely divided along North–South lines. Indeed, it is striking how much of the argument during preparation resembles that from the first conference. The first prepcom, in Nairobi, centred on 'mandates and procedures', as well as reflecting 'the concern of many developing countries that

[110] UNGA resolution 44/228; the date was chosen as June 1992, to coincide with the twentieth anniversary of Stockholm.

[111] Maurice Strong was again chosen as secretary-general. One inevitable consequence of this decision was that the organization and tone of the UNCED preparatory process reflected Stockholm very closely: see Matthias Finger, 'Environmental NGOs in the UNCED Process', in Thomas Princen and Matthias Finger (eds.), *Environmental NGOs in World Politics* (London: Routledge, 1994), 195–6.

[112] *Environment and Development File 1992*, no. 4, July 1990 (Geneva: United Nations NGO Liaison Service).

[113] Nairobi, Aug. 1990, Geneva, Mar. 1991 and Aug. 1991, and New York, Mar. 1992.

their priority of development should not be lost on the environmental agenda'.[114] At the second prepcom, in Geneva, things hardly seemed to have changed at all with the United States opposing 'large unspecified amounts of financial transfers and compensation', and stating that any funds would not be new but diverted from existing development assistance.[115] This gathering reviewed the growing mountain of documentation provided by the secretariat and established a third working group (on legal and institutional issues).

At this stage, fifteen months before the summit, conference preparations largely concentrated, as with Stockholm, on an Action Plan and a Declaration. The former was a document of awesome size (500 pages, 40 chapters) which—as *Agenda 21*—became one of the centrepieces at Rio. The latter started life as the 'Earth Charter' and was initially promoted as an inspirational document designed to be the 'timeless expression of a bold new global ethic'.[116] Consisting of twenty-seven principles, it eventually came to reflect—in a more overt way than in 1972—the political divisions between North and South.

In addition to these two main objectives, three other international environmental projects became linked with the conference. The first was a Framework Convention on Climate Change (FCCC), the second a Convention on Biological Diversity (the 'biodiversity treaty', or BDT), and the third a putative Convention on Forests. Although only climate change was originally envisaged as part of the UNCED process (to be negotiated on a separate track), all three documents eventually became associated with the conference and caused more controversy at Rio than either the Declaration or Agenda 21.

The FCCC was developed by an Intergovernmental Negotiating

---

[114] Michael Grubb *et al.*, *The Earth Summit Agreements* (London: Earthscan/RIIA, 1993), 9.

[115] *Earth Summit Update*, no. 1 (July 1991) (Washington, DC: Environmental and Energy Study Institute), 3. This *Update* records, with a startling sense of *déjà vu*, that the one substantive American proposal to prepcom II was that UNEP's executive-director should head an Environmental Coordinating Board based in New York rather than Nairobi. It is true, however, that the stances of both 'blocs', North and South, were more differentiated than in 1972.

[116] Koy Thompson, 'The Rio Declaration on Environment and Development', in Grubb *et al.*, *The Earth Summit Agreements*, 85.

Committee (INC) established by the United Nations General Assembly in 1990.[117] Climate change had been an increasingly public issue during the 1980s. The scientific community, NGOs, and several well publicized environmental problems, had helped to maintain its high profile and, in 1988, governments urged UNEP and the World Meteorological Organization (WMO) to set up an Intergovernmental Panel on Climate Change (IPCC) to assess the scientific and policy implications of global warming. This group was the principal—although not the only—forum in which data and predictions were produced. Its reports increased international concern and G7 summits in both Paris (1989) and Houston (1990) endorsed the principle of a climate change convention. Finally, the UN General Assembly passed a resolution in December 1990 setting up the INC to produce such a convention for signing at Rio.

The INC met five times before Rio, beginning in February 1991, and eventually hammering out a compromise in May 1992. The convention proved highly contentious, especially over the issue of 'targets and timetables' for carbon dioxide emissions which set the United States and the European Community at loggerheads with each other. Simmering disagreements between the North and the South also persisted through four INC sessions during which the convention remained heavily bracketed. Indeed, at the fourth negotiating meeting, the G77 split so badly that it officially announced it had ceased to act as a unified group.[118] It was only after the INC's chairman, French diplomat Jean Ripert, produced a whole new negotiating document—without brackets—that, after much wrangling, and the explicit threat that President Bush would not attend the conference, the EC acceded to American requests to drop stricter language on CO_2 limits.[119]

The Convention on Biological Diversity was a UNEP-sponsored project which had originally, and ironically as it turned out, been proposed by the United States. It became, under the determined advocacy of UNEP's retiring executive-director Mostafa Tolba, a far-reaching and ambitious attempt to regulate all aspects of the international trade in fauna and flora. This had implications for the

[117] See Daniel Bodansky, 'Prologue to the Climate Change Convention', in Mintzer and Leonard (eds.), *Negotiating Climate Change*.

[118] Ibid. 66–7.

[119] Peter M. Haas, Marc A. Levy, and Edward A. Parson, 'Appraising the Earth Summit: How Should We Judge UNCED's Success?', *Environment*, 34/8 (1992), 13.

emergent biotechnology industry—which US companies dominated—as well as for intellectual property rights and financial
transfers. The UNEP negotiating sessions on this convention between 1990 and 1992 expanded its scope still further and, when the
final document was placed before delegates in Nairobi in May 1992,
the USA refused to sign because:

. . . officials felt that the financial mechanism represented an open-ended
commitment with insufficient oversight and control; that the benefit-shar-
ing provisions were incompatible with existing international regimes for
intellectual property rights; and that the requirement to regulate the
biotechnology industry would heedlessly stifle innovation.[120]

The final project was a forest convention. The United States
made determined efforts to press this initiative and received little
success. Some believed it was a disingenuous attempt to deflect
attention away from climate change and biodiversity, others
thought it was a repetition of resource imperialism with the richer
North telling the poorer South not to exploit its raw materials at the
same time as refusing to acknowledge the North's own historical
contribution to global warming.[121] The 'convention' made it all the
way to Rio by which time it had become simply a 'statement on
forest principles', an unpleasing and fairly unconvincing set of general propositions with no force, legal or otherwise.

The first two prepcoms had been largely procedural in nature
even though resolving questions about the agenda for discussion
and the division of labours often reflected deeper disputes. However, it was with the third and fourth prepcoms that these underlying tensions really came to the surface as political divisions
emerged much more starkly. With many organizational questions
settled the business of detailed negotiation could no longer be
avoided.

At Geneva, the task was to begin preparation of Agenda 21. The
document's vast size and scope meant much of the material represented draft papers submitted by governments and NGOs and
simply imported unchanged into the whole. Negotiation was thus a

---

[120] Ibid. 14.
[121] The South was firmly united in talking of the North's 'historical responsibility'
for climate change. See Delphine Borione and Jean Ripert, 'Exercising Common
but Differentiated Responsibility', in Mintzer and Leonard (eds.), *Negotiating Climate Change*, 83.

tortuous business with delegates forced to wade through a mass of general material with uncertain legal and political implications. The sheer amount of text meant each chapter of the Agenda included something for almost every nation to both agree and disagree with and this proved to be the case, leaving the document riddled with bracketed sentences and paragraphs for later settlement. Out of sixteen agenda items, only four (atmosphere, oceans, forests, and wastes) reached the negotiating stage at prepcom III.[122] Little or no progress was made on the Earth Charter. This left much for the final prepcom which became known as 'the New York Marathon'.

The negotiations at New York centred on Agenda 21 and the Earth Charter and, despite considerable disagreement, both were forwarded for approval to Rio (with some text in brackets). The most notable omission, however, was a chapter for the Agenda on financial resources. This had proved impossible to secure with the gulf between the North and the South as wide as ever. According to the *Earth Summit Update*, the G77, (representing 128 countries), had broken-off negotiations on the final day as no progress was being made, in its opinion, on the question of 'adequate new and additional funds, covering the full incremental costs [of Agenda 21 activities] with no reallocation of existing multilateral or bilateral financial flows'.[123]

Numerous details were at issue including Southern demands that industrial countries commit themselves to reaching the UN target of 0.7 per cent of GNP for Overseas Development Assistance (ODA)—in addition to new environmental aid—and that institutions other than the World Bank's Global Environmental Facility (GEF) should distribute environmental money. Even though various linguistic compromises were sought, the EC, together with the USA, Japan, Canada, Australia, and New Zealand, were judged to be too committed to the GEF by Southern countries and thus the latter terminated negotiations, deciding instead to go to Rio with their own draft intact.

This North–South dispute also weakened the forest principles document under discussion at New York. The final text, which ran to only eight pages, still had twenty-three paragraphs or

[122] *Earth Summit Update* (Special Supplement) (Oct. 1991), 1.
[123] Ibid. no. 8 (Apr. 1992), 1, 6.

subparagraphs in brackets and was described by the New Zealand delegate as 'garbage'.[124] Even though the document was to be non-binding, there was a deadlock between the United States, which still opposed extra funding for world forest conservation, and several developing countries, led vociferously by Malaysia, which upheld the notion of national sovereignty by objecting to language suggesting that forests were somehow in 'the interests of the world community'. Even though some Southern nations viewed a forest agreement as the major, if not the only, point of real leverage against the North, and especially the United States, Malaysia's position actually hardened during the negotiation and it began to object to some provisions it had previously accepted.

NGOs were highly visible during this preparatory process. The fears of the scientific community had been instrumental in raising the profile of environmental problems, especially global warming, and interest groups, both nationally and internationally, had sponsored meetings and conferences to discuss appropriate policy responses. In addition, NGOs became heavily involved in lobbying at the prepcoms before Rio. After being granted excellent access to negotiations at a ministerial conference in Bergen in 1990, these groups pressured Maurice Strong for similar participation in the run-up to Rio.[125] Their demands included thirty seats at the negotiating table for the independent sector. Strong was unable to deliver the quality of access they demanded, however, and they were barred by the first prepcom from having a negotiating role throughout the process.[126] As a concession, the UN General Assembly did agree to allow non ECOSOC-accredited groups to join the UNCED process and by the end of prepcom IV there were 1,420 registered.

Many of these groups worked hard to pressure delegates, or even to secure membership on their national delegations. They provided alternative scientific and political analyses, submitted written papers and were even allowed to speak at times to the prepcom

---

[124] Ibid. 7.

[125] Finger, 'Environmental NGOs', 197.

[126] Some delegations had good NGO representation, even though the end result might still have been disappointing for environmentalists. For a case-study of NGO involvement in Canadian and British preparations for Rio, see Alison Van Rooy, 'The Altruistic Lobbyists: The Influence of Non-governmental Organizations on Development Policy in Canada and Britain', D.Phil. thesis, University of Oxford (Apr. 1994), ch. 7.

plenary sessions. This role centred on the provision of information, a circumscribed activity seen as a poor second-best by many groups which felt entitled to a negotiating seat. Indeed, according to Matthias Finger, NGOs were disappointed that Strong and his staff clearly valued this informational, 'input', role but continued to resist involving the groups in substantive decision-making. As with 1972, the pressure group aspect of NGO activities was de-emphasized by the UNCED secretariat.[127]

In terms of sheer size and numbers, NGOs were much more evident than in 1972. This visibility masks an absence of impact, however. In the end, it remained some of the biggest international—and more often than not American—groups which achieved the best access. These were often perceived by other NGOs, either radical Northern ones or Southern ones, to have been co-opted and therefore to have become too sympathetic to governments.[128]

Because of the secretariat's control over accreditation and procedure for prepcoms, and the power of governments to resist initiatives on NGO access, it is hard for these groups to gain positions of influence at conferences themselves. This is compounded by the fact that many, though by no means all, official positions are already clearly enunciated before the negotiation commences. In other words, the international arena is unlikely to provide better spoils than the national process. This did vary across negotiations, of course. According to Hugh Faulkner, executive-director of the BCSD, the climate change negotiations provided better access than either the UNCED process or the BDT conferences.[129] NGOs worked hard to highlight government backsliding, to inform the public and the negotiators of alternatives, and above all to raise popular consciousness of the need for remedial environmental action. There are few examples, however, of direct and substantive impact on actual decisions.

Prepcom IV at New York eventually forwarded a heavily brack-

---

[127] Business groups, especially the Business Council for Sustainable Development, appear to have had slightly better access. The BCSD was set up by Stephen Schmidheiny, a Swiss industrialist, who was appointed an advisor by Strong. Schmidheiny recruited many top business figures to his Council and they provided advice on the potential economic impact of both problems and solutions.

[128] Finger, 'Environmental NGOs', 209–10.

[129] Hugh Faulkner, 'Some Comments on the INC Process', in Mintzer and Leonard (eds.), *Negotiating Climate Change*, 230.

eted Agenda 21 and Declaration, together with the statement on forest principles, for further consideration at Rio. There they were joined by the two conventions. The number of points at issue in all these documents was substantial but they overwhelmingly centred on North–South issues (finance, technology, equity, sovereignty over resources).

CONCLUSION

The environmental movement in the United States has grown sizeably since the early years of international environmental politics. Membership is numbered in the many millions and a high profile on environmental issues has been advantageous for many individuals (most notably Al Gore). According to David Vogel:

... environmental organizations have remained extremely influential: they now represent the core constituency of the public-interest movement. The political significance of the environmental movement is not simply measured by the size of its membership, the degree of public support for its objectives, or the number of lobbyists, lawyers, and political organizers it employs—though by all these measures, the resiliency of the environmental organizations over the last two decades has been remarkable. It is rather that ... the environmental movement has been able to articulate an alternative view of how the quality of life in America ought to be judged and, at the same time, to provide a range of concrete benefits to large numbers of Americans.[130]

Genuine legislative successes have been achieved since the mid-1960s. The Clean Air Act has been strengthened and, despite the acrimony involved in its passage in 1990, it continues to be a landmark piece of legislation. The NEPA of 1969 created the EPA which continues to be one of the most formidable agencies for monitoring compliance with environmental regulations in the world. Action has been taken on water quality, ocean dumping, and the disposal of toxic waste. In the 1980s, despite Reaganite retrenchment, the Endangered Species Act was extended (1982) and a major bill for water-pollution control was passed over a presidential pocket veto (1986).[131] In addition, according to

---

[130] Vogel, *Fluctuating Fortunes*, 294.
[131] Ibid. 262, 278.

environmentalist Brock Evans, vice-president for national issues at the National Audobon Society, saving forests represents one of the movement's principal achievements.

We almost totally won that issue. If there ever was a hopeless lost cause it was the idea of protecting any more of America's giant ancient forests as late as 1990. Now we're in a position where they're hardly cutting any more out there. We went to court, we got lawsuits, we got injunctions. Then we had to weather the political counter-attack in the Congress, we had to be strong enough to withstand all the efforts that were made to overturn the laws, but we held our ground. President Bush made a major issue of it during his election campaign in those states, Clinton fought back and he won both states.[132]

There were of course defeats, as well as victories, and government spending on the environment was cut heavily during the Reagan years. What one can say with certainty, however, is that a strong and vocal environmental movement now constitutes a major player on the domestic political scene. In addition, many of the areas in which these groups have been involved entail an international dimension, and it is clearly not the case, as the following chapter will show, that these groups lack interest in the external sphere. What will be evident, however, is that their resources and influence make a substantially less impressive impact on the making of foreign policy.

[132] Interview with author, 8 Apr. 1994. The states were Oregon and Washington.

4

American Preparations for the Rio Conference after 1990

The early stages of preparation for Rio were similar to Stockholm. An interagency task force was set up under ambassador Robert Ryan of the State Department's Office of Oceans and International Environmental and Scientific Affairs (OES). Called the US UNCED Coordination Center, it was based at the CEQ in order to facilitate communication—the CEQ having been charged, under chairman Michael Deland, with the task of producing the USA's national report. This co-ordination centre drew its members from many other federal agencies and departments and provided the focal point for preparations on the declaration, Agenda 21, and the forests convention (not climate or biodiversity). State was also responsible for leading the delegations to negotiations on these latter conventions. These different avenues of preparation (UNCED co-ordination, climate, biodiversity, forests) were channelled through the head of IESA, E. U. Curtis 'Buff' Bohlen, and then through Robert Zoellick, who in 1991 was both counsel to the State Department and Under-Secretary of State for Economics.[1]

As the process unfolded, however, intrastate bargaining spilled over increasingly into more informal contacts. The major players from the White House, EPA, and State would confront each other on a day-to-day basis. For State this meant, principally, Zoellick, for the EPA, Reilly, and for the Oval Office, Boyden Gray, OMB director Richard Darman, and his deputy, Bob Grady, chairman of the Council of Economic Advisers, Michael Boskin, along with chief-of-staff John Sununu and, following his resignation, domestic-policy advisor Clayton Yeutter. In addition, towards the end of the

---

[1] Zoellick formally had responsibility for OES, but was even more heavily involved because Secretary of State James Baker excused himself due to a potential conflict of interests. The absence of Baker, whose views were moderate, whose political instincts were acute, and who had the clout to challenge John Sununu, further weakened the position of administration activists like William Reilly.

process, the White House Council on Competitiveness—chaired by Vice-President Dan Quayle—became more openly involved, principally on the issue of biodiversity.

It was these several officials who formulated policy in an atmosphere often tainted with acrimony and intense disagreement. They competed with each other—especially on climate and biodiversity where the White House was most involved—to turn their preferences into policy and to persuade the President, with his most trusted confidant, James Baker, absent, of the soundness of their advice. On the Declaration and Agenda 21, however, some progress was made.

THE RIO DECLARATION AND AGENDA 21

In the case of Agenda 21 and the Declaration, the most senior state officials were relatively uninvolved with the process of detailed negotiation. Although they remained responsible for the general orientation of policy, they were content to allow the State Department to operate secure in the knowledge that the issues under discussion were devoid of binding commitments.

This had implications for the American NGO community. They enjoyed better access to the officials in OES and a relationship was able to develop from which both sides gained something. State received information and feedback while environmentalists were drawn closer to the point at which routine decisions were made. This wasn't access in any formalized way to the core state, but it did represent better liaison than in 1972.

Indeed, after Rio environmental groups praised both Bohlen and Ryan for their efforts during preparations. This level of interaction did not prevent strong criticism of the administration from many environmentalists, but it did ensure that during negotiations on the Declaration and Agenda 21 a more sympathetic relationship existed between NGOs and the state than characterized climate and biodiversity. This helped to compensate for the absence of the advantages these groups usually enjoyed on the domestic level—membership, money, votes, publicity—which became less potent because access to core state officials was limited and Congress and the courts played less of a role.

The principal international institutions, the UN and UNEP, also affected the process, although in a more ambiguous way. They had been central to maintaining the high international profile of environmental issues and were the principal umbrella organizations for all aspects of the Rio process. However, the attitude and actions of UNEP director Tolba, for example, were cited by some American officials as having positively discouraged the United States from signing an agreement on biodiversity. In addition, Maurice Strong's belief that holding a high-profile environmental gathering in an American election year would be advantageous proved misguided. As Curtis Bohlen recounts, in a good illustration of the impact of the political context, Strong's hopes were misplaced.

I think Rio would have been far more successful if it hadn't happened in a US election year and, obviously, if it hadn't happened in a world recession period. I think Maurice Strong intentionally wanted it in the spring of an election year here because he thought that would put public pressure on the administration but it had the opposite effect. It was at that point that the conservatives were riding high and Bush was trying to placate them, and it all back-fired, I thought, politically, and we would have been able to accomplish much more in a different year.[2]

Raising the prominence of international environmental issues at this time enabled the sceptics, with an election fast approaching, to mobilize arguments about the threat of recession against the prospect of environmental regulation. What they thought and did mattered *more*, they had more *weight* within the administration, than they might have done without this extra ammunition. Indeed, the political context wasn't very promising for the activists at all:

You also have to realize that we were under very severe budget restrictions everywhere, but there was no support in the Congress for funding these kind of activities. Foreign assistance was under great threat in the budget process on the Hill. Mitchell [George], the majority leader, had introduced a bill in the Senate to cut foreign aid so you were dealing with a political situation where there was no support for throwing more money at this kind of issue. It wasn't just the administration at all, but the whole political climate and, of course, when budgets are tight, and there is a recession when Americans are hurting and out of jobs and everything else, you can't get support for throwing money at developing countries no matter how important it is.[3]

[2] Interview with author, 30 Mar. 1994.
[3] Curtis Bohlen, interview with author, 30 Mar. 1994.

Neither the Declaration nor the Action Plan provoked the high degree of internal argument that the two conventions created, and as a result the independence of State Department officials was appreciably higher. In other words, the implications—given the domestic political context—were innocuous enough that the sceptics near the core remained relatively uninterested. The one area where concrete concessions did become an issue—finance—proved virtually impossible to negotiate successfully.

Despite this leeway, State still negotiated within a set of guidelines derived from the clear unacceptability of certain options to senior officials in the White House itself. The views of these sceptics were ably represented within the State Department as well. In one example, recounted by an NGO representative on the US delegation to prepcom III, Gareth Porter, delegation-head Bohlen was confronted by an aide to Bob Zoellick, Chris Dawson.

She was considered more or less the enforcer for the White House on the delegation. Everybody knew she was the conservatives' representative. Indeed, at one point she tried to countermand the head of the delegation [Bohlen] on an issue relating to how the US would respond to G77's position paper on, I believe, finance. And she did that not just in front of me, as an NGO representative on the delegation, but also in front of a member of Congress, and congressional staff, which I thought was entirely inappropriate and it created a good deal of uproar.[4]

This story also illustrates a central facet of the NGO : State relationship. As Bohlen and Ryan provided the main focus for environmental groups, the degree to which they were constrained by the policy conflict among senior officials directly affected the efforts of the NGO community as well because their institutionalized access was almost always at this relatively junior level. This mattered less when the policy concerned was non-controversial because the lack of senior state interest gave flexibility to State. But the more impact a policy threatened, the higher up the interagency process it would go, and the keener interest senior figures would take. In this regard, of course, those nearest the core of the state had considerable power.[5] Gareth Porter explicitly recalls the prob-

---

[4] Interview with author, 4 Apr. 1994. Gareth Porter was director of the international program at the Environmental and Energy Study Institute (EESI), in Washington, DC.

[5] It is worth comparing this account with that offered by Rosenau.

lem for NGOs of weakened administration officials who were constrained on certain issues and 'knew what their brief was'.

It ruled out a vast array of potential proposals. Most of the proposals they
wanted to make would be automatically ruled out, they knew that. So
there was not much room for NGOs to influence the US on specific
proposals.[6]

Porter was told by Dawson, for example, not to pursue a relatively minor proposal he wanted to advance in the forest discussions. She told him an interagency meeting would be required in
Washington and not only that he should drop it but also that he was
not to try to get any other delegation to present it, a demand Porter
considered unnecessary and 'egregiously antagonistic' to an NGO
representative.

It is one thing to say don't go criticizing the United States for this position,
which I am perfectly willing to live by, but she was essentially saying,
you're neutered, forget it, you have no role here. So I was ready to
withdraw from the delegation because I felt my ability to pursue things
that I felt important as an NGO delegate was being essentially cut off.[7]

This neatly demonstrates one dilemma associated with better
access for NGOs. Because access to governments can be restricted,
established groups face a trade-off between gaining proximity to
power and losing a degree of independence. They become identified with the formulation of a decision, and perhaps even its implementation, and are therefore less free to criticize it (so-called
'insider' groups). The other option is to retain the opportunity for
radical criticism while eschewing closer ties with government ('out-
sider' groups). One is more able to achieve less, or less able to
achieve more. In the case above, as it happens, Bohlen told Porter
to feel free to pursue his proposal without the need for a referral to
Washington.

Despite the non-committal nature of the UNCED documents,
Zoellick and Bohlen had sought early agreement from the White
House on the general thrust of policy. Bohlen recalls:

The White House never got involved really in Agenda 21, just on a few
issues. Early on we got agreement from the White House on what the US

---

[6] Interview with author, 4 Apr. 1994.
[7] Ibid.

initiative should be, where we should focus our efforts, and we just pursued that. As long as we kept off sensitive issues it wasn't a problem. I think both Bob Ryan and Zoellick, and I, all felt the less that went to the White House the better.[8]

In fact, Bohlen considered it one of his roles to be 'a buffer between UNCED staff and the politicians, and to try and give them as much leeway as possible'.[9] The advantage of getting general support for the direction of policy—and maintaining this overall line—was that the White House could be kept out of the detailed negotiations. This proved particularly important on Agenda 21 because the decision-making process in the executive had slowly deteriorated over the months following prepcom III in August 1991. This development proved more troublesome on climate and biodiversity because the White House was more heavily involved. On Agenda 21, in contrast, the confusion at the centre of the state which emerged after December 1991 enabled more junior officials to exercise greater discretion.

The principal change within the White House which occasioned this deterioration was the resignation of George Bush's combative chief-of-staff, John Sununu, in December 1991. A man of strong views and forceful personality, Sununu had been the linchpin in the decision-making process across most issues.[10] He had taken a special interest in climate change because, as a trained engineer, he claimed to find the scientific analyses of the environmentalists deeply unconvincing.[11] Sununu was replaced as chief-of-staff by transport secretary Samuel Skinner. At the same time, the former agriculture secretary and Republican National Committee chairman, Clayton Yeutter, entered the White House as domestic-policy advisor and assumed responsibility for the environment both at home and abroad.

The problems associated with this change at the core in early 1992 are outlined in detail by Bob Zoellick.

---

[8] Interview with author, 30 Mar. 1994.   [9] Ibid.

[10] His impact on the climate change process was significant. For example, it emerged that a speech George Bush gave to an Intergovernmental Panel on Climate Change (IPCC) meeting in Washington in Feb. 1990 had been 'changed' by Sununu (who denied he had as a result 'toned it down'). This reflected the struggle already underway between sceptics and activists (see *New Scientist*, 125/1703: 23).

[11] EPA director Reilly recalls that Sununu had his own computer simulation programme on climate change into which he would enter the latest data himself (interview with author, 14 Apr. 1994).

There wasn't a well-organized White House process to try to force people to come to some reconciliation of different positions. The views were very strongly held. I had to go over a number of times to say look, I'm doing the negotiations. Now, at the end of the day, if you don't want to do this, fine, I'll drop it, I've got zillions of other things to do. But if you want to try to reach an agreement, and you're willing to say here's the parameters in which we can work in, then here's my strategy on how to do it. But, in part, it was hard to get a decision from people on 'what do you really want, what are you willing to live with?' I kept trying to force that on the system and once Skinner came in, with Scowcroft's help, we created a process around Yeutter to try to do that. Then I would go to these meetings and say okay, we're about ready to go to this conference, I need to know this. Yes or No? Then everybody would talk around and they'd expend their political venom on this, that, or the other thing, and I would say, well, that's nice, but do I do this, or do I not do this? Frankly, I had a lot of frustration with that process. Put it this way, if we'd had those processes in dealing with the other foreign-policy issues for three-and-a-half years we wouldn't have had all the successes we had.[12]

At the centre of this process sat the President, a consensus politician who rarely tried to press his own personal opinions into the process and relied heavily on his cabinet. It is, of course, clear that a more activist president could have weighed in decisively on such an issue and, indeed, the final decision was always George Bush's. But the argument tended to circle around him, to be played out in meeting after meeting by Gray, Reilly, Yeutter, Darman, and Zoellick. Without James Baker to work for consensus in private, the President, with his inclination against extremism, was left to hope his aides reached a satisfactory solution. This was a difficult task for a man 'whose every bone was moderate':

When he had people around him that were basically taking more extreme right views I think it made him uncomfortable. In a sense he didn't want to challenge his own staff or tell Boyden Gray, who was an old family friend for many years, to bugger off. On the other hand, by leaving them to their own devices he made it damn hard for somebody to try to reach a solution that would please his own inclinations and that would help him politically.[13]

The absence of either a strong lead or evidence of a firm inclination from the President enflamed the intrastate battle further.

[12] Interview with author, 13 Apr. 1994. Zoellick later moved to the White House, in Aug. 1992, as deputy chief-of-staff.
[13] Bob Zoellick, interview with author, 13 Apr. 1994.

The key areas of dispute in Agenda 21 related to chapters on funding, and to the implications for intellectual property rights and the biotechnology industry. These were left in abeyance by the UNCED process until the final two prepcoms. A few, acrimonious, issues remained in the Rio Declaration and most of the work in the State Department was undertaken by lawyers seeking to avoid wording which conceded important international precedents like 'the right to develop'.

Prepcom III was held in Geneva in August 1991. In preparation for this meeting the UNCED secretariat circulated option papers calling, among other things, for the eradication of poverty by the year 2000 and the creation of jobs in 'ecologically stressed' areas. In response, the US co-ordination centre released a document rejecting these demands and stating that 'the United States will oppose specific and unrealistic demands for the elimination of poverty' and that neither poverty nor environmental projects 'can be addressed effectively through large unspecified resource transfers'.[14] There was some fruitful discussion in areas like ocean policy and land resources but, on financial resources generally, the G77 insisted on its draft forming the basis for discussion, and on the creation of a new funding institution separate from the World Bank-based GEF. Both of these issues, together with the question of technology transfer, were adjourned for discussion at the final prepcom, in New York.

The absence of senior level involvement had allowed the UNCED Coordination Center to prepare well for this last prepcom.

We had a really first-rate professional team. Our delegation to any prepcom would average probably 45–50 people including people who were really expert on each of the issues. The computer system that Ryan set up was absolutely fantastic. In New York, at the last prepcom, we had an entire room just filled with computers and word processors where we could call up every document from all the previous prepcoms and we could instantly make changes. There's no question in my mind we were better prepared than any other delegation in the world. When we went into those prepcom negotiations we had clear positions on everything.[15]

In other words, left to their own devices the State-led co-ordination

---

[14] *Earth Summit Update*, EESI, no. 2 (Aug. 1991), 1.
[15] Curtis Bohlen (who headed the delegation), interview with author, 30 Mar. 1994.

centre was able to provide the USA with clear and coherent positions within the parameters set by more senior White House officials. Successes at prepcom IV centred, therefore, on areas which did not cross these boundaries.

The US delegation enjoyed a rocky ride during the five weeks of the final prepcom. Not only were they locked into tough discussions with other governments, they were under constant criticism from elements of the American NGO community who even 'hijacked' a reception at the United Nations given for the US delegates by an NGO co-ordinating group, US Citizens' Network on UNCED (based in San Francisco). More than fifty US activists surrounded Robert Ryan and 'demanded that the voices of environmental victims and the poor be heard', adding that: 'Your report card shows FFF'.[16]

Under pressure from domestic lobby groups and other governments, as well as from the United Nations, the State Department was making it clear well in advance that it would resist any proposals it did not agree with and would use the same device as in 1972—interpretive statements—to disassociate itself from specific measures. Official State Department press briefings before New York reiterated that no 'new and additional resources' would be forthcoming, and a State spokesman derided an UNCED paper on changing energy consumption patterns as a 'statist, central economic planning response'.[17]

The USA's own proposal for institutional changes centred on amalgamating three existing UNESCO programmes under the title of the 'sustainable development committee', thereby avoiding the creation of a new UN body. Other delegations had a more ambitious new unit, a sustainable development 'commission', in mind.[18] Although disagreement existed on many parts of the two UNCED documents, it was the apparent stubbornness of the G7 (with the USA a prominent member), especially on funding, which cast the longest shadow over the whole two-year process in advance of New York and provided the focal point for criticism both from within and from outside the process.

---

[16] *Crosscurrents*, (an independent NGO newspaper for UNCED), no. 3, p. 12.
[17] *Earth Summit Update*, no. 7 (Mar. 1992), 3.
[18] Ibid. 2. UNEP also had an interest, of course (see Mark Imber, 'Too Many Cooks? The Post-Rio Reform of the United Nations', in *International Affairs*, 69/1 (1993), 56.

Despite the inauspicious approach to this final prepcom, however, large parts of both Agenda 21 and the 'Earth Charter'—which was retitled the Rio Declaration on Environment and Development—were forwarded to the conference proper in nearly finished form.[19] The major exception was the chapter of Agenda 21 which mattered most—on financial resources—where negotiations had foundered on the appropriate level of overseas development aid the North should provide and the appropriate mechanism for distributing it. Within the Declaration, paragraphs blaming the North and Northern consumption patterns for environmental degradation were dropped and a compromise was reached on the question of the 'right to development'.[20]

On Agenda 21, progress was made and the United States did prove flexible in several important areas especially when Bohlen conceded, in late March, a week before the prepcom finished, that the USA did *recognize* the need for new and additional resources (which remained a long way from saying it was going to provide them). In a speech to the plenary on 24 March, Bohlen told delegates that the industrialized countries had to generate new and additional resources from various sources, public and private, since existing financial resources were insufficient.[21] This paralleled a G77 initiative—later withdrawn—that these resources would only be *part* of the financing mechanism for Agenda 21 (rather than the entire $125 billion annual cost the UNCED staff was estimating).[22] The United States had been spearheading Northern opposition to a G77 proposal for a wholly new fund to finance Agenda 21, with Bohlen arguing on 18 March that the proposal showed:

. . . a great deal of inflexibility on the part of the G77. It's unbalanced, one-sided, and seems to by and large ignore the many good suggestions made last week, many of which had wide support.[23]

According to Dan Abbasi, a reporter for the *Earth Summit Times* at the negotiations, the seemingly new commitment from

[19] The renaming of the Earth Charter as the more modest 'Rio Declaration' reflected the consistent desire of the South to depart from a concentration solely on environmental problems.
[20] *Earth Summit Update*, no. 8 (Apr. 1992), 2.
[21] *Earth Summit Bulletin* (published by Island Press), 26 Mar., 1/19: 1.
[22] Existing ODA spending world-wide totalled $55 billion annually.
[23] *Crosscurrents*, 19 Mar. 1992, p. 4. The suggestions to which he referred concerned a Chinese proposal for a 'Green Fund' within the GEF.

the United States was not, in fact, as promising as it at first appeared.

If you look at the actual language that Bohlen used, and I went up and asked him after this, they clearly built in a lot of protections in that they could say that the resources could come from public or private sources, and that of course opens up 'well, we think it would be a great idea if the private sector would do a job of channelling money' . . . that kind of language. And there was also that 'escape hatch' language down in Rio itself.[24]

These linguistic concessions had little concrete effect because the USA and the G77 remained at odds, in finance chapter negotiations, over the former's refusal to accept that 0.7 per cent of GNP should be a minimum aid target. The European Community also proved as resistant as the United States to Southern demands and, according to the *Earth Summit Update*, it was actually the Europeans' refusal to accept a diminished role for the GEF, as the initial distributor of environmental funding, which caused the G77 to terminate talks until Rio proper.[25]

By the end of the long and arduous negotiations at New York much of the Declaration and the Agenda were agreed. Although very real differences existed on the finance chapter—as well as with the details of any technology transfer, the form of any new environmental unit in the UN, and on sections within the Agenda dealing with lifestyle and consumption patterns—progress had been made.

This was, however, the easier part of the process. The UNCED documents had no legal bite and governments were not committed to pursuing any recommendations contained within them. This is not to say they were treated without caution by delegates. The example of negotiations in other areas, like ozone, and the wariness many governments displayed in putting their names to potentially precedential developments, imbued the discussions with real significance. This was one area, for example, where NGOs might be quick to pounce after the conference, informing the public of the implications of actual commitments (where they could be

[24] Interview, 9 Apr. 1993, World Resources Institute, Washington, DC. In addition, Ryan made it clear to the *Earth Summit Update* (no. 9 (May 1992), 2) that the USA remained steadfastly opposed to committing a specific level of 'new and additional funding' for Agenda 21.
[25] *Earth Summit Update*, no. 8 (Apr. 1992), 6.

discerned) and, more embarrassingly for governments, providing evidence of backsliding.

In the American case, those involved with detailed negotiations were more specifically environmental officials and they were able to operate without constant senior oversight. The story with the conventions was different; they had costly, legally binding implications. Thus the preparation process for climate and biodiversity brought central state officials into the heart of the argument.

CLIMATE CHANGE AND BIODIVERSITY

According to George Bush's EPA administrator, William K. Reilly, there may never be a presidency which discusses climate change so often and at such a senior level. Contrary to the image some have portrayed of an administration unconcerned by the issue of global warming, senior Bush officials spent many hours debating the issue right down to things as specific as the validity of various pieces of conflicting scientific evidence. Chief-of-staff John Sununu took a deep personal interest and lined up with budget director Richard Darman and president's counsel Boyden Gray against Reilly, who spent his four White House years arguing constantly for positive environmental actions against these sceptics. In the 'middle', officials like Bob Zoellick, OMB associate director Bob Grady, and even national-security advisor Brent Scowcroft, became involved in the process of trying to establish a clear policy.

The process of policy-making on these two issues supports the state-centric argument in several consequential ways. Firstly, NGO pressure was most keenly felt in terms of its impact upon one major element of the political context: public perception of the administration (of its general conduct, as well as its attitude to the environment). The 'firestorm' of criticism groups stoked up against the state was a key dimension of the intra-state negotiation. Activists could point to the degree of public dissatisfaction as a reason to act, sceptics could argue that it reflected the pro-Democratic bias of environmental groups thus rendering concessions counter-productive.

To gain publicity for environmentalism was not enough, therefore. In 1972, the value of getting environmental votes gave activists a powerful bargaining weapon and more leeway in policy choice. In 1992, the strength of environmental protest against the Bush administration was such that it actually *weakened* advocates in the core state because their arguments about the 'value' for the President of pursuing a pro-environmental stand lacked credibility.[26]

The fact that the core state was able to restrict access forced interest groups to establish contacts at a level below where crucial choices were made. However, the alternatives proposed by environmentalists—even if advanced 'upwards' by these junior state officials—entered into a new policy arena at the more senior level where other concerns were aired forcefully by powerful advocates and where, most crucially, information, including prognostications about possible environmental disaster and prescriptions to avert it, had to be 'cashed out' in *political* terms. It was only met with sympathy by activists and conciliators (those who encouraged compromise). The sceptics challenged and discounted the arguments of their opponents in this more rarified atmosphere, presenting an alternative case and deploying powerful resources to support it.

The point to bear in mind is that NGO-sponsored initiatives and information still has to be persuasive in a policy debate where it is seen, not as the 'objective' presentation of facts, but as ammunition for one side in the struggle to prevail. Much as many scientists and interest groups perceive themselves to be neutral, to be representing a 'public' interest which should trump the political process, in the core state this information is perceived as weighted in favour of a particular outcome. It is seen as being in the service of pro-environmentalism and it thus faces considerable resistance.

This sceptical opposition is not to be understood simply as the representation of a 'business' interest, the common alternative to more altruistic or 'social' forces. On ozone depletion, for example, the principal business coalition, the Alliance for Responsible CFC Policy, had long since opted to support international regulation when key state sceptics (like Hodel, Sununu, and Darman) were still pushing forcefully to prevent concessions.[27]

---

[26] Before his early death, Republican campaign strategist Lee Atwater had provided some support for Reilly by arguing that the environment was an issue where the administration might retain women voters who disagreed with the party's stance on abortion.

[27] Before his own departure, chief-of-staff Sununu reportedly threw the chairman of Dupont, Edgar Woolard, out of his office, refusing to listen to his views on

Thus, the promotion of an economic perspective does not characterize the state as a whole, only certain sections of it, and even then it is not simply a crude reflection of what 'business' seeks.[28] Dan Quayle's competitiveness council had to manœuvre to outwit its opponents, and to secure an anti-biodiversity administration line. Its victory was in no sense a foregone conclusion. It was helped by some elements of the political context like, for example, the fears about declining American competitiveness which had coloured the debate about industrial policy since the 1980s. As a counterbalance, however, there was confusion about whether all parts of the biotechnology industry were necessarily against the biodiversity treaty.

The political context provides the backdrop to policy arguments. Electoral support, the vocal environmental movement, the state of the domestic economy all comprise the stuff of intrastate debate. It is through this channel that NGOs and business can impact most significantly when the core state is centrally involved. Even Congress was reduced to passing a largely symbolic resolution in an attempt to persuade George Bush to go to Rio—in itself not a particularly ambitious objective. Indeed, the activities of many societal or peripheral state actors were addressed to this end, and yet Bush's refusal to attend was a bargaining tactic employed deliberately and with forethought. He changed his mind (if he ever even intended not to go) because the bargain had been secured not because of mounting societal pressure.

A further implication of the following section is that the activities of international institutions and other governments had an ambiguous impact. The former were the subject of considerable suspicion by sceptics and, as noted, Mostafa Tolba's actions decreased the chance of a biodiversity treaty being signed by the United States.[29]

administration environmental policy and giving him a lecture in return; Gordon Binder (Reilly's chief-of-staff), interview with author, 4 Apr. 1994.

[28] Insurance companies, for example, often support more radical preventive measures on the environment for fear they will be forced to pay out because of unpredictable climatic change. The 'allegiance' of these service-sector businesses—who create little direct pollution—needs more careful consideration than that of old-style industrial corporations with large investments in plant and existing production processes.

[29] For all that the USA was suspicious of Tolba, this was balanced by the G77's wariness of the UNEP executive-director. Southern states feared he was concentrating too much on issues of primary concern to the North and was instrumental in

The UN, UNEP, the EC, and Southern governments, all provided a further avenue for NGOs to try to work their preferences into the process. Again, however, their success in this regard was often limited to information provision and to agenda definition. This is not a negligible aspect of interest-group activity. But it does mean their success is dependent on other actors, the 'sovereignty-bound', possessed of more formal power, being able to prevail. It is also a complex political process. Some Southern countries, and even Southern NGOs, were wary of Northern NGOs which they perceived as privileging the environment over development and thus of representing a diluted version of the Northern position.[30]

Finally, the process of policy-making itself demonstrates the central explanatory importance of intrastate competition between sceptics and activists who both believed quite clearly that their own course of action was to be preferred. Some thought the President should go to Rio, some did not, and they argued the point until a resolution was reached. They argued about signing a climate change convention, they argued about signing a biodiversity convention. Although the political context was central to this process, it was the intrastate debate itself that constituted the crucial factor in policy explanation.

Climate Change

Climate change was the international environmental issue which dominated discussion within the Bush White House. While it was biodiversity which, in May and June 1992, sparked the most intense political reactions, climate was considered at length by the administration for several years prior to Rio. Even before the formal intergovernmental process began in 1991, the findings of the IPCC had been taken up by activists within the state after scientists and the NGO community worked to establish action on greenhouse emissions as part of the international environmental agenda. As

depriving him of a major role in the UNCED process (Porter and Brown, *Global Environmental Politics*, 50).

[30] In the development field, according to Ian Smillie, Southern NGOs seek both financial and moral support from their Northern counterparts but are wary of interference and the imposition of 'second-hand Northern regulation' (Ian Smillie and Henny Helmich (eds.), *Non-Governmental Organisations and Governments: Stakeholders for Development* (Paris: OECD, 1993), 14).

noted, it was partly a concern about setting a climate change precedent which persuaded sceptics to oppose an international ozone-depletion agreement in both 1988 and 1990.[31]

Dominant among the sceptics until the end of 1991 was chief-of-staff John Sununu. He believed those advocating CO_2 control were pursuing a hidden agenda which was anti-growth and anti-development. He tied environmentalists in with those European governments which stood to benefit from any economic restrictions imposed on the United States. His view of Rio was as a kind of forum for international blackmail. As he explains:

I think the whole idea of the Rio conference was to corner the world leaders, particularly the president of the United States, in an election year, and to force them to make a decision that, on a more rational basis, they might not make.[32]

Sununu had been an engineer and he was comfortable disputing the scientific basis of the case for global warming as well as the policy implications. Indeed, he was highly critical of the technical naïvety of politicians and believed more research was essential to establish the merits or otherwise of threats to the earth's climate. The scientific 'ammunition' which both sides deployed reflected an important if ambiguous role for scientists. Pluralist authors, in the 'epistemic communities' literature for example, make much of their influence, Peter Haas maintaining that they become 'strong actors at the national and transnational level', and that:

Members of transnational epistemic communities can influence state interests either by directly identifying them for decision-makers or by illuminating the salient dimensions of an issue from which the decision-makers may then deduce their interests.[33]

However, complexity and uncertainty have marked the issue of climate change from its inception and, as a result, the state has been faced with often contradictory scientific analyses. Even though a vague and very general consensus emerged in the early 1990s, the conservatives in the state were always able to marshall sceptical

[31] Benedick, *Ozone Diplomacy*, 151.
[32] 'The Political Pleasures of Engineering: An Interview with John Sununu', *Technology Review* (Aug./Sept., 1992), 25.
[33] Haas, 'Introduction: Epistemic Communities and International Policy Coordination', 4.

research to counter the activist's case. As Eugene Skolnikoff has argued:

When it comes to difficult, costly, detailed economic and political choices, scientific experts will be testifying in opposition to one another.[34]

Thus, Sununu and other sceptics could usually find, and could even promote, respected scientific support for their arguments. Even though 700 members of the American National Academy of Sciences (NAS), including forty-nine Nobel Prize winners, wrote to George Bush in 1990 urging him to take steps to combat global warming, a report by the George C. Marshall Institute, prepared by several eminent scientists, argued that more research be undertaken because other reasons—besides increases in greenhouse gases—could explain temperature rises.[35] In other words, 'science' is not simply an objective commodity within policy deliberations, it serves as a resource for state officials to argue their respective cases.

Sununu's sceptical attitude extended most importantly to budget director Richard Darman and president's counsel Boyden Gray. Both considered the climate change convention (negatively) as 'an international Clean Air Act', both had been involved with the process of deregulation since the early days of the first Reagan administration, and during 1991 and 1992 both vigorously expressed deep scepticism about the whole Rio process. Darman and Reilly had a poor personal relationship motivated in part by the former's belief that Reilly leaked details of private discussions to the press in order to bolster his position. Reilly's chief-of-staff, Gordon Binder, describes the attitude of Darman and Sununu in the following terms.

They all had that notion that EPA and environmentalists were bunches of eco-cowboys, you know, and that no cost was too great, no problem too small, to require regulatory intervention. That was where they

[34] Eugene B. Skolnikoff, 'The Policy Gridlock on Global Warming', *Foreign Policy*, 79 (Summer 1990), 87.
[35] *New Scientist*, 125/1703 (10 Feb. 1990), 23. The George C. Marshall Institute has generally been sceptical about climate change giving succour to the conservatives. Scientists there have not only rejected the warming hypothesis but criticized the evidence-gathering methods partly in order to demonstrate that there is no 'scientific consensus' as such (see 'Hot Air in Berlin', *National Review*, 1 May 1995, 18–22).

were coming from, and they translated all this on the international level as well.[36]

Gray's attitude towards the EPA, meanwhile, is illustrated by the following anecdote.

The White House's traditional view of EPA is of an incipient monster grasping for total control and lusting in its heart for an Orwellian world run by regulators in which 'everything that is not forbidden is required'. White House counsel Boyden Gray used to entertain his colleagues with a dark tale of environmental mischief, as he posed the rhetorical question: 'How can the Russians destroy America? Should they subvert CBS and the *New York Times*? Or infiltrate the CIA and the Pentagon?'. 'No', he would say, 'all they need to do is get control of EPA. There are enough levers in the Clean Air Act to wreck the whole economy.'[37]

Gray did not, however, evince total scepticism and he became publicly identified with a conservative but flexible position known as 'no regrets'.[38] In company with a member of Vice-President Dan Quayle's competitiveness council, David Rivkin, Gray outlined administration policy in the following terms in 1991.

In view of the uncertainties underlying the global warming debate and the limits on available resources, the administration has embraced a balanced policy of adopting those environmental measures that reduce greenhouse gas emissions while providing concrete environmental benefits. This approach has been termed a 'multiple objective steps' or 'no regrets' policy. Action taken in this area should be based upon the long-term outlook, 'taking into account the full range of social, economic, and environmental consequences of proposed actions for this and future generations'.[39]

---

[36] Interview with author, 4 Apr. 1994.

[37] William K. Reilly, 'I'm Gonna Make You a Star: A New Approach to Protecting the Environment in America and Around the World', prepared text of lecture delivered at the Institute for International Studies, Stanford University, 9 Feb. 1994, p. 11.

[38] This 'no regrets' idea—to enact measures on climate change only if they were good for the environment more generally as well—was initially outlined in a less conservative speech by Secretary of State James Baker to the first session of a US-chaired IPCC working group held in Washington in Feb. 1989. The speech infuriated Sununu, however, and Baker reversed himself in 1990 and thereafter withdrew from the fray (see William A. Nitze, 'A Failure of Presidential Leadership', 192–3). Nitze was formerly deputy assistant secretary of state at OES and head of the US delegation to the IPCC meetings during 1989.

[39] C. Boyden Gray and David B. Rivkin, 'A "No-Regrets" Environmental Policy', *Foreign Policy*, 83 (Summer 1991), 52.

The conservatives also had an institutional advantage within the core state in that the OMB had oversight of the formal relations between government agencies and departments, and Congress. Bob Grady describes its role as 'the long arm of the law':

Any federal agency that wants to testify on Capitol Hill, for example, has to clear their testimony with us. Any agency that wants to promulgate a regulation has to clear the regulation with OMB. Any agency that wants to even send a letter to Capitol Hill has to clear that with OMB. When a bill comes to the floor of the House or the Senate it's the OMB who prepares the statement that says the administration is for or against it and, here's why. When a bill comes to the president to be signed it's the OMB that sends him the memo that says sign this bill or veto it.[40]

The sceptics' position contrasted with that of those in the administration who were more activist, most importantly Reilly. He believed that the projections for reduced greenhouse gas emissions—especially after the passage of amendments to the Clean Air Act—meant the USA could and should sign up to a climate change agreement in which it agreed to stabilize its emissions of carbon dioxide at 1990 levels by the year 2000.[41] As he told a congressional hearing after Rio, the USA's net reductions in emissions meant a level between 1.5 and 6 per cent above 1990 output, not quite stabilization but 'closer than many of our competitors are likely to come'.[42] In addition, Reilly says he would have been inclined to sign the biodiversity treaty and then use its financial mechanism to manage implementation—much in the way he believes other governments (and now the Clinton administration) have done.[43]

Indeed, Bob Grady also argues:

I think we should have endorsed targets and timetables because my own view is we could have met them and will in fact meet them by virtue of the

[40] Interview with author, 8 Apr. 1994. Grady was seen by some as dangerously moderate. One author maintained: 'The normal OMB check on environmental imperialism was neutralized by Mr Bush's appointment to the OMB review post of Robert Grady, another environmental true believer' (Fred L. Smith, Jnr. (founder of the Competitive Enterprise Institute), 'Carnival of Dunces', *National Review*, 6 July 1992, 31).

[41] Interview with author, 29 Mar. 1994.

[42] Hearing before the Senate Committee on Foreign Relations, 18. Sept. 1992, Y4 F 76/2, senate hearing 102–970, p. 38.

[43] Interview with author, 29 Mar. 1994.

quite meritorious policy measures that have been enacted in the United States over the course of twenty years.[44]

The administration had evidence, in fact, that the USA was likely to meet the 1990 levels requirement by the end of the century. A ten-page memo produced by a four-agency working group for the State Department—entitled 'US views on global climate change'—showed CO_2 could be cut by 7–11 per cent without difficulty. As the *Washington Post* remarked: 'Treaty advocates within the administration gained strength in recent days by citing a new analysis that showed that carbon dioxide reductions were possible at relatively little cost to the economy.'[45]

The central issue, then, between the sceptics and the activists was over the question of targets and timetables. The treaty being developed by the INC called for a reduction of CO_2 to 1990 levels by the year 2000 ('stabilization'). For the sceptics, any formal regulation was unacceptable. This was compounded, however, by the relatively greater importance of fossil fuels to the United States compared with Europe. The insistence by the EC that the treaty targeted CO_2 rather than a comprehensive reduction in all greenhouse gases further enflamed White House rejectionists. Thus it was over 'targets and timetables' that the battle was fought.

The chief negotiator for climate change was Robert Reinstein, deputy assistant secretary for environment, health, and natural resources at the State Department. He worked closely with Bohlen and especially Bob Zoellick who was responsible for liaising between the White House and State. As noted, the White House was interested in climate change from the beginning and the leeway which State had been granted on Agenda 21 was absent. Although interagency discussions continued at staff levels, the main points of contention were settled by the principals in Cabinet meetings and informal discussions within the White House itself.

Zoellick, whose background was in economics, enjoyed a degree of trust from Darman and Gray and he manoeuvred during the

[44] Interview with author, 8 Apr. 1994.

[45] *Washington Post*, 25 Apr. 1992, A1, A11; 2 May 1992, A6. See also *Science*, 256 (22 May 1992), 1138. The director of the Office of Technology Assessment told a congressional hearing that many non-Draconian measures were available for reducing CO_2 but after the year 2015 they would 'inevitably' rise again unless commercialization of non-fossil fuels took place on a major scale (Senate Foreign Relations Committee hearing, 18 Sept., pp. 53, 56–63). For a critique of the ten-page memo see Peter Samuel, 'Fog from Foggy Bottom', *National Review* (25 May 1992), 36.

early stages to create some room for negotiation. Well aware that the administration conservatives were against targets and time-tables, he and Reinstein adopted a realistic approach to the nego-tiations. This involved starting without lofty aims or concrete commitments but with a pragmatic assessment of what was feasible—the lowest common denominator. According to Zoellick:

Part of the problem is that the process of negotiating also created political animosity going into Rio because you can't give your bottom line as the first thing so we had to take a lot of criticism for that.[46]

The question for the administration was how to secure a treaty without targets and timetables in the face of opposition from, prin-cipally, the EC. A decision was taken to use the issue of George Bush's attendance at Rio as an explicit bargaining ploy to force the Europeans into a concession. As Zoellick confirms:

That was a point of leverage for the global climate change negotiations. Helmut Kohl and others, John Major, wanted him to be able to come and so that was one of the things I held out—I said 'we ain't going unless we get this treaty', and so that became a point of leverage.[47]

The absence of the world's principal polluter and most powerful state from such a global gathering would have detracted consider-ably from the importance of the occasion for all concerned, damp-ening the atmosphere, devaluing the agreements, and reducing the political capital which could be derived from it. Thus, the attend-ance of the President at Rio became the other half of the targets and timetables issue and these two questions became, to all intents and purposes, the focus of climate change negotiations.

Several officials thought that the President always intended to go to Rio, not least Bob Zoellick who claims he was 'basically negoti-ating with a chimera. I created leverage where there wasn't lever-age.'[48] This is confirmed by Reilly and by the chairman of the CEQ at the time, Michael Deland, who recalls:

I had several discussions with him [Bush] about it and there was never any question in my mind from as early as December of the preceding year that he would go.[49]

---

[46] Interview with author, 13 Apr. 1994.
[47] Ibid.
[48] Ibid.
[49] Interview with author, 21 Apr. 1994.

The sceptics within the state were equally adamant, however, that the President should refuse to go to Rio. We have already seen Sununu's view of Rio and, after his departure, the new domestic-policy advisor, Clayton Yeutter (installed February 1992), shared his scepticism—even about the wisdom of holding the conference at all.

I was persuaded that there was no way the United States could win in that setting. It was simply going to provide a forum for other countries to take advantage of the opportunity to let the United States be the 'villain' of environmental policy, including some of our European friends. In addition, there was no question but that the media that would be in attendance in Rio would likewise have that same basic viewpoint and we were just inevitably going to be battered in the media as well.[50]

The final INC meeting to agree a climate treaty was planned for the first week in May 1992. The arrival of Yeutter had, however, complicated matters as he sought revisions in negotiating positions which had already been established by Zoellick and Reinstein in previous months. Zoellick had worked directly with Reinstein, aware of the fact that Bohlen was 'seen on this issue as not being "reliable" by some people in the White House'.[51] Indeed, Zoellick appointed Reinstein—who had experience in trade, energy, and economic issues—with one eye on the sceptics in the administration, 'so he could meet various constituencies that we had to develop internally'.[52]

Reinstein and Zoellick narrowed down the issues for which interagency agreement was essential and Zoellick concentrated on getting those agreed by the White House through both formal and informal channels. As we have seen, the departure of Sununu exacerbated the problems of decision-making within the administration and these key State officials found it increasingly difficult to get consistent directions. As the process neared completion, Gray

---

[50] Interview with author, 5 Apr. 1994.

[51] Interview with author, 13 Apr. 1994. Zoellick goes on to say: 'I don't want to put a guy in a position where he's going to get killed by people, shot in the back, as the one trying to negotiate the position.'

[52] Ibid. Yeutter argued, in an interview on 5 Apr. 1994, that his existing acquaintance with Reinstein, and the close supervision he could exercise over the process in New York, contributed to his ability to oversee the project and therefore to its satisfactory conclusion from his point of view. That these things were not true of biodiversity—negotiated in Nairobi—in part explains the failure of those talks, he maintains.

and Yeutter put forward even more forcefully the view that whatever happened on climate George Bush should not go to Rio.

At a set-piece debate within the Roosevelt Room in the White
House in April 1992 (before the treaty was agreed) the President
listened to the arguments both for and against attendance. Boyden
Gray forcefully put the case for refusal, recalling that 'I was the
only person who had the courage to say you shouldn't go.'[53] The
argument for was put by Bill Reilly with some support from Brent
Scowcroft, George Bush's national-security advisor.[54]

Gray's argument for non-attendance was forthright. He recalls
telling the meeting that 'it would be a disaster'.

It is in the interests of every other country to beat up on the United States
and you have the echo chamber of senator Gore who went down there and
started beating up on it too. How can you possibly win? Tim Wirth was
horrified. I remember getting a call from him down there . . . [he] came to
Bush's defence because he thought it was so outrageous that an American
delegate would be attacking his own president. All of that was
anticipatable.[55]

As well as this internal dispute about the President's attendance,
outside the state societal groups were working hard to try to push
George Bush into going to Brazil. Environmental and other interested 'social' groups combined to form two organizations. The first,
the Citizens' Network, provided information and received feedback from hundreds of different groups throughout the USA. The
second, the Consortium on Action to Protect the Environment
(CAPE '92), was comprised by six senior interest groups (including
the Sierra Club, the National Audobon Society, and the National
Wildlife Federation) and worked on lobbying the administration
in Washington. The NWF undertook, as part of the Citizens' Network, to organize the 'go to Rio' campaign.

NWF vice-president for international affairs, Lynn Greenwalt,
recalls his organization heading the operation to 'try to get George
Bush hectored into going to Rio'. A campaign of major cinema
advertisements, televised conferences, full-page newspaper ads,
and write-in protests was used to convey the idea that the only

[53] Interview, 7 Apr. 1994.
[54] Scowcroft was appalled, according to one official, that Darman and Yeutter
were proposing the USA should attend a major conference and be the only country
not prepared to sign a treaty designed to 'save the planet'.
[55] Interview with author, 7 Apr. 1994.

heads of state not going to Rio were Saddam Hussein, Colonel Gaddafi, and the President of the United States. As Greenwalt says of NGO strategy:

Sometimes you use a carefully sharpened and very carefully chosen stiletto, sometimes you swing a brick, and in the case of getting George to go to Rio, heaving a big brick was chosen as preferable and more likely.[56]

Congress too, was making an effort to persuade the President to go. In July 1991, forty-two senators wrote to George Bush urging him 'to give UNCED a high priority on your agenda. Without such immediate leadership action we stand to lose both the opportunity that UNCED presents and the goodwill of the many nations which look to America for leadership.'[57] In February 1992, seventy-four House members wrote to the President calling on him to agree to stabilization, and to attend the summit. Then, in April 1992, resolutions were passed by both the House and the Senate opening the way for a joint resolution designed to commit the President to attend the Rio Conference.[58] The most ambitious congressional attempt to influence the administration came, however, with the Global Climate Protection Act. Sponsored by California democrat Henry Waxman, it was designed to force the United States to accept the goal of stabilization.

As chairman of the House subcommittee on health and environment, Waxman told congressmen: 'It is time that Congress stepped in to mandate that the United States take a more responsible position—just as we did in 1990 when the Bush administration was unwilling to support strengthening the international program to protect the ozone layer.'[59] Offered on 2 April 1992 as an amendment to the national energy bill, Waxman's legislation enjoyed some bi-partisan support as it urged an end to the administration's 'irrational opposition' to targets and timetables.[60] This resolution came much too late in the negotiating process, however, and it had barely been introduced before Reinstein secured a deal which the administration accepted. Despite this, Waxman's efforts did have an impact in the White House.

---

[56] Interview with author, 15 Apr. 1994.
[57] 25 July 1991. The letter was co-written by Senators John Kerry (D-Mass.) and Robert Kasten (R-Wis.).
[58] *Earth Summit Bulletin*, no. 8 (Apr. 1992), 3.
[59] Ibid. 1.   [60] Ibid. 3.

One of the sceptics' arguments against agreeing to targets and timetables was that, in contrast to the governments of many other nations, the United States executive would be forced to honour its agreements by virtue of congressional legislative power. In other words, it would be committed to implement any treaty.[61] This was counterposed with the attitude of other states, especially within the EC, who told Bush officials they would sign the treaty and then worry about how diligently to honour it. The sceptics, consequently, drew support from the claim that the USA might be the only conscientious implementer of the climate treaty. Reilly, on the other hand, made a contrasting argument out of the possibility that the USA would be the only non-signer. He feared the USA would end up isolated as the only nation to refuse to sign treaties aimed at saving the planet. Thus not signing entailed costs as well.

The question of Waxman's legislative efforts was addressed explicitly by the President in a remark to Boyden Gray during the Roosevelt Room debate. Reilly recalls it as follows:

One of the points he [Gray] made was that if we go, we make any commitments at all, it's not like other countries making commitments, all of a sudden we'll find that Waxman has taken this over and has legislated a requirement in the law. That's the point at which Bush said, 'Wait a minute, Waxman isn't running this government. Since when are we living in fear of Waxman? Let's decide what we need to do on the merits here and not worry about Waxman.'[62]

The question of George Bush's attendance therefore depended on three things—his own inclinations (seemingly in favour), the climate change treaty being agreed (also achieved successfully), and the political wisdom of his attendance (to which interest-group pressure applied most directly). This last point was, however, the least weighty consideration. Indeed, of the three reasons for attendance, only the latter can be eliminated without seriously

[61] The writers in *Double-Edged Diplomacy* assess the extent to which being domestically 'tied' enhances the credibility of one's bargaining position. On the whole they are sceptical, suggesting that chief executives prefer greater domestic flexibility (see Evans, 'Building an Integrative Approach', 399–403).

[62] Interview with author, 14 Apr. 1994. An article by Paul A. Gigot in the *Wall Street Journal* poured scorn on those in the administration who are 'green as grass'. He feared Waxman would 'stampede' his 'Clinton–Reilly' type bill through Congress leaving Bush facing a veto fight (24 Apr. 1992, 16). The *Journal*'s opinion pages often betrayed considerable sympathy for the sceptics.

hampering an adequate explanation of the affirmative decision the President eventually made.

The deal which was finally struck on climate change—on 9 May 1992—came a long way towards the American position. It was brokered by INC chairman Jean Ripert of France who secured agreement of the parties on the 'circuitously worded goal of returning their greenhouse-gas emissions to "earlier levels" by the turn of the century'.[63] This rather vague aim is complemented by the following objective:

stabilization of greenhouse-gas concentrations in the atmosphere at a level that would prevent dangerous anthropogenic interference with the climate system ... within a time frame sufficient to allow ecosystems to adapt naturally.[64]

The final, fifth, session of the INC was split into two halves and the first, in February 1992, failed to reach agreement. The second began at the end of April 1992 with Ripert introducing an unbracketed compromise text which formed the basis of discussions (as he had been urged to do by a high-level meeting between key delegations in Paris in mid-April).[65] Constant high-level meetings were required as the USA and the UK hammered out language on stabilization but this initially failed to find favour with some Southern delegations, especially India.[66] Eventually, however, acceptable text was secured, and the treaty concluded.

[63] Haas, Levy, and Parson, *Appraising the Earth Summit*, 13. The NGO newsletter at UNCED, *ECO*, described the final agreement as 'True Trash!' (see Matthew Paterson, 'The Politics of Climate Change After UNCED', in Caroline Thomas (ed.), *Rio: Unravelling the Consequences* (London: Frank Cass, 1994), 175). This newsletter was seen by some as essential evidence of NGO influence at Rio, largely because it 'arrived at the breakfast-tables of the negotiators almost every morning before the beginning of the negotiations' (see Atiq Rahman and Annie Roncerel, 'A View From the Ground Up', in Mintzer and Leonard (eds.), *Negotiating Climate Change*, 249).

[64] Haas, Levy, and Parson, *Appraising the Earth Summit*, 13. The *Earth Summit Update* claims Bush rang German chancellor Helmut Kohl personally to 'persuade him to drop a demand for targets and timetables' (no. 9 (May 1992), 1).

[65] Bodansky, 'Prologue to the Climate Change Convention', 61–70.

[66] Ahmed Djoghlaf argues that the climate negotiations were not a successful time for the G77 which only managed one unified position paper through the entire process; 'The Beginnings of an International Climate Law', in Mintzer and Leonard (eds.), *Negotiating Climate Change*, 105. But see Mukund Govind Rajan, 'India and the North–South Politics of Global Environmental Issues: The Cases of Ozone Depletion, Climate Change and Loss of Biodiversity', D.Phil. thesis, University of Oxford (1994), for an alternative view.

According to Curtis Bohlen, Zoellick made an 'extremely hard sell' in the White House to convince Yeutter and Darman that this compromise would be an acceptable final settlement and, accordingly, Reinstein agreed to the language on 'earlier levels'. This final treaty was not enough, of course, to satisfy those who would have preferred no agreement, but it did represent something of a negotiating success for the United States.[67] The *Wall Street Journal* described is as a 'considerable coup' and praised Bob Zoellick for devising the non-attendance ploy thus winning the administration 'concessions beyond their fondest hopes'.[68] Even John Sununu, now out of office, was moved to concede: 'I think the agreement came out reasonably correct: it is a comprehensive approach, without specific targets.'[69]

The conservatives in the White House were also relatively content. In a letter to Congress, which was leaked, Clayton Yeutter pointed out with some satisfaction that: 'There is nothing in any of the language which constitutes a commitment to a specific level of emissions at any time.' He added that the word 'aim' had been carefully chosen for the treaty so as not to imply any kind of timetable, and that the USA would do its fair share only because it already had a domestic process in place, 'not because of any compulsion emanating from this proposed document'.[70]

The President quickly announced he would now go to Rio, and preparations were begun to assemble a delegation. The political climate was running heavily against the administration, however, with unremittingly bad publicity portraying Bush as either wrongheaded or indecisive. This made life very difficult for the activists. For example, when Reilly met with senior environmentalists in May, and they offered to try to generate some public support for the embattled EPA chief, he had to tell them that it wasn't a credible promise, that things had gone too far. The sceptics in the White House had all the ammunition they needed to argue that environmental groups—and the media—would not give positive coverage to a Republican government on this issue.[71]

This was the situation towards the end of May, the moment when

[67] Nitze 'A Failure of Presidential Leadership', 188.
[68] *Wall Street Journal*, 27 May 1992, 1.
[69] Sununu, 'The Political Pleasures of Engineering', 25.
[70] *Boston Globe*, 13 May 1992, 1, 9.
[71] William K. Reilly, interview with author, 29 Mar. 1992.

the biodiversity issue was approaching resolution. The competitiveness council was now fully involved and, according to Reilly,
budget director Richard Darman was telling the President that the
non-signing of the treaty would be no more than 'a two-day story'.
In fact, in Reilly's graphic phrase, it was 'a real train wreck'.[72]

The Biodiversity Treaty

Although efforts to protect biodiversity predated negotiations in
the late 1980s, the concerted attempt made after 1987 to produce a
more comprehensive convention represented a qualitative change
from earlier, less integrated, endeavours. The initial push for a
treaty to protect global biodiversity was started by the United
States itself.[73] The original proposal was, however, to integrate or
rationalize existing international agreements on areas like trade in
endangered species and the protection of tropical forests. What this
became, by 1992, was a far-reaching treaty which sought among
other things to impose limitations on the commercial use of products derived from biological sources like plants and animals.

The sceptics in Washington, (and in other Northern capitals),
feared that the emergent biotechnology industry—led by US
firms—would lose billions of dollars from the making of agricul-
tural, industrial, and pharmaceutical products.[74] By requiring the
sharing of technological developments, changes to laws on intellectual property rights (IPRs) and patents, and new and additional
funds for finance, the treaty played on several areas of existing
sensitivity not just in American foreign policy but also in the South.

Indeed, IPRs were already a source of contention between the
North and the South, especially between India and the United
States, the latter having targeted India for punitive trade sanctions
in retaliation for what the Americans saw as an 'unfair' refusal to
implement patent standards.[75] The USA argued that the competi-

---

[72] Interview with author, 29 Mar. 1992.

[73] Abby Munson, 'The United Nations Convention on Biological Diversity', in
Grubb *et al.*, *The Earth Summit Agreements*, 75.

[74] The USA dominated the emerging biotechnology industry. In 1985 it had 372
firms engaged in this area of the economy compared with 137 in Japan and a total of
115 in France, Britain, Germany, and Italy combined (Calestous Juma, *The Gene
Hunters: Biotechnology and the Scramble for Seeds* (London: Zed Books, 1989),
108–17).

[75] See Rajan, 'India and the North–South Politics of Global Environmental Issues', 241–54.

tiveness of its firms was being undermined by lax IPR regimes in other states, and it sought tighter international agreements under the auspices of both the GATT and the World Intellectual Property Organization (WIPO).

It is important to bear in mind, therefore, that arguments about IPRs, about technology transfer, and about the distribution of benefits from biotechnology, impacted upon an area of international relations which was already highly contentious and played directly on the political fissure between North and South. In addition, the sceptics already had the advantage of a contextual opportunity with Congress having supported trade retaliation. The status quo on intellectual property rights in the United States was near to the conservatives' position giving them an institutional edge over activists who wanted a biodiversity treaty and were prepared to compromise to get it.

On biodiversity, one important new actor was also involved in the treaty process from its inception: UNEP. Under its second executive-director, Mostafa Tolba, who was soon to retire, the negotiations on a treaty, quite pedestrian in the late 1980s, became galvanized into a drive for an all-inclusive convention. Initially, an expert working party was set up by UNEP in 1988. This met three times prior to July 1990 before undergoing two transformations, its final incarnation being as a fully-fledged Intergovernmental Negotiating Committee (INC). This latter body met five times between June 1991 and May 1992, at the headquarters of UNEP in Nairobi, to hammer out a binding convention.[76]

Although the White House, less involved than on climate, kept a careful eye on State Department negotiations in Kenya, and despite the deeply divisive issues under consideration, State managed to keep the US centrally involved throughout the unusually hasty process.[77] Indeed, the speed which characterized the development of the BDT was attributed to Tolba's desire for UNEP—somewhat marginalized in the whole UNCED process (for which there was, of course, a separate secretariat)—to play a larger role. Tolba

[76] Munson, 'The United Nations Convention on Biological Diversity', 75–6.

[77] In this case, with strong negotiating positions held on all sides, the absence of more senior-level involvement played to the sceptics' advantage because it meant little or no political effort was expended trying to pressure other governments domestically (rather than in Nairobi) to relent and make further concessions at UNEP (see Richard N. Gardner, *Negotiating Survival: Four Priorities after Rio* (New York: Council on Foreign Relations Press, 1992), 12.

would have been an obvious choice for UNCED secretary-general but he was replaced at the last minute by Strong, a change for which the USA had pressured.[78] Tolba used the BDT, therefore, as the focal point for his drive to raise UNEP's profile in the process, pressing it into the Earth Summit preparations with sufficient speed to enable a signing ceremony to take place at Rio.[79]

The determination on the part of the South to secure Northern concessions gave the arguments about biodiversity a similar ring to those from Stockholm. The key to the dispute was the question of who benefited, and who *ought* to benefit, from technological developments derived from genetic resources originally found overwhelmingly in the South. In essence, the South 'owned' the genetic material, Northern corporations used it to great commercial advantage, and thus the G77 insisted on a firm affirmation of its ownership of the initial resources.

The developing countries moved to place access to plant genetic resources under the principle of sovereign control by states, thus forcing corporations to negotiate with the state itself for access to resources.

In addition:

... the developing countries were not willing to rely entirely on commercial deals between companies and national governments. They wanted the biodiversity convention to commit the industrialized countries to ensuring that companies taking advantage of developing countries genetic resources shared their profits equitably and gave the source countries access to technologies developed from those resources.[80]

As we have seen, a dispute over patent legislation was already under way and, for the United States (and other Northern countries), the BDT was not an arena in which it was prepared to compromise its existing stand. Despite this, the South persisted in arguing that IPRs were a barrier to the transfer of biotechnology, originally developed from Southern resources, on preferential terms (a key Southern demand). Although these hopes

[78] Finger, 'Environmental NGOs', 195.

[79] According to Mark Imber, Tolba was well known for 'single-mindedness in the promotion of the work and role of UNEP' ('Too Many Cooks?', 62).

[80] Gareth Porter, *The United States and the Biodiversity Convention* (Washington, DC: EESI Papers on Environment and Development, Nov. 1992), 5. Rajan, 'India and the North–South Politics of Environmental Issues', chs. 7 and 8, is a comprehensive guide to the perception of these issues in the South.

were foundering on US opposition, and also against the objections of other Northern countries like Germany, Britain, and
Japan, by the time of the final, and most consequential, meeting
in Nairobi, concessions so significant had been made that
'some delegations from industrialized countries concerned
with the text told the US delegation that they now found it
acceptable'.[81]

A further sticking point was the question of the dispersal of
funds targeted to aid in the preservation of biodiversity. As we
have seen in relation to climate change, the South had already
failed to establish a new body (to circumvent the GEF) from being
named as the responsible organ for the distribution of the money
(on climate, it had secured UNDP involvement in the GEF as a
concession). The GEF was mistrusted by the South because it was
administered by the World Bank, and it was keen to establish the
'parties to the convention' as the administrators, giving each state
one vote and thus giving itself an overwhelming majority as in the
UN General Assembly. The USA would not be able, therefore, to
prevail on questions of funding. The South—having moved ground
on patents—dug its heels in even more firmly on this financial
question. Such was the context of the final confrontation in early
May 1992.

Although senior White House officials had not been debating biodiversity in the way they had been exercised by climate
change, sceptics—especially in the Vice-President's Council on
Competitiveness—had been keeping an eye on developments.[82]
During the negotiation process this had manifested itself in increasing stalemate within the interagency meetings, and in the close
supervision of State officials working on the the treaty in Nairobi.
Curtis Bohlen recalls attempts by the department of Interior and
the competitiveness council to prevent anything affecting the
biotechnology industry from getting into the draft convention. In
addition, State's negotiator in Nairobi, Eleanor Savage, was telephoned regularly by a member of Clayton Yeutter's staff, Teresa
Gorman, to check that Bohlen's reports of developments were
accurate and that the White House's conservative position was
being maintained. Bohlen recalls:

---

[81] Porter, *The United States and the Biodiversity Convention*, 8, 13.
[82] Abby Munson, 'Genetically Manipulated Organisms: International Policy-
Making and Implications', *International Affairs*, 69/3 (1993), 499.

Teresa was not going to take my word for it necessarily and wanted to be sure that the liberals at State didn't stray from the party line.[83]

Thus the conservatives remained vigilant throughout the negotiation process, the competitiveness council having tried already to derail the process. In a memo for the Vice-President's chief-of-staff, Bill Kristol, two council members set out in detail what they saw as the 'major problems' with the biodiversity convention. The memo lists nine deficiencies in the draft treaty including concern about the need for major revision of domestic laws, biotechnology regulation 'in a manner totally unacceptable to the US', preferential transfer of technology, and an inadequate funding mechanism. They concluded:

The current draft convention is so extensively flawed that it is highly unlikely that the sufficient corrective action could be accomplished at a single negotiating session, and thus, any final convention that might be completed in May would remain seriously flawed. The problem for the Administration is how to avoid a flawed final convention resulting from the May meeting either by a significant redraft or reaching agreement to hold further negotiating sessions.[84]

These conservatives were helped in this endeavour by several factors; the seniority of other sceptics in the White House, a broad consensus on IPRs, volatile anti-Republican environmentalism, and the fact that their adversaries had already spent political capital getting agreement on climate change. As Bob Zoellick recalls:

Our freedom of maneuver was less because in a sense I had spent a lot of political chips within the administration to get the global climate one done, it was not going to be easy to go back and the way that they [UNEP] did the negotiation really didn't give me any freedom to go back.[85]

Echoing this observation, Curtis Bohlen describes the atmosphere in the administration during the two weeks after the treaty was signed:

---

[83] Interview with author, 30 Mar. 1994.

[84] White House Council on Competitiveness Memo (14 Apr. 1992) to Bill Kristol, from David McIntosh and John Cohrssen, titled 'Major Problems with the Draft Convention on Biological Diversity'. McIntosh was the director of the competitiveness council and Cohrssen, an expert on biotechnology.

[85] Interview with author, 13 Apr. 1994.

By the time we got the final document back it was only three weeks before Rio, everyone was frantic getting organized for Rio, and there was no time to do a really detailed analysis and then convince the competitiveness council and the interior department that maybe this was something that should be signed politically even though it was not a good document. But Yeutter's principal staff person on this [Gorman] was extremely close with the interior department and the competitiveness council; the conservatives had a lock on this. What was interesting was that when I talked to Zoellick about it he said, 'There's nothing I can do about this one. I went to the mat on climate change with the conservatives and I cannot do it again.'[86]

The cost of the limited success the activists enjoyed on climate change was therefore a diminution in their influence over biodiversity.

In addition, we have already seen the impact of the negative domestic political context; it gave ammunition to the conservatives and prevented the activists from being able to argue that pro-environmental measures made good electoral sense. As Bob Zoellick notes, 'when the environmental community seems to be inflexibly against you then it is harder for someone with a moderate position to prevail'.[87] In addition, the entry of Ross Perot into the presidential race gave the sceptics an extra boost. They were able to argue strongly that in a three-way contest the Republican party had to play to its base which meant supporters who were largely anti-regulation and pro-business, as well as being less sympathetic (although often not *un*sympathetic) to the environmental movement.[88]

The international political context was also running against the United States, most importantly because it had locked horns throughout the pre-Rio process with both its Northern partners and the South. The North was, to an extent, to gain some small revenge for conceding on climate by abandoning the USA, at the last minute, on biodiversity, while the South remained determined not to give any further in Nairobi. The USA was thus left isolated. Indeed, the domestic context worsened for activists as May wore on because of three domestic decisions which all went against the environmentalists, thus fuelling protests against the administration still further.

[86] Interview with author, 30 Mar. 1994.
[87] Interview with author, 13 Apr. 1994.
[88] Gardner, *Negotiating Survival*, 10.

First, a long-awaited decision was taken not to reduce the logging of primary-growth forests in Oregon thus signing the death warrant of the spotted owl to which the trees were home.[89] Secondly, Bush's 1988 election pledge to ensure 'no net loss' of wetlands was effectively broken. A competitiveness council redefinition of wetlands was accepted which opened up to development as much as half of that previously so designated. Thirdly, the President also ruled for Quayle over Reilly by accepting that under certain circumstances air pollution rules were to be relaxed enabling companies to exceed permits without prior government approval.[90]

With the activists in such a precarious position already, the final negotiation at UNEP headquarters did little to help their cause. State's room for manœuvre was highly restricted and Bohlen's account of the final stages in Nairobi reflects his frustration.

After the final negotiation, Tolba, in a very high-handed manner, rammed all this through. He was determined to have something ready for signature and he didn't care what was in it as long as he got it done. He went to such lengths as—on one of the key financial issues—convening a special group one evening to talk about it where an effort was made to reach compromise and we found out right afterwards that it was all just a façade, he had already sent the draft to the publisher to be printed. At the final day on which this thing was to be adopted our delegation didn't see the final document till an hour before. Up till then it had all been handled by different working groups . . . and nobody understood how all these were going to tie together. It was just a horrendous way to run a negotiation and I think the result speaks for itself.[91]

Both Zoellick and Reilly corroborate the essence of this account, with the latter emphasizing how marginalized Tolba had become after climate change was put on a separate track.[92] Bohlen felt progress had been made in the final days of the negotiation and

[89] This decision was taken by the so-called 'God Squad', seven officials who by law have the power to allow a federal activity to continue even if it jeopardizes an endangered species. The 'ayes' won 5–2 led by interior secretary Manuel Lujan. The two 'noes' were Reilly and the representative from Oregon (Gordon Binder, interview with author, 4 Apr. 1994).

[90] *Boston Globe*, 12 May, 3; *International Herald Tribune*, 21 May, 3.

[91] Interview with author, 30 Mar. 1994.

[92] The point here is not about Tolba's views—the South was set against further concessions and was prepared to see an agreement signed without the USA as a participant—but that his actions had a knock-on effect on the intrastate process thereby weakening activists.

that, with a little more time, and perhaps one more INC session, a better agreement could have been reached which the USA could have signed.

Despite Tolba's actions, the power of activists may already have been too low. The final stages of the negotiation reflected an impasse, between the USA and the South, with the sceptics in control in Washington, determined and able to resist compromise, and the South, led by Malaysia, resolving to implement the convention as it was even without US support.[93]

This argument was simply more grist to the mill of the conservatives. Given time, it is possible that a compromise could have been negotiated in Nairobi which might have served to deflect the sceptics' fire, enabling State to push through an agreement. As it was, the USA was faced—after 22 May—with an effective *fait accompli* and thus a choice between isolation and concession.

Some, Reilly most notably, did put the argument for signing. He thought it would be possible to agree to the treaty and then use the funding mechanism to exercise some control. OMB associate director Grady also thought it possible to sign and then haggle about the details.[94] Reilly also feared that the United States would end up as the only non-signer, in contrast to the beliefs of others like Zoellick who thought that Britain and Japan would also reject the treaty. As Curtis Bohlen recalls the decision not to sign:

I don't think anyone thought it was a good treaty . . . It would have taken tremendous effort to take it to high enough levels and get people to agree to sign it and he [Zoellick] just wasn't willing to . . . His actual words were 'We'll have to let the conservatives have this one.' At that point no one had done a real political analysis of the potential fallout if the US wound up being alone. Also at that point there were about five or six other countries in Europe who were strongly opposed to it and told us they probably wouldn't sign it. Of course political pressure eventually turned them all around so we were left isolated.[95]

In discussions at Rio, several heads of government told the President that they agreed with him about the problems within the treaty but were forced to sign due to pressures from green parties

[93] Porter, *The United States and the Biodiversity Convention*, 8.
[94] Interview with author, 8 Apr. 1994.
[95] Interview with author, 30 Mar. 1994. The *Earth Summit Update* (which may, of course, have got its information from State) confirmed that the EC and Japan were likely to reject the treaty ((May 1992), no. 9, p. 1).

at home.[96] Even President Clinton's decision to sign contains the caveat that the treaty be 'fixed' during the legislative process with the addition of interpretive statements (see Chapter 5).

In the final session in Nairobi, State tried to establish a compromise whereby they could agree to the treaty but with reservations or interpretations. At the time this was deemed unacceptable for a binding convention and thus, within the White House, the conservatives were triumphant. The week of discussion made little difference. As Clayton Yeutter recalled when asked whether the President had been consulted directly during this period (before the final decision): 'I don't remember whether we brought him in at that time or not. It would not have been an important question at that point because the US position was very clear.'[97] With the conservatives fully in control of the issue, with Darman telling the President it would be a 'two-day story', and with the US representatives at State having nothing to offer as a stall to keep the issue alive, the President was advised not to sign the treaty, a decision announced in a State Department press release on 29 May which proclaimed, 'the United States does not and cannot sign an agreement that is fundamentally flawed merely for the sake of having that agreement'.[98]

The reaction to this decision was immediate and predictable, given the prevailing political context and the fact that the conference itself started just five days later. As a result, the publicity attending the arrival in Brazil of thousands upon thousands of journalists, NGOs, and government delegates centred on the American announcement that it would not sign one of the two conventions. This adverse reaction may even have been exacerbated by the administration having leaked the news late on a Friday in order to miss Saturday deadlines.[99] In Michael Deland's words, the public relations aspect of the May 1992 decisions was 'an absolute disaster'.[100]

[96] Interview with CEQ chairman Michael Deland, 21 Apr. 1994.

[97] Interview with author, 5 Apr. 1994. Yeutter's view of the treaty is uncompromising and he believes the Clinton administration has erred in signing it. He maintains: 'There is language in the biodiversity treaty on technology transfer to third world nations that is just appalling.'

[98] Press release, Office of the Assistant Secretary, US Department of State, 29 May 1992.

[99] *International Herald Tribune*, 1 June 1992, 2.

[100] Interview with author, 21 Apr. 1994. To accept that the state received negative publicity for a decision doesn't affect the argument for state autonomy.

The interplay of forces within the state itself was such that the sceptics, having agreed a compromise on climate, were dominant on biodiversity. The prevailing political contexts served to bolster this dominance. As illustrated nicely in the following quotation from the *International Herald Tribune*.

Like a float on a fishing line, Mr Reilly's life in the administration has been up one week and down the next. Lately, administration fish stronger than he are trying to tug him completely out of sight.[101]

FORESTS

The initiative on forests was the one area in the UNCED process where the United States attempted to lead. Public and scientific concern was considerable, and although this would not have been enough on its own to place the issue at the top of the USA's agenda, a consensus was forged within the administration that even something as far-reaching as a forests convention was desirable. This was for two principal reasons.

First, the nature of the issue was important. A reduction in logging was probably the ultimate in 'no regrets' policy-making; it had implications for wildlife habitat and thus biodiversity protection, climate change (trees absorb CO_2), aesthetic environmental quality, and desertification. This is not to say that the sceptics were in favour of ceasing large-scale logging, far from it. They were aware, however, that action on trees was the most cost-effective option available. In addition, saving the environment might mean planting a billion trees but many of them could, of course, be harvested in the future. Also, planting trees was a good way of graphically demonstrating in very solid and quantifiable terms the administration's commitment to the environment. And, finally, the proposal as it emerged from the intrastate process left 'primary' forests out of the equation, allowing logging in Oregon and

---

What matters in a 'state-centric' explanation is that the state can be shown to be the central player, rather than that it makes popular decisions. As we will see, this public relations 'disaster' then feeds back into the political context at Rio itself.

[101] 3 June 1992, 2.

elsewhere to continue unabated while new trees were planted to make up the numbers.

Secondly, the issue of forests struck right at the heart of the Southern consensus on other areas of international environmental protection. It was one thing to criticize the United States for failing to honour its obligations by reducing CO_2 emissions or helping to preserve biodiversity, quite another to agree that one's own state would reduce the exploitation of its most valuable natural resource and thus risk hampered development. The divisiveness which the question of forests caused led many critics of the USA to suggest it was entirely a smokescreen designed to deflect attention away from climate. Alternatively, others maintained it was a subtle bargaining ploy; aware that the South would be unlikely to agree to limit deforestation, the USA could then draw concessions from the South in return for letting the issue drop.

Growing international concern about deforestation had been a feature of the 1980s. International institutional developments included a Tropical Forestry Action Plan (TFAP) and an International Tropical Timber Organization (ITTO), initiatives which took in bodies as diverse as the UN Food and Agriculture Organization (FAO), the World Bank, and UNCTAD.[102] By the end of the 1980s, the issue had been forced onto the international agenda by NGO and public pressure and, as a result, it was addressed by the Houston summit of the G7 in 1990. The various elements of the political context came together in the United States to give the activists an opportunity: action on trees was not necessarily economically disadvantageous, domestic concern was high, and it promised good public relations and even electoral gains. At Houston, therefore, George Bush proposed to the other major industrial nations that they should work together to establish a convention to slow down the rate of deforestation.

In the words of Gareth Porter:

It was explained to me that it was Bob Grady at OMB and the head of the forest service . . . [who] got together and cooked up this idea and presented it to the White House. The thought was that . . . it would be a framework convention with no specific commitments to anything that would cost money. Then if protocols were elaborated it would be on the basis of

[102] Francis Sullivan, 'Forest Principles' in Grubb *et al.*, *The Earth Summit Agreements*, 160.

commitments to planting trees—that we should get credit in some fashion for planting trees—and the administration already had a bill . . . that would plant something like several million trees over a period of years. Somehow or other we'd get credit for doing something we were already going to do anyway . . . And, of course, the White House loved that. So that's where they threw their influence, into trying to create something new, and that was the only case that I know of where the United States was offering some new initiative and, of course, that was shot down by developing countries at prepcom II.[103]

In 1991, as a follow-up to Houston, the USA distributed a proposal on forests which had, as its goal, the need for global co-operation to 'conserve, maintain, restore and enhance the biological diversity of forested ecosystems . . .'.[104] This proposal was marked by a glaring omission, however, in the lack of any explicit mention of primary or 'old-growth' forests. In other words, it left the door open for the continued large-scale logging of existing forests in the American Pacific Northwest while compensating with replanting schemes. The spotted owl, as we have seen, would still be threatened under such a plan. Congress was asked, in a resolution jointly sponsored by Senator Al Gore and Representative John Porter (R-Ill.), to override this limited approach and include the protection and sustainable management of primary forests.[105] The attitude of developing countries, meanwhile, was that forests should be dealt with as part of Agenda 21 because the issues to which they gave rise were inseparable from problems associated with the global environment as a whole. Thus developments elsewhere always impacted on forest negotiations, often adversely.

The process of negotiating this convention did take place within the UNCED machinery but it was clear by the end of prepcom II that a binding convention was infeasible on forests, the gaps between the parties were too wide and the interests too divergent. The parties agreed to go for something more plausible and, by prepcom III, the forests convention had become 'negotiations on a non-binding statement of forest principles'—a substantial shift. During this third session, developing countries—led by India and

---

[103] Interview with author, 4 Apr. 1994. During the 1988 campaign, Grady had coined a popular phrase for the President about addressing 'the greenhouse effect with the White House effect'.
[104] *Earth Summit Update*, no. 1 (July 1991) 1.
[105] Ibid.

Malaysia—stuck to their demand that national discretion in forests policy was of paramount importance.[106] Even though this was a principle which the US, *prima facie*, would have been expected to endorse, and certainly had in other negotiations, there was support for the idea—being advanced by Canada—that objective standards (or 'internationally accepted guidelines') could be established. Disagreement was intense and deep and thus the text forwarded to prepcom IV was both short and heavily bracketed. In fact, the attitude of the South (the G77) actually hardened between prepcoms III and IV.

This development was in response to US intransigence on finance and technology. Because forests were seen as an area of leverage for the South, the poor progress made in these other areas caused Southern states, especially Malaysia and India, to take a firmer line with the North and even withdraw some tentative concessions. Indeed, Malaysia made it quite explicit at prepcom IV that, as trees were such an important part of the CO_2 cycle, absorbing the gas (as 'sinks'), and producing oxygen, a failure to reach a deal on targets and timetables would mean no deal on forests.[107]

This last point was recognized by the CAPE '92 group which was highly critical of the forest principles draft which emerged from New York, calling it 'hollow'. The group's statement did accept, however, that because forests were important to the White House, 'some countries have held the forest principles "hostage" until the USA relents on other Earth Summit issues'.[108] The USA, meanwhile, was being quite resourceful in trying to prise apart G77 unity. Malaysia, accounting for half the world's tropical timber exports, had infuriated several African delegations by ignoring their views. The Americans offered support for a (bracketed) African proposal—in Agenda 21—to establish a desertification convention in return for African support on forests.[109]

With the failure to achieve anything more than a heavily bracketed text in New York, many nations greeted with surprise and

---

[106] Stanley P. Johnson claims: 'Malaysia and India said "no" firmly on the first day of the Conference and went on saying "no" to the bitter, very bitter, end', *The Earth Summit: The United Nations Conference on Environment and Development* (London: Graham and Trotman/Matinius Nijhoff, 1993), 108.

[107] *Crosscurrents*, no. 5 (16–18 Mar.), 6.

[108] *Earth Summit Update*, no. 9 (May 1992), 6.

[109] Ibid. 5.

suspicion a US initiative—made just two days before Rio—to provide extra financing for world forest protection. This came as part
of a White House counter-offensive, a four-point plan for moving
forward from UNCED. The initiative included a $150 million in-
crease in US bilateral forest aid and a commitment to pursue a
doubling of world-wide forest assistance from $1.35 million to $2.7
million. Existing US assistance was already $121 million, claimed
the press release, further pointing out that the President's 'America
the beautiful' initiative to plant a billion trees a year was 'the
most ambitious reforestation program undertaken by any country'.[110] This proposal was also argued to be a better approach
to conserving biodiversity (than the convention) by some White
House officials, which merely served, in the words of *Earth
Summit Update*, to underline the 'go-it-alone, defensive nature of
the initiative'.[111]

Scepticism was high about this forests initiative even though it
had some history in the Bush administration. Some thought it was
to deflect attention, some to constitute an ineffective alternative to
better biodiversity schemes, some to provide a new bargaining
chip. The fact remains that, as the part of the UNCED process with
the lowest profile, forests were always dependent on developments
elsewhere and this remained as true at Rio as it had beforehand.
The United States could push for a 'world forests partnership'—
as Reilly had done at a meeting in Munich of G7 environment
ministers—but too many other states were much more interested in climate and biodiversity.

CONCLUSION

NGOs generated much anti-Bush publicity throughout the
UNCED process even though their institutionalized access was
always at a more junior level. Used to a degree of potency domestically, with the opportunity to litigate against transgressors,
they now found that their main political weapon—pressure on

---

[110] *White House Fact Sheet*, released by White House press office, 1 June 1992, pp.
1, 4.
[111] no. 10 (July 1992), 8. The President wrote personally to other G7 leaders
extolling the virtues of his forests initiative for preserving biodiversity; *Financial
Times*, 2 June 1992, 1.

Congress—was relatively ineffectual. Thus, in the absence of enforceable international legislation, another avenue of impact was effectively closed. The environmentalists outside the state objected to almost every element of executive policy—they wanted a stringent climate treaty, an agreement on biodiversity, more flexibility on financial aid for green projects—and yet their efforts actually caused the state to harden its position against their wishes.

The activists had struggled to prevent this. Bohlen and Ryan were praised in congressional testimony for their efforts in regard to US policy. In a hearing before Congress, the chair of CAPE '92, Fran Spivy-Weber, complained that State spent almost a year with no staff but that Bohlen and Ryan were 'very open to working with non-governmental groups'. She argued, however, that the government gave access but 'no substance' and that:

Non-governmental groups have found it extremely difficult . . . to get access to the government's substantive papers . . . In order to avoid a lot of time-wasting debate over some issues, if we were brought in on the preparation—in an informal way, if not a formal way—of these papers, perhaps we could avoid a lot of the debate that might take place later on.[112]

The inadequacy of the resources given to the OES to carry out its obligations—which also, of course, crucially affected NGOs for whom this was the key point of access—was stressed by Bohlen in a remarkably frank comment before Congress. Asked if his bureau was adequately funded, he replied:

I have to say, coming from the private non-profit world, I am appalled at the dearth of resources in the department. The budget for my bureau has been stagnant for five years at roughly the $1.5 to $1.6 million level, despite the quadrupling of our responsibilities. But this is the problem the whole department has. We do not have the funds to do the job we are called upon to do.[113]

There is plenty of criticism in these hearings but, as we have seen, the only substantive piece of legislation on climate change—which would almost certainly have faced a veto, if, indeed, it was ever

---

[112] 'United Nations Conference on Environment and Development', hearings before the Subcommittee on Environment of the House Committee on Science, Space and Technology, 7 May 1991, Y4.Sci 2 102–43, p. 48.

[113] Hearing of the Subcommittee on Human Rights and International Organizations of the House Committee on Foreign Affairs, 17 Apr., 24 July, 3 Oct. 1991, Y4 f76/1 En 8/6, p. 40.

passed—was dropped once the executive forged a deal, despite the fact that Waxman's bill intended to mandate acceptance of targets and timetables. By the end, even Democratic senators like Al Gore were telling Republicans they would not criticize the President for taking another foreign trip (as they had done over his disastrous visit to Japan) if he would agree to go to Rio.

As for the business community, much support was forthcoming for the President.[114] The Association of Biotechnology Companies (ABC) wrote to the President on 18 May and 10 June to offer the full support of its three hundred members (which were spread, according to its press release, across twenty-seven nations). In the first letter, the ABC president Forrest H. Anthony told George Bush that biotechnology was worth $4 billion a year and that patent protection was essential. In the second, William E. Small, executive director, told the President: 'We know that you will find an un-friendly reception in Rio. If it is of any solace, we are with you on this issue and support you all the way. Also, bear in mind what is happening in Rio is nothing short of a diplomatic mugging.'[115]

It was a common refrain of Al Gore's during this period that the wealthy and the powerful had a back door into the White House through Dan Quayle's competitiveness council. At Rio he made much of this societal link and argued that it explained US resist-ance to more activist environmental policies. But the evidence for this compact is scant. Those who were sceptical in the administra-tion came into office—under Reagan and Bush—espousing a pro-business, anti-regulation philosophy that they already believed in. This was the essence of their political creed—allowing the free market to work and, often paradoxically, providing the best oppor-tunities they could to enable American business to thrive.

Once inside the state, however, they faced a challenge from other more activist forces. They needed to struggle and manœuvre to triumph, to use the political contexts for their own best advan-tage. On climate change, for example, they managed to water down the language but they couldn't prevent the USA from endorsing

[114] Some maintain that the business community was not united on its attitude to biodiversity but a closer examination shows that this fissure was comprised of little more than groups like ABC saying it supported 'the gist' of the treaty, something George Bush was quite prepared to admit as well (see 'Industry Surprised by Firm US Stance on Biodiversity Treaty', *Nature*, 357 (11 June 1992), 428.

[115] Association of Biotechnology Companies, Connecticut Avenue, Washington, DC; letters to President George Bush, 18 May and 10 June 1992.

the principle of a climate convention. This was a compromise fought out between factions within the state. As Gareth Porter maintains: 'I know that business was responding to the White House rather than the other way around. Business supported the White House rather than the White House supporting business. Specifically the vice-president's office.'[116]

The pressure interest groups can exert on congressmen is often considerable and domestic groups have had some success. But the principal weapons at their disposal—financial donations, write-in protests, anti-incumbent campaigns, litigation—are less valuable when the issue plays to the strengths of the core state itself. Congress is much more on the outside of foreign environmental issues and this closes off the most valuable avenue for environmental groups. Secondly, the courts—through which much domestic implementation can be pursued—rely largely on US domestic law. Thus, unless Congress has been moved to pass the required legislation, international precedents are of much less value to societal groups than domestic legislation. Thirdly, the core state is *physically* insulated because the State Department and the White House, which dominate these issues, are very difficult to access. The activities of Mostafa Tolba and the UNEP secretariat were also unhelpful. In its determination to secure an agreement, it progressively narrowed the room for manœuvre on which the moderates within State were relying. They needed to be able to compromise in Kenya in order to gain any leverage in Washington.

[116] Interview with author, 4 Apr. 1994.

5

The Rio Conference, its Aftermath, and the First Clinton Administration

The Earth Summit was an extraordinary gathering by any standards. As many as 178 countries were represented in some way and more than 100 heads of state and government made the trip to Rio. The number of press representatives topped 8,000 and there were thousands of official delegates. The number of non-governmental entities represented was nearly 7,500 with NGO delegates numbering more than 17,000. The Brazilian authorities poured thousands of troops onto the streets, closing roads and re-routeing traffic to facilitate the easy transfer of delegates between the NGO's Global Forum, based in the city itself, and the Riocentro—where governments met—which was purpose-built a considerable distance outside Rio.

The Forum played host to a huge variety of interest groups and celebrities from all over the world. NGO delegates, meanwhile, spent much of the two weeks arguing with official delegations (when they could reach them an hour out of Rio), passing their own treaties on numerous subjects, and generally campaigning vigorously for a higher profile for environmental issues.[1] Their anger was usually aimed at the traditional targets. The World Bank, for example, had its stand at the Forum attacked, its leaflets burned, and its signs changed to read: 'The People's Bank'. Meanwhile, as one author, argues:

Expressing strong opposition to the intransigent American position on most of the environmental issues at UNCED was one of the few consistent activities during the Earth Summit.[2]

As with Stockholm, however, the Forum ran into financial trouble and fell $2 million short of the amount required to settle all its

---

[1] Security checks were tight at Riocentro which served to prevent any but the best accredited NGOs from getting near to delegates.

[2] Adam Rogers, *The Earth Summit: A Planetary Reckoning* (Los Angeles: Global View Press, 1993), 74.

bills. The shortfall was made good by donations from celebrity individuals and institutions—the UNDP, for example, gave $1.3 million. Thus the Forum survived for the duration of the conference.

The official opening of the conference proper was scheduled for Wednesday, 3 June but the influx of visitors began two days earlier. During this period, as delegations became acquainted, worked informally on the documents, and settled into their allocated space in the Riocentro, rumours began to circulate about the compromises and initiatives that developed countries had brought with them to impress the assembled nations. The most prominent concerned alleged new US initiatives on forests and biodiversity, and a rumour that the Japanese—whose delegation was very large—intended to offer billions of dollars in new environmental aid in a bid to mark out a position as the global leader in this non-military field.

Although neither of these developments came to pass in quite the way envisaged, it was true that the USA—led in Rio by William Reilly—was trying to negotiate changes in the biodiversity treaty which would enable it to sign. As the official speeches began this behind-the-scenes effort was in full flow. It was to be revealed in a blare of publicity not in Rio but in New York, as the sceptics on the competitiveness council finally destroyed any possibility of the USA signing the biodiversity treaty.

THE REILLY MEMO

Even though the US position in late May seemed fairly clear, the tension between conservatives and activists was still very real. This manifested itself in contrasting ways: frantic final preparations which brought the White House into contact with the issues State had handled in Agenda 21, a suggestion Reilly should not lead the delegation, and an understanding between Reilly and Clayton Yeutter on the biodiversity treaty. It was the latter which caused the biggest headache for the Bush administration.

The decision that George Bush should go to Rio was made definitively in early May. This left just three weeks for State and the White House to decide on the size and character of the delegation.

The result was a certain amount of chaos.[3] As Bohlen recalls in detail, White House involvement in Agenda 21—the main focus of the conference proper and, with the declaration, the subject of the principal issues which remained—meant new ideological battles as well as an organizational nightmare.

Once the president decided to go to Rio that changed everything. All these people at the White House that had paid no attention to Agenda 21 began to get involved. They never understood it. From a policy point of view they never understood what Rio was all about. They never understood that what we were talking about was sustainable development. All the time we were in Rio Bush was on the campaign trail still talking environment versus development. I mean, just totally at odds with what Rio was all about.

He continues:

Someone in the White House decided they better review who we were sending down on the delegation so they asked for a list and I sent over the list and I guess a few agencies complained they weren't getting their people on. So then the White House staff asked every agency to send them a list of who they should send down to Rio. And, of course, everyone wanted to go down to Rio and all of a sudden the White House staff had a list of all the requests from different agencies which was twice the size we could accommodate.

Finally, he criticizes Clayton Yeutter for the confusion which ensued from this unwieldy process:

First of all he didn't decide who was going to head the delegation until the eleventh hour. Then he literally didn't clear the final delegation list until three days before. I had just taken it on myself to authorize a lot of people to go anyway. Otherwise we wouldn't have had time to get travel arrangements and everything. It was just typical of a total inability to reach a decision. And the other thing that I found extraordinary was that you have a chief-of-staff [meaning Yeutter] dealing with this kind of an issue which he clearly wasn't capable of. You can't imagine what a frustrating experience it was.[4]

There was no obvious alternative to Reilly to lead the US delegation even though there was a suggestion that Yeutter himself

---

[3] In contrast to 1972, the Congress sent separate delegations from the House and Senate, the former led by George Miller (D-Ca.) and the latter by Al Gore.

[4] Interview with author, 30 Mar. 1994.

considered assuming the task. At Rio itself, Bohlen tended to handle the negotiations (despite losing his voice for several days) while Reilly handled press and public relations. As Bohlen recalled:

Bill was just fabulous. Thank God we had him. At one point Yeutter wanted to go down as head of the delegation. That would have been an absolute disaster for the US. Not only did he not know the subject but he doesn't have Bill's credibility, or Bill's gift for dealing with the press. And, of course, Bill knew many of the other environmental ministers which was an enormous help.[5]

After being named as delegation head, Reilly secured from Yeutter an understanding about the biodiversity treaty which gave the EPA chief some hope that the USA might still find a way to sign. The two men agreed that if Reilly could negotiate language changes which would satisfy the administration then it was still possible the United States would give its assent. The result was a brief to negotiate in Rio itself. As Clayton Yeutter confirms:

He had certainly been given the mandate to try because, in fact, that mandate came from me. Bill's instructions were that he was to stay in close coordination with me during the Rio meeting and if he was able to develop language that would be satisfactory to us, on biodiversity or anything else for that matter, he was to submit it to Washington DC and we'd give him a quick response as to whether it was a 'go' from our standpoint. And, of course, that was what was done and he did give it a good try and then it was just most unfortunate that it leaked out and torpedoed any chance of working it out.[6]

Reilly took this opportunity seriously and immediately set about trying to secure the required language. The treaty was to be opened for signing on Friday, 5 June giving him little time. On the morning of the second day (Thursday) he announced to the press that 'we have prepared specific language that would satisfy our concerns'.[7] These semantic changes had been conveyed to Yeutter through diplomatic channels the evening before. In a confidential memo, addressed personally to Yeutter, Reilly explained his activities to the domestic-policy chief. As the communication was dated 3 June it is clear Reilly had made progress before the summit even officially began. He told Yeutter:

[5] Interview with author, 30 Mar. 1994.
[6] Interview with author, 5 Apr. 1994.
[7] *New York Times*, 5 June 1992, A6.

As I indicated last night, Brazil has offered to try to 'fix' the Biodiversity Convention so that the United States could sign it. I have serious doubt whether the Brazilians can get others to accept a fix, but I have indicated a willingness to let them try . . . In response to the Brazilian request for changes the United States must have to be willing to sign we have produced the attached list . . . The changes proposed, while not making everyone in the U.S. government totally happy, would address the critical issues that have been identified. They are worth a last examination.[8]

The reaction this memo caused among the sceptics in Washington was immediate. As one unofficial source told the *New York Times*, Reilly's memo 'caused a little commotion'. The source continued: 'The response was what you'd expect. A flat no.'[9] In fact, the highly confidential memo caused more consternation than this simple verbal rejection implies. Reilly's proposal was copied to relevant officials in the White House but was almost immediately leaked to the *New York Times*, an action which had three consequences: an end to the possibility of the USA signing the treaty (the sceptics' intent, of course), an internal inquiry ordered by an irate President, and an improvement in the public stock of the embattled EPA chief in Rio whose own administration now seemed to be prepared to humiliate him.

The most important consequence was the end of negotiation. What had started out as a low-profile attempt to establish a compromise was now the talking point of the conference. Conservatives within the White House missed no opportunity to make it clear Reilly did not speak for the administration when he suggested that the proposed language changes were acceptable. By forcing the issue into the spotlight they presented senior officials with little alternative but to stick to existing policy. The *New York Times* quoted one of these conservatives:

'The modifications were minor and it was communicated to Reilly that this doesn't come close to fitting the bill,' said a senior White House official who asked to remain unidentified. 'Clayton called him and said no way. The feeling here is that he was trying to present an option and that's his role. We'll just have to give him more guidance.'[10]

---

[8] Memo reprinted in appendix to joint hearings before the House Committee on Foreign Affairs and the House Committee on Merchant Marines and Fisheries, 26/ 27 Feb. and 21 and 28 July 1992, Sudoc no. Y4 F76/1. The list includes seven suggestions for changes to grammar and wording.
[9] *New York Times*, 5 June 1992, A6.   [10] Ibid.

Despite the adverse effect the leaking had on the chances for compromise, Darman even tried to blame Reilly for it. According to Gordon Binder: 'At a senior staff meeting on Friday when everyone was screaming . . . Darman was trying to create this notion that Reilly had leaked the memo himself to gain publicity. Yeutter said that Bill was only following his instructions.'[11] George Bush was furious at the leak which not only undermined the head of the US delegation but also made his administration appear confused and, worst of all, rudderless. At a press conference on Friday afternoon to announce an inquiry and to pledge his full support for Reilly (whom he had already telephoned), Bush told the assembled reporters they might help by revealing who had leaked the document. The President felt 'deep-seated outrage' according to Michael Deland. He told the delegation members when he arrived in Rio that the leaker would be 'hung at high noon'.[12]

Gordon Binder claims Reilly was 'as steamed and as angry and as upset as he has ever been; very, very dejected'. The episode was not the personal disaster for Reilly that it might have been, however, as Binder describes:

As word of the story got around he was turned into a folk hero so within twelve hours, by Friday morning, people were coming up to him and congratulating him and telling him what a great job he was doing. People were complementing him for the way he had stood up under all of this. He became a symbol of the forces of good against the forces of darkness.[13]

The fact remained that any chance of US compromise on the treaty had evaporated. Even if the leak backfired, creating sympathy for Reilly in other delegations and with the President, the treaty was opened for signing on Friday which meant negotiating time had expired, not with a last-ditch deal but in a blaze of adverse publicity.

The conservatives were already well in control of this issue, as we have seen, and even without the leak they would probably have carried the day. Yet, a shrewd piece of political skullduggery had

[11] Interview with author, 4 Apr. 1994.

[12] Interview, 21 Apr. 1994. The FBI held an inquiry into the leak but, according to Reilly, could only trace it as far as the competitiveness council—members of which had as a matter of course seen the memo—not to any individual. Thus, the leaker remained unexposed.

[13] Interview, 4 Apr. 1994.

further outmanoeuvred Reilly. Its larger consequence, however, was its poor reflection on the Bush White House. The *Washington Post* maintained: 'In Washington folkways, the leak cost Reilly points in political oneupmanship. But in diplomatic circles here [Rio], the main casualty was U.S. prestige.'[14] According to the *New York Times*, meanwhile:

. . . the Bush administration appeared divided and paralyzed by ideology and political concerns, reinforcing the perception that in an election year it is incapable of facing up to new foreign policy challenges.[15]

With the conference now three days old the United States had managed to retain its dubious position as the centre of attention. As Reilly told Yeutter in the ill-fated memo, 'the U.S. refusal to sign the Biodiversity Convention is the major subject of press and delegate concern here'.[16] By Friday, 5 June, both conventions were open for signing so no further changes were possible. Arguments were still fierce in the remaining UNCED documents where the USA was also under fire, especially over its attitude to finance (in Agenda 21) and to the forest principles. The publicity it was receiving was unremittingly bad. It was no exaggeration to say that the Bush administration was seen by many to represent 'the forces of darkness'. The thousands of US citizens in Rio as NGO members marched in protest carrying signs saying 'You're embarrassing U.S.' The newspapers and television were full of anti-US rhetoric from NGOs and formal denunciations from other governments. An NGO poll named the US as the prime villain in respect to environmental issues and George Bush was even being described by some as the 'antichrist'. The leaking of the memo had given this cauldron of invective a further stir. It was, in one commentator's words, 'a little hand-grenade' tossed by the conservatives.[17]

The response to this onslaught is instructive and it serves to further demonstrate the importance of the sceptics in the White House. The negative press coverage was being beamed into the homes of ordinary Americans constantly and public criticism of the

---

[14] *Washington Post*, 18 June 1992, 16.
[15] *New York Times*, 15 June 1992, 1.
[16] Appendix to joint House hearings, Sudoc no. Y4 F76/1.
[17] Richard Schrader, 'The Fiasco at Rio', *Dissent* (Fall 1992), 432. This fits conveniently, of course, with the metaphor of political contexts providing *ammunition* for core state officials.

administration within the USA was growing according to a *New York Times*/CBS poll.[18] The response of the administration in Washington, however, was actually to go on the offensive by promoting its isolation as a sign of leadership and integrity. Electoral strategists began to see advantages in a kind of 'imperial defiance' which, needless to say, terminated any lingering hopes the activists had about securing last-minute deals in Rio.

THE WHITE HOUSE STRIKES BACK

The White House began its offensive with several attacks in Washington on the summit itself and on the motives of the USA's erstwhile Northern partners. In a televised news conference on Friday, a newly defiant George Bush told the nation that he would not be pushed around:

I'm going on the offence, not the defence . . . I am the one that is burdened with the responsibility to find a balance between sound environmental practices on the one hand and jobs for American families on the other . . . If they don't understand it in Rio, too bad.[19]

This new mood was evident on the Tuesday of the second week at Rio when White House officials—who refused to be named—continued to carry the attack by criticizing Japan and Germany. The officials told the *New York Times* that these countries were only opposing the United States as a 'politically correct' way of 'displaying their status as emerging world powers'.[20] This was described as 'guilty developed-world logic' and for good measure, the officials cast doubt on the sincerity with which some nations intended to carry out their treaty obligations. The conference was also derided as a 'circus'. The *Earth Summit Update* records the comments of Bob Zoellick at a Washington press briefing on 9 June when he criticized Japan and Germany for their attempt

[18] Of the 1,374 adults polled just before the summit began, only 9 per cent thought it might produce substantive results while 47 per cent did think it might 'help a little'. This lack of genuine optimism was linked, by the *New York Times*, with the President's low ratings on the environment with a startling 70 per cent saying the President had been 'insincere' in his expression of support for environmental issues (*New York Times*, 11 June 1992, 13).

[19] *Independent*, 6 June 1992, 1.

[20] *New York Times*, 10 June 1992, 6.

to gain credibility as world powers by opposing the United States.[21]

In the *New York Times* of the 12 June, the day that President Bush spoke in Rio itself, one Republican adviser 'fumed':

Japan's out there killing whales and running driftnets, for God's sake, while we've got the world's toughest environmental laws and we're twisting ourselves into knots over how many jobs to abolish to save a subspecies of an owl.[22]

Finally, as he stood on the steps of Airforce One, George Bush told reporters: 'I am determined to protect the environment, and I am determined to protect the American taxpayer. The days of the open cheque-book are over.'[23] This echoed a campaign speech the President had given on the eve of the California primary, on the weekend of 30/31 May, when he told a rally: 'We cannot shut down the lives of many Americans by going to the extreme on the environment.'[24] Even though this more combative approach was entirely in keeping with the dominance of conservatives within the White House, campaign strategists also found some solace in Bush's new role as a 'global maverick' which they believed would show him as a tough leader unafraid of being isolated on a point of principle. This would play well against Ross Perot, they thought.[25]

This new verbal offensive was not adopted by the delegation in Rio itself. American delegates were trying to negotiate deals with the very countries that the administration in Washington was publicly criticizing. Indeed, the US delegation in Rio was receiving support—both symbolic and substantive—from other Northern nations.[26] At the beginning of the Summit it was still unclear how many other states would not sign the biodiversity treaty. The most important hold-outs were Germany, Japan, Britain, France, and

---

[21] *Earth Summit Update*, no. 10 (July 1992), 5.

[22] *New York Times*, 11 June 1992, 12.

[23] *Independent*, 12 June 1992, 11.

[24] *Guardian*, 1 June 1992, 1.

[25] *New York Times*, 11 June 1992, 12. The *Times* goes on: 'Administration officials attribute the President's stance ultimately to a long-time struggle within the Administration between environmental moderates and a passionate band of conservatives who view the Earth Summit as a scientifically fraudulent and economically disastrous venture.'

[26] This may well have been partly sympathy for the popular Reilly after his perceived split from the administration.

Canada and the US delegation was still hoping that at least some of those nations might hold the line (none did, but the British were the last to announce a decision to sign). Meanwhile, a deal had been agreed between the USA and Germany to develop economic and technical practices for use in the preservation of the world's forests.[27] In addition, both the Germans and the Australians had given high-profile dinners for the US delegation in order to help them to break their isolation. Curtis Bohlen recalls:

One point I would like to make is how really sympathetic other governments were to the position we were in. I remember one night the Australian minister hosting a dinner that Bill and I went to, and the sole purpose of the dinner was to see—there were probably 20 different delegations there—how these other countries could help the US. The Germans gave a similar event one night too. They didn't enjoy seeing the US so isolated and being so criticized.[28]

Also, in areas like the financing chapter of Agenda 21, the North was still lined up against the South over the question of 0.7 per cent of GNP as a target for aid donations.

The USA was still working behind the scenes to try to draw concessions out of its former allies, most importantly Germany and Japan. Although it was disappointed when they announced (Germany as the conference began) that they would sign on biodiversity, it still continued to work to prevent a Japanese announcement of a big increase in overseas aid at the conference, and to head off an EC plan to commit to targets and timetables publicly at the conference. Whether or not the US pressure made a difference, Japan announced an aid increase significantly lower than expected and EC plans for a statement on climate change were dropped.[29] In addition, *Newsweek*, for example, claimed senior State Department officials were lobbying their EC counterparts, saying that support for the USA's forests initiative would be of great benefit for the President.[30]

[27] *International Herald Tribune*, 1 June 1992, 2.

[28] Interview with author, 30 Mar. 1992. He recalls that some developing countries shared this sense of 'camaraderie'.

[29] For this claim about Japan see Mark Nichols, 'Progress in Rio', *Maclean's*, 22 June 1992, 52. Austria, the Netherlands, and Switzerland were proposing a public commitment to 1990 levels on CO_2 by the year 2000 but they were persuaded against it by other EC countries.

[30] *Newsweek*, 15 June 1992, 31–2.

Opinion within the EC was clearly split, however, on the approach to be taken with the United States. According to the *Earth Summit Times*:

European envoys, saying the American slide into isolation at the Earth Summit had to be halted, said yesterday that they had begun a delicate effort to try to create a more constructive atmosphere for the U.S. delegation and its diplomatic adversaries in Rio de Janeiro.[31]

However, the EC delegation head, Laurens Jan Brinkhorst, told the *Financial Times*:

We're very disappointed with the US decision [on biodiversity]. It will be very sad if it results in a cleavage not just between developed and developing countries but also between developed countries.[32]

And later, during the second week, German environment minister Klaus Topfer, was quoted as saying the USA seemed to be afraid of a 'new communism hidden behind ecology', which he termed 'ecologism'.[33]

The difference in approach of the administration as a whole and of the delegation in Rio is clear. The White House had decided to go on the attack while the delegates in Rio still sought to reach a compromise which would enable the USA to recover some of the ground lost during the run-up to, and first week of, the conference. This is not to say that Reilly and his senior officials were not bargaining hard for changes in Agenda 21 and the Declaration which would make the treaties acceptable to the United States. Reilly announced publicly that the USA would 'try to block a German initiative to get European Community support for the early negotiation of a convention protocol that would establish emissions targets and timetables'. The *Earth Summit Update* continues: 'European diplomats in Rio reported intense U.S. efforts to dissuade them from going ahead with a declaration on the stabilization target and protocol.'[34] The vigour with which the USA

---

[31] *Earth Summit Times*, 6 June 1992, 1. The EST was the official newspaper of record for the UNCED published as a collaborative effort by a group including the *New York Times*, the Japanese Kyoto Fund, and the *Journal Do Brasil*.

[32] *Financial Times*, 2 June 1992, 1. The EC's environment commissioner, Carlos Ripa de Meana, had apparently refused to attend the conference because of the inadequacy of the agreements to be signed.

[33] *New York Times*, 10 June 1992, 6.

[34] *Earth Summit Update*, no. 10 (July 1992), 4–5.

pursued this effort was described in a later congressional hearing as 'shooting sparrows with a cannon', to which Robert Reinstein replied that the threat was bigger than a sparrow and the weapon smaller than a cannon.[35]

The US delegation also tied changes it demanded in Agenda 21 to its eventual acceptance of the Rio Declaration (the USA was the only country to attempt to reopen the text). In addition to Reilly—who took the lead in speaking for the delegation—the other prominent spokesman was one of Zoellick's staff, the deputy under-secretary of state for economic affairs, Michael Young. Even though he took a more conservative and combative line—telling a press briefing, for example, that US isolation on aid targets was 'not a bad position to be in'—this was mild compared with the attacks from Washington.[36] Reilly, meanwhile, was describing the German delegation as 'most helpful' and the Japanese attitude as 'positive'.[37] After the President's combative public statements on protecting American families, Reilly's efforts were described as an attempt to 'keep the door open'.[38]

By the end of the second week—as heads of state and government began to arrive for their set-piece speeches—the shape of the three UNCED documents was still uncertain. Negotiations on forest principles were clearly unlikely to develop into any major piece of international legislation while the Declaration was stuck on several questions including 'the right to develop' and the environmental rights of 'people under occupation' (a reference to the Palestinian issue which also occurred six times in the Agenda). The most crucial arguments were still being joined over the finance chapter of the Agenda.

In the end compromise was reached on all three. A deal was done to eliminate references to 'people under occupation' from the Agenda while leaving a single reference in the Declaration. In the finance negotiations, the North prevailed; having successfully pushed the GEF into a central role in the funding process, it secured language on the 0.7 per cent ODA commitment which spoke of the 'reaffirmation' of that target as a goal. Despite some initial—misplaced—excitement that this meant an American commitment

[35] Senate Committee on Foreign Relations, 18 Sept. 1992, Y4 F76/2, p. 50.
[36] *Earth Summit Update*, no. 10 (July 1992), 5/8.
[37] *International Herald Tribune*, 12 June 1992, 4.
[38] *Independent*, 6 June 1992, 13.

in principle to 0.7 per cent, it became clear that this wording was only acceptable to the USA because it had never 'affirmed' to a target in the first place, thus it considered itself exempt from a reaffirmation.[39] In addition to these concessions, the USA also tabled ten reservations on parts of the Agenda and the Declaration, These interpretive statements, also used at Stockholm, effectively negated any precedent by enabling the USA to argue that it only accepted its own understanding of the meaning of certain paragraphs.

Even though the final, all-night negotiation was still to be concluded on finance at the end of week two, presidents and prime ministers were beginning to arrive in large numbers to make their speeches at the end of the conference.[40] This was to include, of course, the speech by George Bush on the USA's contribution to the international environment. There was an expectant air as the man who had initially declined to say he was coming, and had subsequently become the focus of a torrent of invective, arrived at the summit to sign the climate change treaty and to answer the administration's global critics.

THE SUMMIT'S END AND ITS AFTERMATH

Even though the omens had not been good, George Bush's trip to Rio got off to an even worse start than the administration could have imagined. On 11 June he flew from Washington, DC to Panama where a crowd of protestors was tear-gassed by police and the President was forced to abandon the platform without delivering his speech.[41] He arrived late that evening in Rio and the next morning met a collection of American NGO representatives in his hotel suite at the Sheraton. This meeting involved a frank

[39] See Johnson, *The Earth Summit: The United Nations Conference*, 444–5.

[40] The last negotiating session pitted eight representatives from developing countries against eight from the developed world. They started at 10 a.m. in Rio and finished at 4.30 the following morning. As Curtis Bohlen suggests, 'a lot of this kind of negotiation is stamina. Those who fall by the wayside lose' (interview with author, 30 Mar. 1994).

[41] Boyden Gray recalled that the opportunity to stop-off in Panama—to gain good news coverage after the USA's successful removal of General Noriega—provided a further rationale for those advocating a trip to Rio (interview, 7 Apr. 1992).

discussion of environmental issues and the Bush administration's attitude to them. Accounts differ about the gathering but it seems not to have been the highly charged confrontation that one might have expected. Journalist Dan Abbasi recalls:

I remember my sense was, in talking to some of those NGOs when they came out of the meeting, that I was surprised at how, in a sense, mollified, they'd been by him. I don't know if that was being awestruck at meeting with the president. I wouldn't have expected that of some of them, they were not necessarily a hard-bitten bunch but certainly a savvy bunch who were used to battling the administration. I think I wouldn't have expected this sense of 'oh gee, he was actually much more informed than we thought and seemed to care about the issues but was expressing the difficult situation he was in' . . . I didn't get the sense that there was this attempt to pile-on to Bush when he got there. It seemed like relations were actually pretty good. Bush had just come through Panama and I think he was kind of cowed a little bit too, not wanting to be real high-profile and trying as hard as he could probably to try to appease people. It wasn't like this big moment of confrontation.[42]

Having met with the NGOs, the President was ferried out to Riocentro to make his eagerly awaited speech that afternoon. There had been two speeches prepared for the President, one echoing the strong line taken by the administration in previous days, the other less combative and more conciliatory. It was the latter which the President delivered (the former was described to the *Wall Street Journal* as an 'in-your-face' address).[43] In his presentation—which lasted only seven minutes and left delegates nonplussed by its brevity—the President told the assembled gathering that he had not come to Rio to apologize for the United States which he claimed had an exemplary record on environmental issues. He repeated the pledge on forests and told the packed hall that the USA would be increasing its international environmental aid by 66 per cent above 1990 levels (it was unclear to what extent this included forests money and, most crucially, transfers from other aid programmes). He also told delegates that the USA would cease clear-cutting (the most destructive form of logging).

On biodiversity, George Bush repeated the claim officials had been making that the USA exceeded the requirements of the treaty

[42] Interview with author, 9 Apr. 1993.
[43] *Wall Street Journal*, 15 June 1992, 14.

in terms of the protection of wildlife and habitat. He told the assembly that he was 'standing alone on principle' which was greeted in the hall with a degree of mirth. At its culmination, the speech brought little applause and some chuckling from delegates. Afterwards, Bush told a Brazilian newspaper: 'I am the President of the United States, not the president of the world.'[44]

The overwhelming feeling after this event seems to have been one of anti-climax. As Dan Abbasi recalls:

He gave a speech that was not well or poorly received. It was just kind of 'there it is'. If I had written the front-page story that day in the *Earth Summit Times* I would probably have focused more on other folks . . . It wasn't the story of the day necessarily. It was kind of, 'Bush came, he made a speech, no big surprise, he didn't change his mind.'[45]

The summit was over, and the weary American delegation returned home. Back in Washington, however, the controversy just would not go away. For example, one potent administration critic, Al Gore, had so impressed Bill Clinton by his performance in Rio he was persuaded to choose the Tennessee senator as his presidential running-mate. Thus, Gore continued to attack the administration for its positions on environmental issues as he had criticized Bush and Sununu in his book *Earth in the Balance*.[46] Before Rio he alleged the President had abdicated leadership and passed-up business opportunities inherent in the biodiversity treaty. He argued:

The positions the U.S. has taken at UNCED are not the delegation's fault. The delegates are quite professional and I have the deepest respect for them. But the policies of the Administration, chiefly President Bush, have much to answer for. This has been a disgraceful performance. It is the single worst failure of political leadership that I have seen in my lifetime.[47]

This message about the opportunities for US business was

[44] Rogers, *The Earth Summit*, 172–5.

[45] Interview, 9 Apr. 1993. The end of the summit was also overshadowed by the non-appearance of the Japanese prime minister, Kiichi Miyazawa, caught in an acrimonious domestic debate about sending troops on peacekeeping missions.

[46] Al Gore, *Earth in the Balance: Forging a New Common Purpose* (London: Earthscan, 1992), 174, 175. Gore said of Bush '. . . here is a man who sees twenty-year-old technology at the supermarket checkout line and looks like an ape discovering fire' (Senate Committee on Foreign Relations, 18 Sept. 1992, p. 30). In the campaign, of course, Bush dubbed Gore 'Mr Ozone'.

[47] Steve Lerner, *Beyond the Earth Summit: Conversations with Advocates of Sustainable Development* (Bolinas, Calif.: Commonweal, 1992), 15.

echoed in a September Senate hearing during which Gore traded punches with ardent Republican supporters like Jesse Helms (N. Carolina) and Mitch McConnell (Kentucky). He told them that the USA could create millions of jobs by 'leading the environmental revolution'. At the same hearing, Reilly argued that the only thing he would have done differently about US policies was to 'sell them better'.[48]

Reilly it was who remained at the centre of controversy within the administration on this issue. First, his apparently contrived exclusion from a post-Rio meeting with NGOs led the president of the biggest, the National Wildlife Federation's Jay Hair, to storm out in protest. He demanded Michael Deland's resignation after the CEQ chairman expressed regret that Reilly would not be able to attend. Hair told the meeting that Deland knew Reilly had only been invited the night before, making it impossible for him to attend.[49]

Secondly, on 15 July, Reilly sent a memo to all EPA employees in response to a 'welcome home' message thousands of them had signed on his return from Rio. The greater part of the memo was devoted to a listing of US achievements and Reilly's sincerity is unmistakable. However, two paragraphs in particular caught the imagination of the press and elevated the EPA chief once more onto the front pages. In the first, Reilly described his experience at Rio, especially in relation to the leaked memo.

For me personally, it was like a bungee jump. You dive into space secured by a line on your leg and trust it pulls you up before you smash to the ground. It doesn't typically occur to you that someone might cut your line!

In the second paragraph, Reilly ruminated about why the conference has been such a public-relations failure for the USA.

Another key question, frankly, is why did the United States play such a low-key defensive game in preparing for Rio? We assigned a low priority to the negotiations of the biodiversity treaty, were slow to engage the climate issue, were last to commit our President to attend Rio. We put our delegation together late and we committed few resources. No

[48] Senate Committee on Foreign Relations, 18 Sept. 1992, pp. 17, 50.
[49] *Los Angeles Times*, 20 June 1992, A18.

doubt this contributed to the negative feelings towards the United States.[50]

It took a couple of weeks for the press to pick up the story but when it did it provided headlines to dismay a President seeking re-election. The *New York Times* headlined the story 'Bush aide assails US preparations for Earth Summit' and interpreted it as an effort by Reilly to try to 'restore his standing' among environmentalists (pointing out that it was also useful ammunition for the Clinton/Gore team).[51] In a telephone response to the story, Reilly explained:

We prepared for Rio in the midst of political and economic preoccupations that were a distraction. The preparation clearly suffered. This was a public relations disappointment. I set out in this memorandum to explain why we received such criticism.[52]

In a letter to the *New York Times* two weeks later, Reilly criticized its story as a 'distortion of the intent and content of my memorandum', concluding his letter: 'A fair reading of the memo makes clear that the conference was a success for the United States and for the environment.'[53]

In the memo, and in Reilly's response to its publication, one can see the frustrations of the UNCED preparatory process and, given the information contained in this and previous chapters, the story which underlies them. By August the administration was in the thick of an election campaign, the result of which had at one point looked like a foregone conclusion. By this time the stresses and strains of the Rio preparatory process were partially submerged in the collective effort of trying to get the President re-elected.

THE CLINTON ADMINISTRATION

If twelve years of Republican presidency had seemed like night

---

[50] Memo, from William K. Reilly, to all EPA employees, subject 'Reflections on the Earth Summit', 15 July 1992. Reilly claimed the press unfairly portrayed US efforts, and that 'we experienced a public relations set-back internationally, counting on the notion that lonely defiance has its champions at home, and when it is principled it is often vindicated by history'.

[51] *New York Times*, 1 Aug. 1992, 1; see also *Washington Post*, 1 Aug. 1992, 13.

[52] *New York Times*, 1 Aug. 1992, 1, 9.

[53] Ibid., 15 Aug. 1992, 18.

without end for American environmentalists, the election of
November 1992 brought them a glorious sunrise. The new Vice-
President, Albert Gore, Jnr., was the author of a best-selling book
on the global environment; the new EPA administrator was his
former Senate aide and Florida's most senior environmental official, Carol Browner, and the new Secretary of the Interior, Bruce
Babbitt, a former governor of Arizona and president of the League
of Conservation Voters, had impeccable environmental credentials. The World Resources Institute's Rafe Pomerance, and environmentally friendly Senator Tim Wirth, seemed destined for
senior State Department positions while a founder of the NRDC,
and a high-profile activist, Gus Speth, headed the President's transition team on the environment.[54] According to Mark Dowie:

For most of December 1992 the American mainstream environmental
movement was in a state of near ecstasy. At every opportunity, the president elect was publicly bear-hugging the most environmentally sensitive
vice-president in American history . . . At the Environmental Ball, held in
Washington the night before the presidential inaugural, enviros had tears
in their eyes.[55]

Despite the choice of Reilly to head the EPA, and the passage of
amendments to the Clean Air Act, the Bush administration had
found it impossible to get good press from interest groups and the
public relations debacle of Rio was simply the final nail in the
coffin. As a former president of the World Wildlife Fund and
the Conservation Foundation, and a young operative at the CEQ in
the early days of institutionalized environmental policy-making,
Reilly might well have been an acceptable choice for Democrats as
well. Under Bush, he and other sympathizers within the core state
were simply outgunned. The intrastate environmental faction under Clinton was now much stronger at more senior levels and
societal environmentalists could secure access right to the heart of
the administration.

---

[54] Even the deputy budget director, Alice Rivlin, had been chair of the governing
council of the Wilderness Society for four years (Will Nixon, 'Bill and Al's Green
Adventure', *E Magazine* (May/June, 1993), 33).

[55] Mark Dowie, *Losing Ground: American Environmentalism at the Close of the
Twentieth Century* (Cambridge, Mass.: MIT Press, 1995), 177. As Dowie points out,
this was despite the League of Conservation Voters ranking President Clinton—on
environmental issues—seventh out of the seven Democratic candidates who initially
stood in New Hampshire (p. 279 n. 2).

In keeping with the argument made so far, this scale of societal involvement should be understood as providing potent ammunition for Gore, Browner, and Babbitt to push for more activist environmental policies. In domestic policy-making, we have seen that Congress and various societal interests are more prominent, possessing opportunities for influence not readily available internationally. In foreign policy, by contrast, the state has more leeway and decisions should, as a result, demonstrate the hallmarks of the intrastate process, and even then the core state much more than the periphery. Overall, available evidence on the Clinton administration until 1996 fits this picture reasonably well.

Activists within the state began with high hopes and several initiatives were launched on the international and domestic environment. The USA made a firm commitment to cut CO_2 to 1990 levels by the year 2000 (the core of the Bush administration's objections to the climate treaty) and a decision was taken to sign the biodiversity treaty (although not without important reservations). Domestically, decisions were announced to institute higher charges for mining and grazing on public land, to restrict logging, to develop an energy tax, and to raise EPA to formal cabinet status as a Department of the Environment. The green credentials of senior state officials shone out through these policy goals. Implementing them was another matter, however, with both domestic and foreign measures falling victim to congressional resistance. It is here, therefore, that the story of the Clinton administration takes on a more interesting character and where arguments for the overlap of international and domestic politics find some purchase.

It remains differentiation within the state which explains outcomes, and the nature of the struggle within the core state which explains national policy goals, but the difficulties of implementation become more pertinent. The United States stood committed internationally to cutting CO_2; the territorial state's signature was still wet on the treaty and it was ratified by Congress. But enacting the measures required to bring this about proved tougher and activists within the core state had to work hard against not just congressional resistance but those within the administration, the President not least among them, who were either less committed or—as with the Bush sceptics—unconvinced of the desirability of certain environmental goals.

In examining congressional testimony, for example, what is

remarkable is how little accent the Clinton administration put on environmental issues for their own sake, and how much on the potential competitive benefits to the United States. Although it is clear that much of this language was designed to persuade Congress, it casts important doubt on the extent to which the activists within this greenest of presidencies ever actually secured a stronger intrastate position than Reilly and Bohlen under George Bush. Ironically, this reflected a crucial contextual change attendant upon the election of Bill Clinton.

The environmental movement began to lose ground—in terms of money and members—precisely at the moment when the election of Gore as Vice-President meant environmentalists backed off a little and waited for things to happen. Thus the societal ammunition available for activists within the core state was reduced from the outset. It is too early to say whether or not this delay was what fatally weakened the chances for more radical environmental successes, yet it was only with the election of a more aggressively anti-environmental Congress in 1994 that the activists really began to make ground within the administration.

Even before Bill Clinton became President, there was a degree of public fatigue with environmental issues claims Michael McCloskey of the Sierra Club. This loss of interest—consistent with a broad reading of the issue–attention cycle—changed the domestic political context even before the election of a President whom many environmentalists believed was much more their man. As McCloskey says:

The amount of coverage on the environment as an issue waxes and wanes. From about 1986 to 1992 it received a huge amount of coverage. It built up in the late eighties, reached a crescendo in 1990, and then it began to ebb quickly, but then Rio . . . as Stockholm, we went through exactly the same cycle from seventy to 72. It culminated in 1970—the build-up of the late sixties—then it started falling and Stockholm brought it up again and we went through the same profile twenty years later. I think the media was already getting tired of the environmental issue by Rio and then the overwhelming flood of international news pushed it back up again briefly, and then all environmental coverage dropped like a rock. Now we have a sort of new debunking mood, seeing if environmentalists have been lying about everything.

He goes on to describe the links between the new President and reasons for the decline.

To some extent it also is associated with the Clinton administration, or at least expectations that the new establishment was more pro-environmental so the press, always wanting to be critical, was more anti-environmental than the administration. It's about establishing an opposite relationship.[56]

Environmental activists on the inside were not faring much better than those lobbying outside the state. Speaking in 1994, one former EPA official (who declined to be named), argued: 'I'm hard-pressed to see what's different in terms of policy. Morale is low at EPA. It is a peculiar paradox, but morale was very high when Bill Reilly was there partly because the agency had a real strong sense of mission and purpose and they felt they had a leader who was representing their interests and making news a lot.' In arguing that Carol Browner was finding her task difficult, the same official also demonstrated the perverse effects of contextual changes: 'She has had a friendlier White House and more sympathetic colleagues in the cabinet, who are interested in the environment and care about all this, so she has had a tougher time establishing herself. She did not have, particularly, an agenda. She had to mobilize the agency. It's very much in a reactive mode.'[57]

Many critics of the administration's environmental policy have gone much further. Mark Dowie, for example, argues that environmental leaders 'were being particularly careful not to offend the administration because they perceived it, in some degree, to be their only hope for reasonable access to government agencies where they had been cold-shouldered for 12 years'.[58] The result, he claims, was a kind of 'reverse access to the environmental movement', with the President getting the inside track on lobbying as many as ten million voters.[59] Dowie quotes an environmental activist from Oregon, Jeffrey St Clair, claiming:

[56] Interview with author, 7 Apr. 1994.
[57] Interview with author, 3 Apr. 1994.
[58] Dowie, *Losing Ground*, 179–80.
[59] Dowie argues that 'reverse access' paid off handsomely when the President needed to advance NAFTA which many environmentalists abhorred. Nevertheless, Bill Clinton was able to get several mainstream group leaders to actually campaign for it, allowing Al Gore and US trade representative Micky Kantor to argue that the environmental community was behind the agreement (a good illustration of a policy being 'sold' to society) (*Losing Ground*, 185–7). NAFTA was a nice example of social-scientific epistemic non-consensus: a cartoon in *Village Voice* by Mark Alan

Dealing with Clinton ain't like dealing with Reagan and Bush. In fact 'Team Clinton' is much more dangerous, because they know our move-ment inside out. Bush didn't ask for any favors, and none were given, but when St Albert and Brother Bruce [Babbitt] came calling, attention was paid immediately.[60]

The capacity of the new administration to broker agreements led another very vocal critic, Alexander Cockburn, to argue that it had taken a Democrat to persuade major environmental groups to sign 'the articles of surrender' on forests (what he elsewhere called 'Munich in the Redwoods').[61] Cockburn maintains that the admin-istration's emphasis on 'compromise' and 'coercive harmony' to relieve 'gridlock' is 'Clintonspeak' for capitulation, and he argues '. . . gridlock is often a terse way of describing a last-ditch stand by good guys holding off the onrushing forces of darkness'.[62]

Initial Policy Responses

A series of international- and domestic-policy changes were quickly announced by the new administration (the Council on Competitiveness was scrapped immediately). It took three months from Bill Clinton's inauguration for the USA to agree to sign the biodiversity treaty and agree to the target of CO_2 stabilization at 1990 levels by the year 2000. As the *New York Times* reported, however, this decision to agree to stabilize was the result of a new battle within the administration.

Though Mr Clinton had pledged the action during the campaign, his announcement on global warming was an important victory for Vice-

Stamaty titled 'Balance in the NAFTA Debate' had the punchline: '299 experts for/ 299 against'; 14 Sept. 1993, 38/37:22.

[60] Dowie, *Losing Ground*, 190.

[61] Alexander Cockburn, ' "Win-win" with Bruce Babbitt: The Clinton Adminis-tration Meets the Environment', *New Left Review*, 201 (1993), 54 (see also *The Nation*, 23/30 Aug. 1993, 199–200). Dowie's and Cockburn's critiques of the envi-ronmental movement (the latter in his often vitriolic 'Beat the Devil' column in *The Nation*) are similar: that it is too addicted to compromise in Washington (lobbying, deal-making with Congress and big business, corporate sponsorship, etc.), and too WASP and middle-class in its senior ranks (Dowie). Both stress the importance of grass-roots activism, Dowie in particular arguing for broader local and national participation to create a 'social' rather than just an 'environmental' movement.

[62] Cockburn, ' "Win-win" with Bruce Babbitt', 49. John Nielsen argues that Babbitt accepted compromises even the Bush White House were not prepared to countenance (see 'Competing Concerns', *Earth Journal* (Nov./Dec. 1993), 72).

President Al Gore over Treasury Secretary Lloyd Bentsen and Energy Secretary Hazel R. O'Leary, who, among others, had argued that such restrictions would harm American industry.[63]

This argument about signing-up to stabilization had continued right to the last minute with speech-writers uncertain about exactly what the President was going to say. In an extraordinary development, bearing in mind the story of biodiversity as we have seen it, the new President accepted he had misgivings about some of the same issues as the Bush administration and that, remarkably, be would attach an 'interpretative statement' to his signature on biodiversity.[64] The *New York Times* went on to say:

White House officials said the interpretative statement to accompany the biodiversity treaty would assure American companies that they would not have to share technology with developing countries that provide resources for products manufactured by those companies.[65]

In announcing a commitment to stabilization on the eve of Earth Day 1993, the new President told his audience the administration would bring forward a detailed plan by August for reducing emissions to 1990 levels (a cut of about 7 per cent in CO_2 emissions). In the event, this process took several months longer as various agencies wrangled over its details and the plan was only unveiled in October. In it, the President called for the deployment of 'American ingenuity not more bureaucracy or regulation' as he announced a set of voluntary proposals for industry to follow. Good access for the environmentalists, at least as good access as business and far better than they had ever experienced under George Bush, had led to a plan for voluntary actions from private industry.[66]

Within the administration there had been discussion of an energy tax, and Clinton had committed himself on the pre-election trail to raising the required miles-per-gallon fuel efficiency standard on cars. Despite much discussion, this latter pledge never saw

[63] *New York Times*, 22 Apr. 1993, 1.
[64] This statement was drafted after a White House meeting with biotechnology and environmental groups. The principal irony is that the Bush administration might have signed with the use of such statements but they were ruled out in Nairobi.
[65] Ibid. 10.
[66] See J. Raloff, 'Clinton Unveils New Greenhouse Policy', *Science News*, 144/17 (23 Oct. 1993), 263.

the light of day while the proposal for an energy tax—submitted as part of the deficit-reduction package rather than as an environmental measure—failed to materialize as stronger than a four-cent levy on petrol. According to Tom Wicker, Gore 'pushed hard' for a more meaningful tax but 'found little support in or out of the administration'.[67] The administration used provisions under the pre-existing Energy Policy Act of 1992 (passed by the Bush administration) as, in the words of secretary of energy, Hazel O'Leary, 'the keystone of this Global Climate Action Plan'.[68] This meant, in effect, voluntary compliance. Clinton also announced an Executive Order requiring federal departments to buy recycled paper although not without several months of wrangling over the details.[69]

Needless to say, this was not the kind of hard-hitting plan for reducing CO_2 that environmental groups had sought and they criticized the administration on several fronts: the proposal had no mandatory element, no post-2000 dimension and entirely excluded the transport sector—one of the biggest CO_2 producers.[70] Even a New York Times editorial was moved to suggest the Action Plan was nearer to Bush than Gore and that Clinton's effort to enlist industry 'appears far more vigorous than Mr Bush's'.[71] A report from the NRDC soon alleged that the voluntary plan would not be tough enough to meet the USA's obligation of 1990 levels (missing by 70 million metric tonnes of CO_2) as cold weather, industrial

[67] Tom Wicker, 'Waiting for an Environmental President', Audubon (Sept./Oct. 1994), 102.

[68] 'Energy Policy Act 1992 and the President's climate change action plan', hearing before the Senate Committee on Energy and Natural Resources, 10 May 1994, Y4. En2: 103–794, p. 6.

[69] See Barbara Ruben, 'A Long Way from Earth Day', Environmental Action (Winter 1994), 35–6. Ruben gives an interesting account of societal competition about the minutiae of chlorine percentages in the Executive Order and provides good evidence for how access can make a difference in domestic policy as well as about the way one lobby's activities can stimulate a counter-lobby.

[70] Raloff 'Clinton Unveils New Greenhouse Policy', 263; Ruben, 'A Long Way from Earth Day', 34.

[71] New York Times, 6 Nov. 1993, 22. The head of the UK Foreign Office's department dealing with international environmental legislation before Rio, Tony Brenton, also notes the continuance of a 'traditional internal struggle between the economic and the environmental sides of the administration' under Clinton, adding that the latter were 'significantly reinforced by commitments that Clinton had made during his election campaign'—an illustration of the activists gaining from the political context (see Tony Brenton, The Greening of Machiavelli: The Evolution of International Environmental Politics (London: RIIA, 1994), 193).

growth, and cheaper oil, were leading to an increase in CO_2 emissions.[72]

The President was also forced to ask Dupont, the world's largest CFC producer, not to stop producing these ozone-depleting chemicals as quickly as a unilateral Bush initiative had decreed. This retrograde step was linked to the need for the support of Michigan congressmen on health care. As CFC phase-outs meant problems for air-conditioners in cars, a delay was the price.[73] Added to the 'fixing' of the biodiversity treaty, it was clear that the administration activists were on the back foot. Serious domestic environmental policy reverses did nothing to dispel this impression.

The perception that Clinton, and most importantly his interior secretary, Babbitt, were too quick to strike deals in order to claim domestic-policy successes came to be shared by a widening constituency of environmentalists, often leading to near-splits within mainstream groups as more radical activists started to lobby against the administration which was still supported by their superiors. Early 'defeats' included the reversal of a Gore campaign pledge that an incinerator in Ohio would never be allowed to burn toxic wastes, the quick withdrawal of plans for grazing and mining reforms in the West (the speed of which astonished even opponents), budget cuts to the EPA, and talk of relaxing the 1954 Delaney Amendment which mandated no food could be sold in the United States which *might* be carcinogenic however small the risk.[74]

The President planned to introduce the first major institutional shake-up since the NEPA by scrapping the CEQ, raising the EPA to cabinet status, and creating a new White House Office on Environmental Policy (WHOEP) as well as placing an environmental representative on the National Security Council and in OMB. These plans ran into problems, however. First of all, scrapping the CEQ was deeply unpopular with environmental leaders and their response clearly served to undermine Gore's reputation for being able to 'deliver' the environmental vote. After being told by the

[72] Tina Adler, 'Clinton Emissions Plan Under Fire', *Science*, 30 Apr. 1994, 278. This proved to be the case.

[73] Reilly, who joined the board of Dupont after leaving office, remembers Al Gore making the call.

[74] According to James Conaway, Senate 'Rockycrat' Max Baucus from Montana who opposed the grazing rights proposal, was nevertheless still appalled by how easily the President had given in (see Conaway, 'Babbitt in the Woods', 53).

President he had received a letter about the CEQ from 'your friends', the Vice-President allegedly 'read the riot act' to representatives of the Green Group (formerly the Group of Ten), telling them to 'get out of the way' and accusing them of a 'betrayal'.[75]

Secondly, the proposed raising of EPA to cabinet status was frustrated by Congress—as it had been under the Bush administration—and the new WHOEP, under a former Gore aide Kathleen A. McGinty, clearly suffered from proximity to more powerful activists and sceptics. As a new institution, it possessed little stored bargaining power or political capital which could be deployed.[76] With Congress cutting EPA's budget into the bargain, and refusing to elevate the agency (which would have made the administrator a full cabinet secretary), the scrapping of the CEQ simply replaced one established agency with a much newer one and left the EPA with a slightly tarnished reputation.

The one major domestic policy initiative on the environment which the President undertook during his first year in office was on the question of continued logging in the Pacific Northwest's old-growth forests, the 'spotted owl' controversy which had also dogged the Bush administration. In April 1993, the President held an environmental summit in Portland, Oregon, and undertook to work out a plan to appease the various factions. Although a working group produced eight options trading-off logging for habitat protection at varying levels, a ninth option was eventually chosen (the option Cockburn describes as 'Munich in the Redwoods') which allowed continued but reduced logging. Activists like Brock Evans were quoted as describing this as a 'shaky victory' while others set about criticizing the administration heavily, forcing it to go on the offensive trying to sell the policy. Overall, according to Dowie, most mainstream Washington-based groups were persuaded it was an acceptable compromise while local activists were horrified.[77]

Thus the first year of the new administration was marked by

[75] See Tim Beardsley, 'Ecolocation', *Scientific American* (June 1993), 28; and Daniel Glick 'Barbarians Inside the Gate', *Newsweek*, 1 Nov. 1993, 32.

[76] Dowie describes McGinty as 'lightweight' ('The Selling (Out) of the Greens', *The Nation*, 18 Apr. 1994, 514).

[77] Dowie, *Losing Ground*, 189–91. For a detailed account of the policy process see T. H. Watkins, 'The Perils of Option 9', *Wilderness* (Winter 1993), 6–9.

controversy, with heavy criticism of the various measures enacted on both foreign and domestic environmental issues. The 'interpreted' biodiversity treaty, once it was signed by the President, became bogged down in the process of Senate ratification while preparations continued for the first major meeting of the parties to the climate-change convention, to be held in Berlin in April 1995.

Preparations for Berlin

As we saw in Chapter 4, US assent to the climate-change treaty also required some fixing, the most notable element being the choice of the word 'aim' for the stabilization goal. President Clinton's April 1993 announcement turned that aim into a firm commitment, although the voluntary nature of the climate-change action plan and increased energy use after 1992 made it largely unrealizable. Nevertheless, discussions about Berlin within the USA concentrated on what steps were to be taken once the return to 1990 levels had been achieved. This had two dimensions in US policy debates: what firm commitments were now to be required of developing countries, and that would happen after the year 2000 when projections suggested CO_2 emissions would rise again, the most cost-effective efficiency measures having already been undertaken. Thus policy discussions centred around Southern compliance, and most crucially whether or not the United States would commit itself to an emissions reduction goal after 2000.

The State Department retained a central role in these policy deliberations, and both Pomerance and Wirth, his senior, were heavily involved in the preparatory process.[78] In dealing with Congress, for example, their role usually centred on 'selling' administration policy rather than in liaising with congressmen on the content of policy decisions. In a statement before a House energy subcommittee in May 1993, Wirth told this audience that the USA's policy-development process under Clinton differed from

[78] Pomerance was deputy assistant secretary for environment and development, and Wirth, a State Department counselor and under-secretary for global affairs. According to *Business Week*, Wirth had as many as 150 people within State working on the follow-up to Rio ('One Year After Rio: The US Waves a Green Flag', 14 June 1993, 90). Nevertheless, both still operated below the level of senior policymakers.

that under Bush most importantly because 'we take the science seriously'. He informed congressmen:

As President Clinton noted in his Earth Day speech, there will be, by the end of this decade, a $300 billion market for environmental technologies and the United States must capture as much of that market—and the tens of thousands of jobs it will create—as possible.[79]

In other words, there was no environmental imperative: the decision made perfect sense in terms of national industrial competitiveness. In the words of the deputy administrator of the EPA, Robert Sussman:

The Administration seeks to ensure that the US mitigate its share of global emissions of greenhouse gases in a way that enhances our continued competitiveness in the world's economy.[80]

This was clearly just what congressmen wanted to hear, as they had in 1972. The chairman of the Subcommittee on Economic Policy, Trade, and Environment of the House Committee on Foreign Affairs, Sam Gejdenson (Connecticut) told a hearing on climate change:

Tough US actions to stem global warming will help ensure that American firms will move forward with environmentally sound technologies which will not just give us an advantage in the international marketplace but will also give us an advantage in our own productivity here at home.[81]

The concern of some congressmen with the domestic economic impacts of certain proposals, most notably the ill-fated energy tax, went deeper. Representative Donald A. Manzullo (Illinois) told Wirth: 'I think it is immoral to raise gasoline taxes so people use less gasoline.'[82] Despite the need to sell the policy, testimony by

[79] Timothy E. Wirth, 'Developments in US policy toward global climate change', statement to the Subcommittee on Energy and Power of the House Committee on Energy and Commerce, 26 May 1993 (US Department of State dispatch, 4/32 (31 May 1993), 400–1).

[80] 'Energy Policy Act 1992 and the President's climate change action plan', hearing before Senate Committee on Energy and Natural Resources, 10 May 1994, Y4 En 2 103–794, p. 22. Sussman also notes, however, the USA's 'commitment to the world' under the climate-change convention.

[81] 'Administration views on global climate change', hearing before Subcommittee on Economic Policy, Trade and Environment, House Committee on Foreign Affairs, 18 May 1993, Y4. F 76/1 G 51/7, p. 1.

[82] 'Administration views on global climate change', Subcommittee on Economic Policy, Trade and Environment, 18 May 1993, p. 19. Manzullo argued such a tax penalized the poor.

various administration officials still demonstrates the importance attached to environmental issues as issues in their own right. The President's desire that the United States re-establish 'leadership' is frequently mentioned. Rafe Pomerance told senators: '. . . we must use the moral authority that preparation of our own plan gives us to urge other countries to work to meet their own commitments'.[83] At a later House hearing, Susan Tierney, assistant secretary in the office of policy, planning and program evaluation, Department of Energy, argued that the United States ought to cut greenhouse gases so it might:

play a legitimate and credible leadership role internationally in preventing pollution, and in mitigating the accumulation of greenhouse gases in the atmosphere. It is clearly a tough challenge to reduce our emissions to 1990 levels by the end of the decade, but the challenge, if addressed creatively, offers a host of opportunities for American industry.[84]

Finally, in outlining policy immediately before the Berlin Conference, Pomerance argued that a key US aim, 'joint implementation' (see below), was '. . . a triple win, good for the environment, good for the economy, and good for American industry'.[85] At this hearing, not only did some representatives demonstrate their deep scepticism, they also revealed that in essence they simply did not trust the State Department to do what it claimed. Congressmen John D. Dingell (Michigan) repeatedly pressed Pomerance over whether developing countries were actually tied to any firm commitments at all. He concluded:

In other words, we are going to be bound but other countries are not going to be bound. I find that a curious position for a representative of the United States Government to be taking at an international meeting, don't you?[86]

After the conference, Dingell displayed his scepticism (and

---

[83] 'Energy Policy Act 1992 and the President's climate change action plan', hearing before Senate Committee on Energy and Natural Resources, 10 May 1994, Y4 En 2 103–794, p. 26.

[84] 'Global climate change and air pollutants', hearings before Subcommittee on Health and the Environment of House Committee on Energy and Commerce, 4 Aug./26 Oct. 1993, Y4 En2/3 103–71, p. 23.

[85] 'International global climate change negotiations', hearing before Subcommittee on Energy and Power of House Committee on Commerce, 21 Mar./19 May 1995, Y4 C73/8, 104–13, pp. 10–11.

[86] Ibid. 60.

realism) about State Department claims, telling Wirth that State
tended to agree to 'wonderful language' which:

... usually binds us and usually does not fine the foreigners, and it leaves
the United States in the rather embarrassing position not only of having
commitments made to do things and spend money that others are not
compelled to do, but also creates a floor upon which further expectations
of further actions by the United States, usually adverse to the American
interest, must be taken at some future time.[87]

This reflected the fact that once the Congress had ratified a
treaty, like that on climate change, an administration could often
make further commitments without reference back to Capitol Hill.
As Pomerance had told senators about the President's announcement of a US commitment to 1990 emissions levels, '. . . we are very
sensitive to what we should or would have to go back to the Senate
for'.[88]

Although administration witnesses before Congress were fairly
unanimous in their message about the gains to US industry, they
failed to shake congressmen's suspicions that a new post-2000 commitment might be in the offing. There is, however, little evidence to
suggest that this was ever the case, especially as it became clear
relatively quickly that the USA was not going to meet its 1990-by-
2000 emissions target. Berlin was to be the first major meeting of
the parties to climate change at Rio, the treaty having come into
force in 1994 after fifty ratifications. In order to consider options for
a post-2000 regime, the administration established a task force co-
chaired by the office of science and technology policy, the office of
environmental policy, and the national economic council.[89] This
was explicitly designed to solicit advice from within and outside
government. The USA also gave $25 million to various developing
countries to prepare reports on climate change strategies, $430
million to the core fund of the GEF, as well as establishing its own
initiative on 'joint implementation'.

Although the 1992 framework convention provided for joint
implementation, the State Department launched a specifically

---

[87] 'International global climate change negotiations', 21 Mar./19 May 1995, pp.
142–3.
[88] 'Energy Policy Act 1992 and the President's climate change action plan', 10
May 1994, p. 36. Energy secretary Hazel O'Leary told the same meeting the administration had 'no intention to bypass Congress' (p. 36).
[89] Ibid. 26.

American pilot programme in October 1993. It would have allowed heavy polluters such as the United States to 'buy' credits (possibly with technology transfer) to continue polluting from developing countries who would 'sell' some of their pollution 'allowance'. This proposal was popular with sceptical congressmen, and American industry whose representative at one meeting described joint implementation as a 'silver bullet' which would increase US exports and investment.[90]

What concerned several congressmen, however, was not only that the United States intended to accept new commitments to reduce emissions at the Berlin meeting, but that the President's April 1993 announcement on the 1990 target also entailed more than had been agreed at Rio, hence, the discussion with Pomerance about the need for new Senate approval if more goals were to be set. Senator Malcolm Wallop (Wyoming) managed to get Pomerance to accept that ratification of the treaty in 1993 depended on any new 'binding' commitments going back to the Senate but the latter also described the President's April announcement as 'a political commitment'.[91]

Although the administration argued strongly that it had no intention of agreeing to further commitments at Berlin, it seems a disagreement did exist within the core state about the need for such moves. In 1993, for example, Wirth told House members:

The administration is committed to seeing the Convention promptly inplemented and, if necessary, strengthened.[92]

Just before the Berlin Conference, in March 1995, Vice-President Gore accepted that much tougher measures were required after 2000 at the same time as confirming the United States was not going to endorse them.[93] At the pre-conference House hearing, however, Rafe Pomerance told congressmen that the USA supported a 'structure' not specific targets and timetables, and a

[90] Jerry Jasinowski, president of the National Association of Manufacturers, and on behalf of the Global Climate Coalition ('Global climate change and air pollutants', 4th Aug./26 Oct. 1993, p. 64).

[91] 'Energy Policy Act 1992 and the President's climate change action plan', 10 May 1994, pp. 36, 37.

[92] 'Administration views on global climate change', 18 May 1993, p. 5.

[93] R. Monastersky, 'Climate Summit: Slippery Slopes Ahead', *Science News*, 147/12 (25 Mar. 1995), 183.

'mandate' for negotiations, not a regulatory mandate.[94] This was reinforced by Wirth after the conference when he reiterated that the 'Berlin Mandate', issued in Germany, entailed no obligations for any state after 2000. It was simply an agreement to set up a negotiating process.[95]

Immediately prior to Berlin, a ministerial-level negotiation (with the USA represented by Wirth) had taken place in Bonn to try to make some headway before the conference started on 28 March 1995. After the fourteen days of actual negotiation, the final agreement did call for emissions reductions after 2000, and a timetable for them, but accepted that a further meeting (at Kyoto in December 1997) should decide on the exact numbers. The United States was widely seen as holding out on this issue, stressing the need for developing countries to make firm commitments to cut their emissions. Nevertheless, it backed the final Berlin Mandate.[96]

Although the USA was considered more reluctant than the European Union on this issue, an interim meeting in Geneva in August 1996 reversed this impression. According to the *Wall Street Journal*, the USA made a 'sudden shift in policy' to accept legally binding commitments as part of an international treaty, with Wirth arguing the USA had to exercise leadership and put some 'shoulder behind it' while also denying it entailed any specific cuts or timetables (these having to be negotiated within the USA first). The *Journal* described environmentalists as 'jubilant' and industry as 'outflanked' and 'horrified'.[97]

Although evidence is still scarce, this 'victory' for activists within the administration undoubtedly reflected the shift in political context occasioned by sweeping Republican victories in Congress in 1994's mid-term elections. Efforts to roll back environmental statutes caused a backlash which provided just what Al Gore and his sympathizers needed to convince the President to focus on the environment more. This was not enough to rescue the biodiversity treaty from the Senate, however. The ratification process for the

---

[94] 'International global climate change negotiations', 21 Mar./19 May 1995, pp. 36–7.

[95] Ibid. 128–9. Congressional concern about US competitiveness, and about the possibility the United States will be disadvantaged in some way, is truly remarkable in its intensity in this hearing. Here, at any rate, the realist vision—albeit of an economic rather than a military struggle for survival—is alive and well.

[96] *The Times* (London), 6 Apr. 1995, 9; 8 Apr., 14.

[97] *Wall Street Journal*, 18 Aug. 1996, A9A.

BDT passed through its committee stage easily but a concerted last-ditch campaign by the 'Wise Use' movement led to Senator Bob Dole spearheading a Republican blocking coalition thus hampering further progress. According to the *Washington Post*, none of the objectors to the BDT in the foreign-relations committee (where it passed 16–3) mentioned 'sovereignty' but the campaign to block the bill in April 1995 was conducted successfully along these lines.[98]

The Tide Turns (a Little)

The retaking of both Houses of Congress by Republicans in 1994 altered the political landscape appreciably, increasing public sympathy with environmental issues and thereby strengthening those within the White House who were arguing for the President to be more proactive on the environment. As with the Reagan administration in 1981, Republicans brought into office an anti-regulatory message which saw them try to overturn or water down many pieces of legislation.

Things became so difficult that many environmentalists, who had seen the various bills coming up for renewal after 1994 as a chance to strengthen things, now preferred to leave well alone as the Congress wasted no opportunity in trying to weaken existing standards. In addition, new areas of the countryside—most notably the heavily protected Arctic refuge—were deemed suitable for oil and gas exploration. By August 1995, the President was telling Americans that twenty-five years of bipartisanship on the environment were over as Congress tried to gut environmental legislation and allowed 'big company' lobbyists to actually write the bills. He vowed to veto them.[99]

According to Kathleen McGinty, this fight-back did not represent a new policy, just validation for the existing one. It was based, said the administration, on polling data (the ubiquitous Dick Morris) showing increasing concern with environmental issues under the new Congress.[100] By mid-1996, the *New York Times* was

[98] *Washington Post*, 23 Apr. 1995, C2.
[99] 'Remarks on environmental protection in Baltimore, Maryland', 8 Aug. 1995, and 'Remarks on the 25th anniversary of Earth Day in Havre de Grace, Maryland', 21 Apr. 1995, Official Record of the *Administration of William Jefferson Clinton*, p. 1395 and p. 677.
[100] *New York Times*, 5 July 1995, A11.

suggesting that this clash had been the defining moment in terms of the administration's environmental policy, with Congress now 'cowed' a little having learned the power of mainstream environmental groups and the President now clearer that 'wrapping himself in green would pay off politically'.[101]

Under the headline, 'GOP's rollback of the green agenda is stalled by a public seeing red over proposed changes', the *Wall Street Journal* pointed out that many more moderate Republicans in Congress were also concerned about cutting environmental regulations further. The proposal to make deep inroads into EPA's budget would, said the *Journal*, 'cripple enforcement'. Other initiatives, to cut the Superfund (for cleaning up toxic-waste sites, one cause of Anne Gorsuch Burford's resignation under Reagan) and to weaken the 1973 Endangered Species Act, were also openly in dispute.[102]

Despite this 're-ignition' of interest, and the increased ammunition available to activists like Gore and Babbitt there was no large-scale resistance to the moves Congress was making from the White House and, indeed, one or two policy decisions seemed to confirm the pre-1994 trend. For example, to 'save' the Endangered Species Act, the administration weakened some requirements applicable to small-lot holders as a way to generate resistance against Congress's proposal to compensate larger private landholders who suffered. The end result was a weaker act.[103]

Finally, the White House also badly 'miscalculated' in relation to a 'salvage logging rider' Congress attached to a spending bill in mid-1995, initially vetoing it but then relenting. After a very broad court interpretation, logging picked up speed in the Pacific Northwest again and it became clear that some previously protected areas were now vulnerable. 'That was, indeed, our biggest mistake,' Al Gore told reporters.[104]

---

[101] *New York Times*, 31 July 1996, 1, A12. The policy struggle over 'ecology and economy' in the administration prior to 1994 was described as follows: 'The same ambivalence permeated the Cabinet and the White House staff, where there was a constant tension between people who figuratively wore green armbands and those who preferred green eyeshades. There were strong environmentalists and Gore loyalists, but also noncommital number-crunchers and a cadre of political movers and shifters' (p. A12).

[102] *Wall Street Journal*, 26 Dec. 1996, A8. The *Journal* suggests, knowingly, that the White House's interest in the environment might be 're-ignited' by this opposition.

[103] *New York Times*, 7 Mar. 1995, C4.

[104] *New York Times*, 31 July 1996, A12.

CONCLUSION

This final, substantive section of the book is necessarily sketchy given how little good material is yet in the public domain. Much more needs to be known about the process by which positions were adopted on targets and timetables both for Berlin and also for the Geneva meeting which followed it a year or so later. Nevertheless, three tentative conclusions can be reached about the Clinton administration thus far.

First, to note the degree to which, although enjoying excellent access and with activists at the commanding heights, environmental groups failed to institute the kind of revolution they had been seeking. As Dowie argues:

As shifty and unpredictable as he is, Bill Clinton nevertheless provides the mainstream environmental movement a functional proving ground for its heaviest weapon—the lobby. If the environmental lobby, with its 25 years of experience in Washington could not affect a Democratic Congress and a rhetorically friendly Democratic administration, it may never be effective again. By all indications, this is the case.[105]

If the explanation for this is that even such a sympathetic administration simply listened more intently to the business community, it is necessary to explain why any administration passes legislation which is in the environmental interest. Alternatively, a realist explanation about reponses to an anarchic international system misses the deep degree to which the state is differentiated. In the words of Peter Passell, even out of office, Gore and his supporters had been trying to get 'global warming and rain forest protection to the top of the national agenda'.[106] Or, as Ralph de Gennaro of Friends of the Earth said of Clinton's environmental appointments: 'You don't have to convince these people. They get it.'[107] They continued to lobby for these choices once inside the state, but met powerful resistance.

Activists were simply outgunned, with sceptics, harder to find, and more moderate than in the previous Republican administration, nevertheless able to argue that the national economy, congressional concerns about competitiveness, even campaign donations and voter sympathy in key areas, all depended on a less

---

[105] *Losing Ground*, 192.
[106] Peter Passell, 'Economic Science', *New York Times*, 10 Dec. 1992, D2.
[107] Nixon, 'Bill and Al's Green Adventure', 33.

radical stance. As Michael McCloskey puts it: 'Even the best of administrations have counterforces within them.'[108] In this respect, one must also differentiate presidents Clinton and Bush. The former was clearly much more proactive in these areas, not just waiting for the debate to be resolved but weighing-in himself. It was the plaintive wail of many environmental writers that the President just refused to exercise leadership or spend political capital on environmental issues. This rebounded on environmentalists outside the state too, the President's lack of will in this area a portent for their prospects, and his reluctance to use 'moral persuasion' via the bully pulpit a crippling blow.[109]

Secondly, the distinction between domestic and foreign policy remains although the climate-change example is fascinating because it requires domestic legislative changes—such as an energy tax—to realistically meet international commitments. While domestic legislation clearly brought Congress to the fore, in foreign policy it is possible to see the White House and State carving out a deeper US commitment on future climate-change strategy. Here, also, the distinction between policy-making and implementation really begins to bite. The hard reality is that the Clinton administration was unable to push through an energy tax which would have made its commitment to reach 1990 levels by 2000 feasible. One might stress the power of Congress here. However, the tax appears to have been a non-starter and was withdrawn almost immediately. Why a policy would be announced which the administration wasn't even going to try to enact is open to several explanations.

One, for example, might be sheer misjudgement, and the first half of the first Clinton administration was certainly beset by tactical and strategic miscalculations. A more interesting interpretation might relate back to the literature on two-level games. To pronounce a radical policy measure to meet international commitments, secure in the knowledge that it is domestically untenable, provides an explanation for the failure to achieve targets which self-evidently places the blame somewhere else. Notwithstanding

[108] Nixon, 'Bill and Al's Green Adventure', 32.
[109] Wicker, 'Waiting for an Environmental President', 102. He argues that Al Gore's presidential ambitions also prevented him from appearing too 'green' (p. 54). Joan Hamilton argues that Bruce Babbitt was undermined on mining and grazing rights, for example, because it was clear he didn't have the President behind him ('Babbitt's Retreat', *Sierra*, July/Aug. 1994, 57).

the fact that the authors of *Double-Edged Diplomacy* found chief negotiators keen to expand their flexibility, rather than claim their hands were tied, this might be evidence of the latter strategy.

Thirdly, the notion of an envelope is clearly in evidence. In fact, some might be persuaded, along with the realists and even structural Marxists, that the relative continuity in terms of policy performance suggests that the envelope provides evidence of deeper shared motivations based either on institutional characteristics or norm-based socialization. This reduces the ideas and beliefs of both the sceptics and the activists to either 'tone' (rather than substance), rationalization, or simply marginal disagreements centred around a much more extensive and consensual core. For this to be the case, the arguments put forward by various environmentalists within the state must not have a substantive impact on policy. Intrastate struggles then matter much less than identifying the institutions and norms, and the processes of socialization and 'embedding' through which they work. Agency disappears, and structure ascends. Overall, the argument throughout this book is a determined attempt to cast doubt on the inadequacy of this position, both as an explanation for American foreign environmental policy but also as a dead-end for any kind of empirical research.

6

Continuity and Change in American Foreign Environmental Policy

Having established the value of adopting a more institutional conception of the state, the initial argument presented in Chapter 1 stressed that the central actors in American foreign environmental policy remained state officials. Despite tangible societal constraint in the domestic realm, international environmental politics provide an enhanced opportunity for officials to turn their preferences into policy. The disjuncture therefore holds between domestic and foreign policy.

The various elements at work in both the societal and international spheres feed into this process by creating the *context* in which this policy is made. These elements serve to bolster or frustrate coalitions within the state itself. They do this, for example, by influencing the international agenda. However, as we have seen, a set of limits, an 'envelope', exists to limit feasible policy options. This is accepted by state officials with a high degree of consensus because it derives from their very similar social experiences, and is then reinforced by the institutional imperatives of holding national office.

In other words, the argument is for a 'state-centric' explanation which accommodates political developments in operation at the societal and international levels. Although these claims relate specifically to US foreign environmental policy, in the conclusion of a recent collected work on the state and American foreign *economic* policy, one of the editors argues:

Even in the United States, with a political system marked by its fragmentation of political authority and diffusion of power, the shaping and constraining role of state officials and the institutions they inhabit remain considerable. The implication of this conclusion, however, is not that, in a contest of approaches, the state-centred models of foreign economic policy won. The conclusion is not that scholars embracing society and system-centred perspectives should pack their theoretical tents and steal away into the night. In fact, the research presented in this volume suggests a very different message. The most useful analysis explores the interplay and the historically contingent role of international-, societal-, and state-centred variables.[1]

The Stockholm Conference was called at a time when the US state already had significant domestic environmental machinery in place. Even though some efforts were being made to discuss environmental issues at a multilateral level, these were confined to wealthier countries. Thus the UN process inaugurated a change of emphasis, in the United States as elsewhere, and a far broader range of issues emerged onto the international agenda. In the American case, these were dealt with largely through an intrastate process. The State Department played a powerful role, using its insulation from constituency pressures, and its strategically advantageous position at the intersection of other involved departments, to steer the process. It was a constant complaint of societal groups, and even congressmen, that State was hard to access and thus meaningful public input was small.

In addition to State, the CEQ was the other major domestic actor. This body was even more exclusive, made up of only three men—Train, MacDonald, and Cahn—with a supporting staff including William Reilly and Lee Talbot. The main US proposals emerged out of the interplay between the CEQ and State. Even though they both faced some scepticism, even from the President (who was suspicious rather than fearful of the aims of environmentalists), they had three advantages conferred on them by the political context.

First, the high profile of environmental issues made them an important concern for voters and other Nixon aides appreciated this acutely. Thus, activists could override the fears of conservatives by accentuating the good electoral sense of a strong pro-environmental message. Second, Vietnam was causing the administration great concern—publicity at home and abroad was very negative—and activists argued successfully that laying stress on environmental issues would help repair some of the damage done

---

[1] G. John Ikenberry, 'Conclusion: An Institutional Approach to American Foreign Economic Policy', in Ikenberry, Lake, and Mastanduno (eds.), *The State and American Foreign Economic Policy*, 221–2. The paragraph concludes: 'In effect, we need a more encompassing set of reference points that provide guidance in selecting and incorporating the array of explanatory variables.'

by the war. Third, the importance of an external origin for the conference meant the activists avoided an intrastate battle about the principle—it simply confronted the US state and required a policy reaction. In this way, the advantages enjoyed by State and the CEQ were magnified. The issue context also helped: complexity ensured few at a senior level could compete with intrastate environmentalists who were well-versed in such problems; and 'newness' meant few precedents had been established to queer the activists' pitch—vested interests, thus far, were few.

This policy-search had limits, however. These were not constituted by some kind of 'compromise' within the bargaining process whereby two antithetical positions—sceptic and activist—would converge around a median position; it is more accurate to suggest that one side, rather than the other, secured a 'victory' of sorts. The limits came from a shared perspective on certain fundamentals about the American political system. In all their dealings, state officials from either faction accepted that the United States should in some sense benefit from the agreements under consideration. They remained heavily committed to the importance of the domestic sphere, and always mindful of the potential adverse effects of certain courses of action. Some of this awareness was clearly prudential for activists who sought to avoid exacerbating sceptic concerns. But one is struck throughout the story by the absence of radical proposals being fed into the process at the highest level, and by the extent to which both factions supported the American effort to pursue what amounted to international leadership in this field (more so in 1972 than in 1992).

This is evidenced, for instance, by the extent to which state officials in the preparation process emphasized US successes, stressed the predominance of domestic concerns, and subsequently, at the conference, resisted Southern demands for technology transfer and compensation for trading losses because they were subjects 'inappropriate' for such a gathering. State officials assiduously repelled arguments about changes in lifestyle and redistributive justice which would have entailed major transfers from the USA, and other wealthy nations, to the poorer countries of the world. This was unacceptable to both sceptics and activists, representing as it did utilitarianism rather than a pareto improvement.

Support for this argument emerges out of the story of preparations for Rio as well. This is despite, rather than because of, societal developments in the intervening years. As we saw there were at least three developments which might have been expected to curtail the degree of autonomy enjoyed by the state in 1972. First, the tremendous growth in domestic environmentalism in the United States and its increasing professionalism; second, the establishment of new international institutions, especially UNEP; and third, the identification of even more complex and genuinely global environmental issues.

Domestic environmental groups in the United States enjoyed an extraordinary rise in membership and revenue in the twenty years since Stockholm. They now have millions of paying supporters, and have been transformed into well-funded and professional lobby groups. Most have offices, often their head office, in Washington (not a site of particularly remarkable natural beauty), they employ large staffs of lawyers and policy analysts, and they spend a great deal of their time working both in Congress and the courts for either the enactment or implementation of environmental legislation. They are now a firmly established and central component in the domestic-policy process and, in areas like clean air and logging, they have secured real political victories.

Business, too, has responded to the challenge of the environmental movement. Firms and whole industries have become better organized, tackling the environmental movement on television, in the courts, and in Congress. They became heavily involved in the issue of ozone depletion and, indeed, it was business's 'defection' to the regulatory camp which actually undermined the sceptics on ozone in the mid-1980s. Activists were then able to argue forcefully that a central plank of the sceptics' case—the adverse effect on the USA's economic health—was contradicted by the very groups to which they appealed for support. The arguments at the senior state level remained similar—there was little change at the top—but what did alter was the context.

The crude picture of either the state as a whole, or the sceptics in particular, acting merely as the delegates of the business community is at best inadequate. These officials display considerable independence of mind, arguing from more complex motives, and engaging in an intrastate policy struggle they want to win. The sceptics did, in general, emphasize the negative effects that certain courses of action would have on American business interests but, more often than not, this served to reinforce their essential aversion to both multilateral and domestic environmentalism. There is clearly a congruence, and even a sympathy, between sceptics and business (based on some shared ideas and values), but one can't simply discount electoral politics, the pressure from other governments, fears about setting future precedents for US multilateral involvement, personal ideas about the motives of environmentalists and about environmentalism, concern for US prestige, and so forth.

Thus the state in 1992 was subject to a far more sophisticated collection of groups—both business and environmental—with resources, substantial experience in the pursuit of policy, and established lines of communication into Congress. The domestic front had been even more radicalized during the conservative retrenchment of the Reagan era, and the battle over clean air amendments had been waged for the whole of the 1980s. These groups were also much better organized on an international level—a lot was learned from Stockholm and, from the late 1970s onwards, the growth in the size and number of both transnational groups and meetings in the international arena was high.

A better appreciation emerged of the linkages between environmental issues and other concerns (trade, development), as well as of the ties to other countries entailed by the idea of the 'global commons' (acid rain, deforestation, ozone depletion, global warming), meaning that some extra-national dimension became a natural extension. The National Audobon Society, for example, has become involved in helping several foreign environmental groups to fight logging projects (in countries like Finland, Norway, and Russia). According to Brock Evans tactics include sending faxes to harass governments and applying pressure to prominent involved individuals. When it comes to international negotiations, however, his frustration is plain.

I have to say that for myself, as a domestic lobbyist who is used to really strong action and results, and things like that, this whole world of the international arena seemed very arcane. Everything is sort of third or fourth remove from something. You lobby one delegate to lobby the minister to lobby the whole colloquium to maybe get a bracket put around a word. The word is a vague word anyhow, and then it gets in the treaty and then it's ten years, and you probably don't see anything anyway.[2]

    [2] Interview with author, 8 Apr. 1994.

A second development between the conferences was the emergence of a central non-state institutional player: UNEP. Set up at Stockholm, as we have seen, UNEP has been involved in many of the major environmental discussions to take place since the early 1970s. Originally envisaged, by the USA at least, as a fairly modest body to help implement and monitor agreements reached elsewhere, it quickly became a focus of the South's drive for a prominent say in international environmental politics. In the first ten years of its existence it suffered from problems of internal management, lack of executive authority in relation to other UN agencies (it quite explicitly wasn't an 'agency' itself), and a relatively small budget.[3] In the 1980s, however, it played an increasingly active role, most noticeably in relation to ozone depletion and biodiversity.

As Gareth Porter and Janet Welsh Brown point out: 'The agenda-setting function in global environmental politics has been dominated by UNEP because of its unique mandate, growing out of the 1972 Stockholm conference, to be a catalyst and coordinator of environmental activities and focal point for such activities within the UN system.'[4] UNEP effectively became the 'arena' for the discussion of ozone depletion, providing a secretariat, convening both formal and informal meetings and, through Tolba's behind-the-scenes lobbying, trying to pressure for binding commitments. It established a Coordinating Committee on the Ozone Layer in 1977, and also urged support for a 'world plan of action' to tackle the problem.[5] We have already seen how involved UNEP became in the preparation of the biodiversity treaty; in a sense, it was a UNEP process even though the participants were governments, and Tolba was a central figure in actually forging consensus for the final convention.

A third development relates to the arrival of two 'new' issues on the international political agenda. Ozone depletion was an issue in the United States before it was an issue anywhere else and, despite

[3] McCormick, *The Global Environmental Movement*, 109–24; Wapner, 'Politics Beyond the State', 315 n. 12.

[4] Porter and Brown, *Global Environmental Politics*, 48. On p. 49 they list some of the major agreements, including CITES and the ocean dumping convention, with which UNEP has been involved.

[5] Elizabeth P. Barratt-Brown, 'Building a Monitoring and Compliance Regime under the Montreal Protocol', app. 5 to House Subcommittee on Human Rights, 3 Oct. 1991, Y4 F76/En8/6, p. 218. Barratt-Brown was an attorney with the international program at the NRDC.

recalcitrance in the early 1980s, the USA was the most powerful state supporting an agreement after 1985 (in opposition to the EC, an interesting reversal of the situation on climate change). This issue, while of concern to many countries, centred on a known culprit, involved relatively few central actors, and implied limited costs. Global warming, the profile of which was raised considerably by a drought in the USA in 1988, entailed potentially enormous lifestyle changes and brought into stark relief the multitude of ways in which the environment in separate countries was part of a global 'ecosphere', linked-in with fundamental questions about development, trade, and overall quality of life. There was probably no way—given the institutional apparatus now in place—that this most complex of global problems was ever likely to be addressed other than at the multilateral level from the start.

These developments all share the characteristic that they encircle the state. Interest groups worked away both nationally and through international institutions, and other governments. UNEP relieved powerful states of some agenda control and worked as a kind of co-ordinator, 'by building concern and by improving the contractual environment'.[6] The nature of the issues meant they lent themselves to intergovernmental negotiation thereby weakening the purchase that any one government could gain on the process as a whole. In spite of all these developments, however, the US state retained a considerable degree of autonomy when it came to preparations for Rio.

In the first place, the resolution of policy positions is explained most fully by the process of decision-making within the state. Even though the principal UNCED documents were largely the preserve of less senior officials at the State Department, to whom environmental groups had better access, the general thrust of policy came, as we have seen, from the highest levels. There was, it is true, some room for manœuvre inside these parameters and officials used it to work for acceptable compromises with other states. Figures like Curtis Bohlen and Bob Zoellick were prominent in trying to carve out a sphere in which agreements could be reached. It was at this level that societal groups had their best input, liaising through the US UNCED Coordination Center and directly with the principals, the latter attempting to create a more conducive atmosphere for

---

[6] Parson, 'Protecting the Ozone Layer', 64.

consensus, and seeking to protect their discussions from White House oversight. This only proved possible, however, on non-binding documents: the Declaration and Agenda 21.

On climate change and biodiversity things were different. These conventions were legally binding and, as a result, the most senior officials maintained a much more active interest. The decisions to oppose targets for stabilization, and to refuse to sign the biodiversity treaty, were taken in the White House after many months of wrangling and debate. EPA chief Reilly worked hard to convince the President that climate change was an issue on which the USA could reach agreement. He cited the ability of the USA to meet such commitments, and the fact that measures already en-acted would bring the country close to the proposed target, the advantages to the American economy more generally, and the importance of a good position on the environment in terms of votes. Reilly consistently believed that Republicans could gain environmental voters. He was opposed, however, by powerful forces.

John Sununu and Richard Darman formed a strong and united front against climate concessions. They were supported by other heavyweights like Boyden Gray and, after Sununu resigned, by the new domestic-policy advisor, Clayton Yeutter. They argued re-morselessly against stabilization and even against attendance at Rio. This latter point had been a ploy—a very successful one—to get the EC to compromise. However, there were those, Gray and Yeutter most prominent, who still thought George Bush should refuse to attend. These decisions were thrashed out during heated debates in the White House.

On biodiversity, the equally sceptical Council on Competitive-ness had been closely involved and it staged a well-timed and successful effort to pare down the US position in Nairobi, and thus make it difficult to secure any agreement to which the American delegation could assent. They issued a now infamous memo warn-ing of the possibility of a treaty being signed which would severely damage the US economy, and they pushed remorselessly for non-signature. Then, having achieved this, they sank any last hope of a late deal in Rio itself.

Societal groups mattered in this process in three main ways, but they were not central to the explanation of core decisions. They helped establish the agenda; they helped to provide often fiercely critical publicity, thereby greatly increasing awareness and altering the character of the political context; and they provided information for both governments and publics about substantive issues, the talks, and the conference. In this manner, they affected the way in which issues were addressed, the availability of alternative analyses of administration choices, and, most importantly, the fortunes of those within the state who sympathized. The kind of arguments that Reilly was having to make were, however, weakened not strengthened by the actions of environmental groups. His assertion that the Republicans could get environmental votes was quite spectacularly undermined by the constant barrage of criticism. As the intrastate debate unfolded, the sceptics were able to harden their position in the face of unrelenting adverse publicity. That some other states joined this protest simply exacerbated the problem. A more yielding stance on the environmentalists' part might well have improved matters.

Despite the tension between the activists and sceptics, however, there were still some shared elements. The arguments that the South advanced for limits to consumption were much too radical for anyone involved in the policy process at a senior level. The object for American negotiators was to get an agreement which was good for their citizens as well, that would ensure high long-term living standards for the USA. The importance of economic growth, and of the good sense of allowing the market to work in some areas, combined with this objective to form a kind of shared outlook. This was perhaps most evident on biodiversity where both sceptics and activists had reservations.[7]

Overall, the story of Rio thus bears great similarity to that of Stockholm. Despite the growth in societal interest and expertise, the state still retained a dominant position in the policy-making process. Those who argue from a pluralist perspective are quite right to advertise the visibility of societal and international non-state actors, and to stress their role in agenda formation, consciousness raising, and information provision. But they do not make a direct and determining impact on deliberations within the state. This process works more from the top down, with officials using the political landscape laid out before them to garner support for

---

[7] Curtis Bohlen recalls that, to the best of his recollection, no one in the US state really thought it was a good treaty (interview with author, 30 Mar. 1994).

the positions they think the US state should adopt. A much more independent view of the state is required to adequately capture this feature of foreign environmental policy.

The idea of 'epistemic communities', 'networks of knowledge-based experts', is an interesting development in the pluralist literature, yet it too fails to present an adequate alternative to the central importance of the state. Recall the claim that, especially under conditions of uncertainty, the expertise of scientists (principally) moulds the way state officials understand problems. As new issues arise, state officials turn to specialists for help. Thus the primary importance of non-state forces. There is little evidence, however, of these 'societal' figures having a deep impact on the policy process.

They certainly played a role in agenda setting, in relation to climate change and the G7, for example, but their direct access was usually at a low level and, even where scientists presented a tentative consensus for action, their arguments encountered stiff sceptic resistance. There is little to suggest that these figures could shape the evolution of policy so as to reflect their own concerns. Influencing agendas, and providing information and publicity, still remain potent weapons but they do not substitute as an explanation for the policy-making process within the core state. Epistemic communities may form part of an explanation which centres on the state but they are no alternative to it, either as the focus of analysis or as the 'real' determinants of foreign-policy choice. It is possible, however, that their principal long-term contribution may lie in defining problems and solutions such that their interpretation of the nature of the issue comes to be seen as a set of 'objective' facts, and section two below speculates on this.

The realists do not emerge profitably from this analysis either. Ultimately, they would probably claim that international environmental politics are simply too devoid of importance for their particular picture of the state to be of use.[8] Yet, the Rio process did have quite an impact on US prestige and, for all its relatively lowly status, the issue of leadership in environmental politics has provoked interest in both Japan and the EU, especially Germany. This may not be evidence for US decline but it is certainly not evidence

---

[8] See Waltz, 'Reflections on *Theory of International Politics*', 329. For arguments against this position, see Finnemore, *National Interests*, 31–3.

of US strength either. There is little to be said for the claim that the pursuit of a national interest was visible in intrastate politics. Although the position of the sceptics seems at times 'approximately' realist, being conservative, wary, and more nationally oriented, the detail suggests that this does violence to their actual motivations which included scientific doubt, personal animosities, electoral politics, anti-environmentalism, as well as—it is true—a good helping of suspicion about the motives of other states. In addition, the picture of the workings of the inner state, and especially the crucial role societal factors play in explaining intrastate outcomes—a highly 'political' process—demands that some theorization of the state is undertaken. It remains *the*, not *a*, central actor, much as many might wish it were not.

CHANGING CONCEPTUAL PARAMETERS

The argument so far has emphasized continuity. The question remains: what, if anything, has changed over the last thirty years? There are at least three, admittedly modest, developments which suggest themselves: that environmental problems are now seen as 'real' issues, that the 'content' of the issue has been permanently redefined away from an initial pollution-based understanding, and that the need for some collective discussion and consideration of environmental issues is now better established.

The cluster of issues subsumed under the heading 'international environment' now holds a permanent place on the foreign-policy agenda. Even sceptics are forced to accept that they can't avoid engaging with the issue in some form (although some tried in 1992). The network of interest groups and international institutions has ensured the survival and prominence of environmental concerns such that a policy is *required*, with all the attendant calculations about costs and benefits, trade-offs, long-term implications, and the impact of formal institutionalization. This does not mean, however, that the environment will achieve the status of a central issue in foreign policy. As Steve Smith argues:

The world of power, social, political, economic, and academic, is far less conducive to environmental concerns than the last decade's experience might suggest. In this sense the environment shares with gender and race the dubious privilege of being *an* issue in political and academic circles, but

I wonder whether that means anything more than that it is impossible not to pay lip-service to it.[9]

Nevertheless, the firm establishment of environmental issues on the foreign-policy agenda attests to the success of NGOs and perhaps even UNEP in propagating a new set of notions about the environment, similar to those described by Paul Wapner as an 'ecological sensibility', a change in 'the governing ideas that animate societies'.[10] Wapner argues that groups like the World Wildlife Fund and Greenpeace can:

... change the way vast numbers of people see the world—by dislodging traditional understandings of environmental degradation and substituting new interpretive frames.[11]

This argument for a conceptual shift echoes my introduction and links nicely to the idea of the 'social construction' of state interests. If ideas matter, if the way state officials perceive a problem or an issue in relation to other states, and to their own publics, shifts, then state behaviour may also change. It matters crucially how these state officials interpret their environment, what they think is going on, if we want to explain foreign policy.

In Martha Finnemore's argument, for example, great weight is placed on the role played by international norms as 'taught' to states by international organizations like UNESCO. These norms are 'shared expectations about appropriate behaviour held by a community of actors'.[12] Her core claim is that:

... states are socialized to accept new norms, values, and perceptions of interest by international organizations.[13]

Although it seems plausible to argue that constant exposure to new sets of ideas about appropriate norms may inculcate a new 'sensibility' in state officials, in the specific cases under examination here, UNEP, for example, only played a co-ordinating role (see below). It can be seen to have had little impact on 'the state' once one differentiates 'the state' internally. The United States may be

---

[9] Steve Smith, 'Environment on the Periphery of International Relations: An Explanation', in Thomas (ed.), *Rio: Unravelling the Consequences*, 30.
[10] Wapner, 'Politics Beyond the State', 322.
[11] Ibid. 321.
[12] Finnemore, *National Interests*, 22.
[13] Ibid. 5.

an exception here, along with some Scandanavian states and perhaps Germany, in pushing the idea of international environmentalism 'upwards' into the UN in the first place.[14]

It makes more sense to see the activists within the United States trying to use the UN (as they did the OECD and NATO) to pursue 'domestic' foreign-policy goals via international institutional arrangements. Although these may then appear as international norms to other states, the institution provides more of a 'transmission mechanism' than an entity with any independent preferences. It serves as a kind of fulcrum, the use of which allows an act of agency to attain increased leverage. Many non-Western states would undoubtedly view the IMF and the World Bank in precisely this way, as the 'hammers' of liberalism. It may even be the case that these norms make their greatest impact on the 'envelope', the range of feasible options for policy choice within a particular social context.

Nevertheless, to the extent that norm-related activity was visible during preparations for Stockholm and Rio, it was used as ammunition by activists who were in 'the state' in the first place precisely because they were receptive to these sorts of ideas. Once one differentiates the state, one can see that just because 'the state' as a whole refuses to endorse or adopt certain international norms, does not mean that inside the state there are not individuals (or even within society 'waiting' for the call) who already believe in those norms and as yet have been unable to turn them into policy.

Change may come, therefore, either through the envelope, or through the enhanced power of sympathetic officials. As even Hedley Bull acknowledged in noting the rise of environmentalism in the 1970s:

... the argument that the states system is dysfunctional overlooks the possibility that through it a greater sense of human solidarity in relation to environmental threats may emerge. In the long run, it is unlikely that action at the purely state level will be sufficient to cope with environmental dangers, and the functionality of the states system, or of any other form of universal political order, will depend on the emergence of a greater sense of human cohesion than now exists.[15]

A second substantive change over the last thirty years is the

---

[14] A role Finnemore does allow for; see for example, *National Interests*, 47.
[15] Hedley Bull, *The Anarchical Society* (London: Macmillan, 1977), 294–5.

acceptance of a clearer link between environment and development which was the key aim for Southern countries during the
Stockholm process. The first prepcom for Rio was also marked by
a determination on the South's part that 'their priority of development should not be lost on the environmental agenda'.[16]
Apart from the gathering's formal title—the UN Conference
on Environment *and Development*—the key concept which
emerged out of Rio (although coined well before) was 'sustainable
development'.[17]

As part of this process, it is clear that states dealing with international environmental politics have initiated and financed remarkable levels of scientific research to determine the exact causes, and
the possible antidotes, for climate change. This has undoubtedly
strengthened both the idea and practice of an international scientific community and has yielded mountains of data although, as we
have seen, claims to consensus may be premature. One ironic result
of this greater awareness is that some states may discover potential
pay-offs from global warming (more rainfall, or the unfreezing of
the permafrost in Siberia). The degree to which there is uncertainty
about the impact of climate change prevents most states from
knowing, however, and as a result most states express concern.[18]

A final change in which environmental groups have been instrumental is in the establishment of the *expectation* of some international co-operation. This is not a strong norm, and the US
government has been firm in stressing the essential primacy of the
domestic sphere, the limited role for institutions, and the 'discrete-
ness' of environmental issues. This has served to protect sovereignty, showing how much it is the state's to yield. Even in this area,

[16] Grubb *et al.*, *The Earth Summit Agreements*, 9.

[17] UNEP was instrumental in advancing this conceptual shift in the 1970s and
1980s and, in 1987, Mostafa Tolba even published a book on the idea, *Sustainable
Development: Constraints and Opportunities* (London: Butterworth). See Peter S.
Thacher, 'The Role of the United Nations', in Hurrell and Kingsbury (eds.), *The
International Politics of the Environment*, 188–90.

[18] It is widely perceived to be good to gather as much information as possible so
that we can assess the likely impact of climate change, and almost all states support
more monitoring and research. If one envisages this uncertainty acting as a Rawlsian
'veil of ignorance', however, one can see that uncertainty provides an incentive to
reach agreements (on an 'insurance' plan) that will maximize the minimum level of
protection any one state will get. It is better overall if states don't know how they
will do, so they choose the kind of world where everyone will fare reasonably well
(see John Rawls, *A Theory of Justice* (Oxford: Oxford University Press, 1972)).

the American state has been careful to preserve its authority to choose the territorial state's 'national interest'.

However, two developments have taken place: the legitimacy of international negotiations on environmental issues is now firmly secured, and the institutional arena includes organizations and procedures which promote continuous dialogue and interaction. On ozone depletion, for example, the important role played by UNEP is well acknowledged. As Edward Parson has argued:

... it seems that the suasive force of even the earliest negotiations was increased by their being formally authorized by UNEP's Governing Council, rather than arranged *ad hoc* by the activist nations. There are two pieces of evidence: first, those nations who opposed a treaty also opposed the original authorization of negotiations, and subsequently tried once in 1984 to have the authorization revoked prematurely; second, even those nations who most strongly opposed a treaty continued to attend the negotiations throughout.[19]

What has not occurred is any acceptance that international co-operation is the only, the best, or even a necessary way to improve the environment. The United States remains unwilling to yield independent power to any extra-state institution.

As for the future, what the foregoing suggests is that it is in the incremental perceptual changes of state elites that a slow shift towards more international co-operation may, *may*, lie. The way these officials understand the world strongly affects the approach they take in intrastate struggles. Thus, the way they believe the world to be changing is a key element in the development of state practice. As John Gerard Ruggie has argued of the change from feudal communities to the state:

... the mental equipment that people drew upon in imagining and symbolizing forms of political community itself underwent fundamental change.[20]

International norms of the sort Finnemore describes may turn these perceptions into more routine state practice as might international law.[21] Although any changes underway in relation to the

---

[19] Parson, 'Protecting the Ozone Layer', 64.

[20] Ruggie, 'Territoriality and Beyond', 157.

[21] As Louis Henkin claimed, 'Almost all nations observe almost all principles of international law and almost all of their obligations almost all of the time' (*How Nations Behave: Law and Foreign Policy*, 2nd edn. (New York: Columbia University Press, 1979), 47).

United States are infinitely less substantial than those Ruggie describes, over time officials may come to perceive the world differently, and, as a result, act differently in it. The state is highly likely to retain its central role in political developments and so it is in the ideas and practices of those who act in its name that the seeds of change need to be sown.

Bibliography

PRIMARY SOURCES

Interviews

Christian A. Herter, Jnr.: 8 Apr. 1993
Dan Abbasi: 9 Apr. 1993
John W. McDonald: 14 Apr. 1993
Russell E. Train: 5 May 1993; 28 Mar. 1994
Claiborne Pell: 6 May 1993
William K. Reilly: 29 Mar. 1994; 14 Apr. 1994
E. U. Curtis Bohlen: 30 Mar. 1994
Peter S. Thacher: 3 Apr. 1994
Gareth Porter: 4 Apr. 1994
Clayton Yeutter: 5 Apr. 1994
Gordon Binder: 5 Apr. 1994
C. Boyden Gray: 7 Apr. 1994
Michael McCloskey: 7 Apr. 1994
Larry Williams: 7 Apr. 1994
Brock Evans: 8 Apr. 1994
Robert Grady: 8 Apr. 1994
Robert Zoellick: 13 Apr. 1994
Fran Spivy-Weber: 13 Apr. 1994
Lee Talbot: 14 Apr. 1994
Lynn Greenwalt: 15 Apr. 1994
Michael Deland: 21 Apr. 1994

Official Papers and Publications

Nixon Presidential Materials Staff
White House Central Files:
  Federal Government (Organizations)
  Welfare
  President's Office Files
  White House: Environment
  International Organizations
White House Special Files:
  Haldeman Papers
  Ehrlichman

Department of State

Bulletins from 1969 to 1973.
Safeguarding Our World Environment, pub. no. 8630 (1972).
Stockholm and Beyond, pub. no. 8657 (1972).
Other documents and press releases referenced in detail in text.

Congress

'U.S. participation in 1972 United Nations Conference on Human Environment', Subcommittee on International Organizations and Movements, Committee on Foreign Affairs, House of Representatives, 13 Nov. 1969; CIS NO: 70-H381-5.

'International cooperation in the human environment through the United Nations', House Subcommittee on International Organizations and Movements of the Committee on Foreign Affairs, 15, 16 Mar. 1972, CIS NO: 72-H381-30.

'U.N. Conference on Human Environment: Preparations and prospects', Subcommittee on Oceans and International Environment of the Committee on Foreign Relations, the Senate of the United States Congress, 3, 4, 5 May 1972, CIS NO: 72-S381-22.

'Participation by the United States in the United Nations Environment Program', House Subcommittee on International Organizations and Movements, 5, 10 Apr. 1973, CIS NO: 73-H381-13.

'Report on the United Nations Conference on the Human Environment', House of Representatives Committee on Public Works, Sept. 1972, CIS-NO: 72-H642-10.

'United Nations Conference on the Human Environment', report to the Senate by Senator Claiborne Pell and Senator Clifford Case, Oct. 1972, CIS NO: 72-S382-22.

House Subcommittee on International Organizations and Movements, 'Participation by the United States in the United Nations Environment Program', 5, 10 Apr. 1973, CIS-NO: 73-H381-13.

'Review of the global environment 10 years after Stockholm', House Committee on Foreign Affairs, 30 Mar. 1, 20 Apr. 1982, CIS NO: 82-H381-61.

Hearing before the Senate Committee on Foreign Relations, 18 Sept. 1992, Y4 F 76/2, hearing 102-970.

'United Nations Conference on Environment and Development', hearings before the Subcommittee on Environment of the House Committee on Science, Space and Technology, 7 May 1991, Y4.Sci 2 102-43.

Hearing of the Subcommittee on Human Rights and International Organizations of the House Committee on Foreign Affairs, 17 April, 24 July, 3 Oct. 1991, Y4 f76/1 En 8/6.

Joint hearings before the House Committee on Foreign Affairs and the House Committee on Merchant Marines and Fisheries, 26/27 February and 21 July and 28 1992, Y4 F76/1.

'Administration views on global climate change', hearing before Subcommittee on Economic Policy, Trade and Environment, House Committee on Foreign Affairs, 18 May 1993, Y4. F 76/1 G 51/7.

'Global climate change and air pollutants', hearings before Subcommittee on Health and the Environment of House Committee on Energy and Commerce, 4 Aug./26 Oct. 1993, Y4 En2/3 103-71.

'Energy Policy Act 1992 and the President's climate change action plan', hearing before the Senate Committee on Energy and Natural Resources, 10 May 1994, Y4. En2: 103-794.

'International global climate change negotiations', hearing before Subcommittee on Energy and Power of House Committee on Commerce, 21 March/19 May 1995, Y4 C73/8, 104-13.

United Nations

Report of the United Nations Conference on the Human Environment: Stockholm, 5–16 June, 1972, A/conf.48/14/Rev.1 (New York: United Nations, 1973).

Minutes of meetings held by the United Nations General Assembly, ECOSOC, and various preparatory meetings between 1967 and 1973, as well as miscellaneous UN publications, (all referenced in text).

Newspapers and Periodicals

United States

The *New York Times*
The *Earth Summit Times*
The *Washington Post*
The *Boston Globe*
The *Los Angeles Times*
The *International Herald Tribune*
Wall Street Journal

Business Week
Science
Scientific American
Bulletin of the Atomic Scientists
Time
Newsweek
US News and Current Affairs

United Kingdom

The Times

The *Financial Times*

The *Guardian*

The *Independent*

The Economist

Nature

New Scientist

SECONDARY SOURCES

Adler, E. and Haas, P. M., 'Conclusion: Epistemic Communities, World Order, and the Creation of a Reflective Research Program', *International Organization*, 46/1 (1992), 367–90.

Adler, T., 'Clinton Emissions Plan Under Fire', *Science* (Apr. 1994).

Allison, G. T., *Essence of Decision: Explaining the Cuban Missile Crisis* (Boston: Little, Brown, 1971).

——and Halperin, M. H., 'Bureaucratic Politics: A Paradigm and Some Policy Implications', Tanter and Ullman (eds.), *Theory and Policy in International Relations*.

Anderson, B. O'G., *Imagined Communities*, rev. edn. (London: Verso, 1991).

Anderson, J. and Binstein, M., 'Biodiversity Breakfasts', *Washington Post* (6 June 1993), p. C7.

Archer, C., *International Organizations*, 2nd edn. (London: Routledge, 1992).

Ashley, R. K., 'The Poverty of Neorealism', in Keohane (ed.), *Neorealism and its Critics*.

Baldwin, D. A. (ed.), *Neorealism and Neoliberalism: The Contemporary Debate* (New York: Columbia University Press, 1993).

Ball, T., Farr, J., and Hanson, R. L. (eds.), *Political Innovation and Conceptual Change* (Cambridge: Cambridge University Press, 1989).

Barkin, J. S. and Cronin, B., 'The State and the Nation: Changing Norms and Rules of Sovereignty in International Relations', *International Organization*, 48/1 (1994) 107–30.

Beardsley, T., 'Ecolocation', *Scientific American* (June 1993).

Beitz, C. R., 'Sovereignty and Morality', in Held (ed.), *Political Theory Today*.

Benedick, R. E., *Ozone Diplomacy: New Directions in Safeguarding the Planet* (Camb, Mass.: Harvard University Press, 1991).

Bodansky, D., 'Prologue to the Climate Change Convention', in Mintzer and Leonard (eds.), *Negotiating Climate Change*.

Booth, K. and Smith, S. (eds.), *International Relations Theory Today* (Cambridge: Polity Press, 1995).

Borione, D. and Ripert, J., 'Exercising Common but Differentiated Responsibility', in Mintzer and Leonard (eds.), *Negotiating Climate Change*.

Bramble, B. J. and Porter, G., 'Non-Governmental Organizations and the Making of US International Environmental Policy', in Hurrell and Kingsbury (eds.), *The International Politics of the Environment*.

Brenton, T., *The Greening of Machiavelli: The Evolution of International Environmental Politics* (London: RIIA, 1994).

Brown, N., 'Planetary Geopolitics', *Millenium: Journal of International Studies*, 19 (1990), 447–60.

Bull, H., *The Anarchical Society* (London: Macmillan, 1977).

Burtraw, D. and Portney, P. R., 'Environmental Policy in the United States', in Helm (ed.), *Economic Policy Toward the Environment*.

Caldwell, L. K., 'The World Environment: Reversing US Policy Commitments', in Vig and Kraft (eds.), *Environmental Policy in the 1980s*.

—— *International Environmental Policy: Emergence and Dimensions*, 2nd edn. (Durham, NC: Duke University Press, 1990).

Camilleri, J. A. and Falk, J., *The End of Sovereignty: The Politics of a Shrinking and Fragmenting World* (Aldershot: Edward Elgar, 1992).

Cammack, P., 'Review Article: Bringing the State Back In?', *British Journal of Political Science*, 19 (1989), 261–90.

Carson, R., *Silent Spring* (London: Hamish Hamilton, 1962).

Caulfield, H. P., 'The Conservation and Environmental Movements: An Historical Analysis', in Lester (ed.), *Environmental Politics and Policy*.

Clarke, R. and Timberlake, L., *Stockholm Plus Ten: Promises, Promises?* (Earthscan/IIED: London, 1982).

Clifford, J. G., 'Bureaucratic Politics', in Hogan and Paterson (eds.), *Explaining the History of American Foreign Relations*.

Cockburn, A., ''Win-win'' with Bruce Babbitt: The Clinton Administration Meets the Environment', *New Left Review*, 201 (1993), 46–59.

Conaway, J., 'Babbitt in the Woods', *Harper's Magazine* (Dec. 1993).

Conca, K., 'Rethinking the Ecology–Sovereignty Debate', *Millenium: Journal of International Studies*, 23/3 (1994), 701–11.

Dahl, R., *Who Governs?* (New Haven: Yale University Press, 1961).

Dasgupta, C., 'The Climate Change Negotiations', in Mintzer and Leonard (eds.), *Negotiating Climate Change*.

Deudney, D., 'Global Environmental Rescue and the Emergence of World Domestic Politics', in Lipschutz and Conca (eds.), *The State and Social Power in Global Environmental Politics*.

Djoghlaf, A., 'The Beginnings of an International Climate Law', in Mintzer and Leonard (eds.), *Negotiating Climate Change*.

Dowie, M., 'American Environmentalism: A Movement Courting Irrelevance', *World Policy Journal* (Winter 1991–2), 67–92.

—— 'The Selling (Out) of the Greens', *The Nation* (Apr. 1994).

—— *Losing Ground: American Environmentalism at the Close of the Twentieth Century* (Cambridge, Mass.: MIT Press, 1995).

Downs, A., 'Up and Down with Ecology: The Issue-Attention Cycle', *The Public Interest*, 26–9/28 (1972), 38–50.

Doyle, M., 'Thucydidean Realism', *Review of International Studies*, 16 (1990), 223–37.

Dunlap, R. E., 'Public Opinion and Environmental Policy', in Lester (ed.), *Environmental Politics and Policy*.

—— 'Trends in Public Opinion Toward Environmental Issues: 1965–1990', in Dunlap and Mertig (eds.), *American Environmentalism*.

—— and Mertig, A. G. (eds.), *American Environmentalism: The U.S. Environmental Movement, 1970–1990* (Philadelphia: Taylor and Francis, 1992).

Dunleavy, P. and O'Leary, B., *Theories of the State: The Politics of Liberal Democracy* (London: Macmillan, 1987).

Evans, P. B., 'Building an Integrative Approach to International and Domestic Politics', in Evans, Jacobson, and Putnam (eds.), *Double-Edged Diplomacy*.

—— Jacobson, H. K, and Putnam, R. D. (eds.), *Double-Edged Diplomacy: International Bargaining and Domestic Politics* (Berkeley: University of California Press, 1993).

—— Rueschemeyer, D., and Skocpol, T. (eds.), *Bringing the State Back In* (New York: Cambridge University Press, 1985).

Faulkner, H., 'Some Comments on the INC Process', in Mintzer and Leonard (eds.), *Negotiating Climate Change*.

Featherstone, M. and Lash, S., 'Globalization, Modernity and the Spatialization of Social Theory: An Introduction', in Featherstone, Lash, and Robertson (eds.), *Global Modernities*.

—— —— and Robertson, R. (eds.), *Global Modernities* (London: Sage, 1995).

Feraru, A. T., 'Transnational Political Interests and the Global Environment', *International Organization*, 28/1 (1974), 31–60.

Ferguson, Y. H. and Mansbach, R. W., *The Elusive Quest: Theory and International Politics* (Columbia, SC: University of South Carolina Press, 1988).

Finger, M., 'Environmental NGOs in the UNCED Process', in Princen and Finger (eds.), *Environmental NGOs in World Politics*.

Finnemore, M., *National Interests in International Society* (Ithaca, NY: Cornell University Press, 1996).

Freedman, L., 'Logic, Politics, and Foreign Policy Processes: A Critique of the Bureaucratic Politics Model', *International Affairs*, 52 (1976), 434–49.

Gardner, R. N. (ed.), *Blueprint for Peace (Being the Proposals of Prominent Americans to the White House Conference on International Co-operation)* (New York: McGraw-Hill, 1966).

——*Negotiating Survival: Four Priorities after Rio* (New York: Council on Foreign Relations Press, 1992).

Gendlin, F., 'Voices from the Gallery', *Bulletin of Atomic Scientists* (Sept. 1972).

Gillroy, J. M. and Shapiro, R. Y., 'The Polls: Environmental Protection', *Public Opinion Quarterly*, 50 (1986), 270–9.

Gilpin, R., *War and Change in World Politics* (Cambridge: Cambridge University Press, 1981).

Glick, D., 'Barbarians Inside the Gate', *Newsweek* (Nov. 1993).

Goldstein, J. and Keohane, R. O. (eds.), *Ideas and Foreign Policy: Beliefs, Institutions, and Political Change* (Ithaca, NY: Cornell University Press, 1993).

—— ——'Ideas and Foreign Policy: An Analytical Framework', in Goldstein and Keohane (eds.), *Ideas and Foreign Policy*.

Gore, A., Jnr., *Earth in the Balance: Forging a New Common Purpose* (London: Earthscan, 1992).

Gottlieb, R., *Forcing the Spring: The Transformation of the American Environmental Movement* (Washington, DC: Island Press, 1993).

Gray, C. B. and Rivkin, D. B., 'A "No-Regrets" Environmental Policy', *Foreign Policy*, 83 (Summer 1991), 47–65.

Greve, M. S. and Smith, F. L. (eds.), *Environmental Politics: Public Costs, Private Rewards* (New York: Praeger, 1992).

Grieco, J. M., 'Anarchy and the Limits of Cooperation: A Realist Critique of the Newest Liberal Institutionalism', *International Organization*, 42 (1988), 485–507.

——*Cooperation Among Nations: Europe, America, and Non-Tariff Barriers to Trade* (Ithaca, NY: Cornell University Press).

Grubb, M., Koch, M., Munson, A., Sullivan, F., and Thompson, K., *The Earth Summit Agreements* (London: Earthscan/RIIA, 1993).

Haas, P. M., 'Introduction: Epistemic Communities and International Policy Coordination', *International Organization*, 46/1 (1992), 1–35.

——Keohane, R. O., and Levy, M. A. (eds.), *Institutions for the Earth: Sources of Effective International Environmental Protection* (Cambridge, Mass.: MIT Press, 1993).

——Levy, M. A., and Parson, E. A., 'Appraising the Earth Summit: How Should We Judge UNCED's Success?', *Environment*, 34/8 (1992), 7–14, 26–36.

Haggard, S. and Simmons, B. A., 'Theories of International Regimes', *International Organization*, 41 (1987), 491–517.

Hall, J. A. and Ikenberry, G. J., *The State* (Milton Keynes: Open University Press, 1989).

Hall, P. A., *Governing the Economy: The Politics of State Intervention in Britain and France* (Cambridge: Polity Press, 1986).

Halliday, F., *Rethinking International Relations* (London: Macmillan, 1994).

Halperin, M. H. with Clapp, P. and Kanter, A., *Bureaucratic Politics and Foreign Policy* (Washington, DC: The Brookings Institution, 1974).

Hamilton, J., 'Babbitt's Retreat', *Sierra* (July/Aug. 1994).

Hays, S. P., *Beauty, Health and Permanence: Environmental Politics in the United States, 1955–1985* (New York: Cambridge University Press, 1987).

——'Three Decades of Environmental Politics: The Historical Context', in Lacey (ed.), *Government and Environmental Politics*.

Heclo, H., 'Issue Networks and the Executive Establishment', in King (ed.), *The New American Political System*.

Held, D. (ed.), *Political Theory Today* (Cambridge: Polity Press, 1991).

——and McGrew, A., 'Globalization and the Liberal Democratic State', *Government and Opposition*, 23/2 (1993), 261–85.

Helm, D. (ed.), *Economic Policy Toward the Environment* (Oxford: Blackwell, 1991).

Henkin, L., *How Nations Behave: Law and Foreign Policy*, 2nd edn. (New York: Columbia University Press, 1979).

Hermann, C. F., Kegley, C. W., and Rosenau, J. N. (eds.), *New Directions in the Study of Foreign Policy* (New York: Harper-Collins, 1987).

Herter, C. A. and Binder, J. E., *The Role of the Secretariat in Multilateral Negotiation: The Case of Maurice Strong and the 1972 UN Conference on the Human Environment* (Washington, DC: Johns Hopkins Foreign Policy Institute, 1993).

Hogan, M. J. and Paterson, T. G. (eds.), *Explaining the History of American Foreign Relations* (Cambridge: Cambridge University Press, 1991).

Hollis, M. and Smith, S., 'Beware of Gurus: Structure and Action in International Relations', *Review of International Studies*, 17 (1991), 393–410.

Hollis, M. and Smith S., *Explaining and Understanding International Relations* (Oxford: Clarendon Press, 1991).

—— ——'Structure and Action: Further Comment', *Review of International Studies*, 18 (1992), 187–8

Holsti, K. J., *The Dividing Discipline: Hegemony and Diversity in International Relations* (Boston: Allen and Unwin, 1987).

Holsti, O. R., 'International Relations Models', in Hogan and Paterson (eds.), *Explaining the History of American Foreign Relations*.

Holzgrefe, J. L., 'The Origins of Modern International Relations Theory', *Review of International Studies*, 15 (1989), 11–26.

Hrebenar, R. J. and Scott, R. K., *Interest Group Politics in America* (New Jersey: Prentice-Hall, 1982).

Hunt, M. H., *Ideology and U.S. Foreign Policy* (New Haven: Yale University Press, 1987).

Hurrell, A., 'International Political Theory and the Global Environment', in Booth and Smith (eds.), *International Relations Theory Today*.

——and Kingsbury, B. (eds.), *The International Politics of the Environment* (Oxford: Clarendon Press, 1992).

—— ——'The International Politics of the Environment: An Introduction', in Hurrell and Kingsbury (eds.), *The International Politics of the Environment*.

Ikenberry, G. J., 'Conclusion: An Institutional Approach to American Foreign Economic Policy', in Ikenberry, Lake, and Mastanduno (eds.), *The State and American Foreign Economic Policy*.

—— ——Lake, D. A., and Mastanduno, M. (eds.), *The State and American Foreign Economic Policy* (Ithaca, NY: Cornell University Press, 1988).

—— —— ——'Introduction: Approaches to Explaining American Foreign Economic Policy', in Ikenberry, Lake, and Mastanduno (eds.), *The State and American Foreign Economic Policy*.

Imber, M., 'Too Many Cooks? The Post-Rio Reform of the United Nations', *International Affairs*, 69/1 (1993), 55–70.

Inayatullah, N. and Blaney, D. L., 'Realizing Sovereignty', *Review of International Studies*, 21 (1995), 3–20.

Ingram, H. M. and Mann, D. E., 'Interest Groups and Environmental Policy', in Lester (ed.), *Environmental Politics and Policy*.

Jackson, R. H., *Quasi-States: Sovereignty, International Relations and the Third World* (Cambridge: Cambridge University Press, 1990).

Jarvis, A. P., 'Societies, States and Geopolitics: Challenges from Historical Sociology', *Review of International Studies*, 15 (1989), 281–93.

Johnson, B., 'The United Nations' Institutional Response to Stockholm: A Case-Study in the International Politics of Institutional Change', *International Organization*, 26/2 (1972), 255–301.

Johnson, S. P., *The Earth Summit: The United Nations Conference on Environment and Development* (London: Graham and Trotman/ Matinius Nijhoff, 1993).

Jones, C. O., *Clean Air: The Policies and Politics of Pollution Control* (Pittsburgh: University of Pittsburgh Press, 1975).

Jones, R. J. B., *Globalization and Interdependence in the International Political Economy: Rhetoric and Reality* (London: Pinter, 1995).

Juma, C., *The Gene Hunters: Biotechnology and the Scramble for Seeds* (London: Zed Books, 1989).

Katzenstein, P. J. (ed.), *Between Power and Plenty: Foreign Economic Policies of Advanced Industrial States* (Madison, Wis.: University of Wisconsin Press, 1978).

——'Introduction: Domestic and International Forces and Strategies of Foreign Economic Policy', in Katzenstein (ed.), *Between Power and Plenty*.

——(ed.), *The Culture of National Security: Norms and Identity in World Politics* (New York: Columbia University Press, 1996).

Kegley, C. W. and Wittkopf, E. R., *American Foreign Policy: Pattern and Process*, 4th edn. (New York: St Martin's Press, 1991).

Kennan, G., 'To Prevent a World Wasteland: A Proposal', *Foreign Affairs*, 48/3 (1970), 401–13.

Kennet, W., 'The Stockholm Conference on the Human Environment', *International Affairs*, 48/1 (1972), 33–45.

Keohane, R. O. (ed.), *NeoRealism and Its Critics* (New York: Columbia University Press, 1986).

——'Theory of World Politics: Structural Realism and Beyond', in Keohane (ed.), *NeoRealism and Its Critics*.

——and Nye, J. S., Jnr., *Power and Interdependence: World Politics in Transition* (Boston: Little, Brown, 1977).

Khong, Y. F., *Analogies at War: Korea, Munich, Dien Bien Phu, and the Vietnam Decisions of 1965* (Princeton: Princeton University Press, 1992).

King, A. (ed.), *The New American Political System* (Washington, DC: American Enterprise Institute, 1978).

Knorr, K. and Verba, S. (eds.), *The International System: Theoretical Essays* (Princeton: Princeton University Press, 1961).

Kraft, M. E., 'Environmental Gridlock: Searching for Consensus in Congress', in Vig and Kraft (eds.), *Environmental Policy in the 1990s*.

——and Vig, N. J., 'Environmental Policy from the Seventies to the Nineties: Continuity and Change', in Vig and Kraft (eds.), *Environmental Policy in the 1990s*.

Krasner, S. D., *Defending the National Interest: Raw Materials Investments and American Foreign Policy* (Princeton: Princeton University Press, 1978).

—— 'Review Article: Approaches to the State, Alternative Conceptions and Historical Dynamics', *Comparative Politics*, 16 (1984), 223–46.

—— *Structural Conflict: The Third World Against Global Liberalism* (Berkeley: University of California, 1985).

Lacey, M. J. (ed.), *Government and Environmental Politics* (Washington, DC: Woodrow Wilson Center Press, and Baltimore: The Johns Hopkins University Press, 1991).

Landy, M. K, Roberts, M. J., and Thomas, S. R., *The Environmental Protection Agency: Asking the Wrong Questions* (New York: Oxford University Press, 1990).

Lerner, S., *Beyond the Earth Summit: Conversations with Advocates of Sustainable Development* (Bolinas, Calif.: Commonweal, 1992).

Lester, J. P. (ed.), *Environmental Politics and Policy: Theories and Evidence* (Durham, NC: Duke University Press, 1989).

Linklater, A., 'Neo-Realism in Theory and Practice', in Booth and Smith (eds.), *International Relations Theory Today*.

Lipschutz, R. D. and Conca, K. (eds.), *The State and Social Power in Global Environmental Politics* (New York: Columbia University Press, 1993).

Lipset, S. M., 'American Exceptionalism Reaffirmed', in Shafer (ed.), *Is American Different?*.

Little, R. and Smith, M. (eds.), *Perspectives on World Politics*, 2nd edn. (London: Routledge, 1991).

Luchins, D. E., 'The United Nations Conference on the Human Environment: A Case-Study of Emerging Political Alignments, 1968–1972', unpub. Ph.D. thesis, City University of New York.

Lundqvist, L. J., *The Hare and the Tortoise: Clean Air Policies in the United States and Sweden* (Ann Arbor, Mich.: University of Michigan Press, 1980).

McCloskey, M., 'Twenty Years of Change in the Environmental Movement: An Insider's View', in Dunlap and Mertig (eds.), *American Environmentalism*.

McCormick, J., *The Global Environmental Movement: Reclaiming Paradise* (London: Belhaven Press, 1989).

MacDonald, G. J., 'International Institutions for Environmental Management', *International Organization*, 26/2 (1972), 372–400.

McDonald, J. W., 'Global Environmental Negotiations: The 1972 Stockholm Conference and Lessons for the Future', working paper WP-2, American Academy of Diplomacy/Paul H. Nitze School of Advanced International Studies, Johns Hopkins University (Jan. 1990).

McFarland, A., 'Interest Groups and Theories of Power in America', *British Journal of Political Science*, 17 (1987), 129–47.

McInnis, D. F., 'Ozone Layers and Oligopoly Profits', in Greve and Smith (eds.), *Environmental Politics: Public Costs, Private Rewards*.

Mann, M., *States, War and Capitalism: Studies in Political Sociology* (Oxford: Blackwell, 1988).

—— 'The Autonomous Power of the State: Its Origins, Mechanisms and Results', in Mann (ed.), *States, War and Capitalism*.

Marsh, D. and Rhodes, R. A. W., *Policy Networks in British Government* (Oxford: Clarendon Press, 1992).

—— —— 'Policy Networks in British Politics: A Critique of Existing Approaches', in Marsh and Rhodes (eds.), *Policy Networks in British Government*.

Mintzer, I. M. and Leonard, J. A. (eds.), *Negotiating Climate Change: The Inside Story of the Rio Convention* (Cambridge: Cambridge University Press, 1994).

Mitchell, R. C., 'Public Opinion and Environmental Politics in the 1970s and 1980s', in Vig and Kraft (eds.), *Environmental Policy in the 1980s*.

—— 'From Conservation to Environmental Movement: The Development of Modern Environmental Lobbies', in Lacey (ed.), *Government and Environmental Politics*.

—— Mertig, A. G., and Dunlap, R. E., 'Twenty Years of Environmental Mobilization: Trends Among National Environmental Groups', in Dunlap and Mertig (eds.), *American Environmentalism*.

Mitchell, T., 'The Limits of the State: Beyond Statist Approaches and Their Critics', *American Political Science Review*, 85/1 (1991), 77–96.

Monastersky, R., 'Climate Summit: Slippery Slopes Ahead', *Science News*, 147/12 (1995), 183.

Moon, B. E., 'Political Economy Approaches to the Comparative Study of Foreign Policy', in Hermann, Kegley, and Rosenau (eds.), *New Directions in the Study of Foreign Policy*.

Moravcsik, A., 'Introduction: Integrating International and Domestic Theories of International Bargaining', in Evans, Jacobson, and Putnam (eds.), *Double-Edged Diplomacy*.

Morgan, E. P., 'Stockholm: The Clean (But Impossible) Dream', *Foreign Policy*, 8 (1973), 149–55.

Morgenthau, H. J., *Politics Among Nations* (New York: Knopf, 1948).

Morse, E. L., 'The Transformation of Foreign Policies: Modernization, Interdependence, and Externalization', *World Politics*, 22/3 (1970), 371–92.

—— *Modernization and the Transformation of International Relations* (New York: Macmillan, 1976).

Munson, A., 'Genetically Manipulated Organisms: International Policy-Making and Implications', *International Affairs*, 69/3 (1993), 497–517.

—— 'The United Nations Convention on Biological Diversity', in Grubb *et al.*, *The Earth Summit Agreements*.

Nettl, J. P., 'The State as a Conceptual Variable', *World Politics*, 20/4 (1968), 559–92.

Nichols, M., 'Progress in Rio', *Maclean's*, 22 June 1992.

Nitze, W. A., 'A Failure of Presidential Leadership', in Mintzer and Leonard (eds.), *Negotiating Climate Change*.

Nixon, W., 'Bill and Al's Green Adventure', *E Magazine* (May/June 1993).

Nordlinger, E. A., *On the Autonomy of the Democratic State* (Cambridge, Mass.: Harvard University Press, 1981).

Nys, J. *et al.*, 'The Stockholm Conference: A Synopsis and Analysis', *Stanford Journal of International Studies* (1972), 31–152.

Odell, J. S., *U.S. International Monetary Policy: Markets, Power and Ideas as Sources of Change* (Princeton: Princeton University Press, 1982).

—— 'Understanding International Trade Policies: An Emerging Synthesis', *World Politics*, 43 (1990), 139–67.

Parson, E. A., 'Protecting the Ozone Layer', in Haas, Keohane, and Levy (eds.), *Institutions for the Earth*.

Paterson, M., 'The Politics of Climate Change after UNCED', in Thomas (ed.), *Rio: Unravelling the Consequences*.

—— *Global Warming and Global Politics* (London: Routledge, 1996).

Pepper, D., *The Roots of Modern Environmentalism* (London: Croom Helm, 1986).

Piper, D. C. and Terchek R. J. (eds.), *Interaction: Foreign Policy and Public Policy* (Washington, DC: American Enterprise Institute, 1983).

—— —— 'Introduction: Foreign Policy as Public Policy', in Piper and Terchek (eds.), *Interaction: Foreign Policy and Public Policy*.

Pogge, G., *The State: Its Nature, Development and Prospects* (Cambridge: Polity Press, 1990).

Polsby, N. W., *Political Innovation in America: The Politics of Policy Initiation* (New Haven: Yale University Press, 1984).

Porter, G., *The United States and the Biodiversity Convention* (Washington, DC: EESI, 1992).

—— and Brown, J. W., *Global Environmental Politics* (Boulder, Colo.: Westview Press, 1991).

Princen, T. and Finger, M. (eds.), *Environmental NGOs in World Politics* (London: Routledge, 1994).

Putnam, R. D., 'Diplomacy and Domestic Politics: The Logic of Two-Level Games', *International Organization*, 42/3 (1988), 427–60.

Quarles, J., *Cleaning Up America: An Insider's View of the Environmental Protection Agency* (Boston: Houghton Mifflin, 1976).

Rahman, A. and Roncerel, A., 'A View From the Ground Up', in Mintzer and Leonard (eds.), *Negotiating Climate Change*.

Rajan, M. G., 'India and the North–South Politics of Global Environmental Issues: The Cases of Ozone Depletion, Climate Change and Loss of Biodiversity', D.Phil. thesis, University of Oxford (1994).

Raloff, J., 'Clinton Unveils New Greenhouse Policy', *Science News*, 144/17 (1993).

Rawls, J., *A Theory of Justice* (Oxford: Oxford University Press, 1972).

Reilly, W. K., 'I'm Gonna Make You a Star: A New Approach to Protecting the Environment in America and Around the World', prepared text of lecture at Stanford University (1994).

Richardson, J. J. and Jordan, A. G., *Governing Under Pressure: The Policy Process in a Post-Parliamentary Democracy* (Oxford: Blackwell, 1985).

Risse-Kappen, T. (ed.), *Bringing Transnational Relations Back In* (Cambridge: Cambridge University Press, 1995).

Roan, S. L., *Ozone Crisis: The 15-Year Evolution of a Sudden Global Emergency* (New York: John Wiley and Sons, 1989).

Rogers, A., *The Earth Summit: A Planetary Reckoning* (Los Angeles: Global View Press, 1993).

Rosenau, J. N., *The Scientific Study of Foreign Policy* (New York: The Free Press, 1971).

—— 'Pre-theories and Theories of Foreign Policy', in Rosenau, *The Scientific Study of Foreign Policy*.

—— 'Comparative Foreign Policy: Fad, Fantasy or Field?', in Rosenau, *The Scientific Study of Foreign Policy*.

—— 'Introduction: New Directions and Recurrent Questions in the Comparative Study of Foreign Policy', in Hermann, Kegley, and Rosenau (eds.), *New Directions in the Study of Foreign Policy*.

—— *Turbulence in World Politics: A Theory of Change and Continuity* (New York: Harvester-Wheatsheaf, 1990).

—— and Czempiel, E.-O. (eds.), *Governance without Government: Order and Change in World Politics* (Cambridge: Cambridge University Press, 1992).

Rowland, W., *The Plot to Save the World* (Toronto: Clarke, Irwin & Company, 1973).

Rowlands, I. H., *The Politics of Global Atmospheric Change* (Manchester: Manchester University Press, 1995).

Ruben, B., 'A Long Way from Earth Day', *Environmental Action* (Winter 1994).

Ruggie, J. G., 'Review of *The National Interest* by S. D. Krasner', *American Political Science Review*, 74 (1980), 296–9.

—— 'Continuity and Transformation in the World Polity: Toward a Neorealist Synthesis', in Keohane (ed.), *Neorealism and Its Critics*.

Ruggie, J. G. 'Territoriality and Beyond: Problematizing Modernity in International Relations', *International Organization*, 47/1 (1993), 139–74.

Samuel, P., 'Fog from Foggy Bottom', *National Review* (25 May 1992).

Schrader, R., 'The Fiasco at Rio', *Dissent* (Fall 1992).

Segerson, K. and Tietenberg, T., 'Defining Efficient Solutions', in Tietenberg (ed.), *Innovation in Environmental Policy*.

Shabecoff, P., *A Fierce Green Fire* (New York: Hill and Wang, 1993).

Shafer, B. E. (ed.), *Is American Different? A New Look at American Exceptionalism* (Oxford: Clarendon Press, 1991).

Shaw, M., *Global Society and International Relations* (Cambridge: Polity Press, 1994).

Sherman, H. R., 'The Role of the United States Congress in International Environmental Conservation', *Environmental Policy and Law*, 2 (1976).

Skinner, Q., 'The State', in Ball, Farr, and Hanson (eds.), *Political Innovation and Conceptual Change*.

Skocpol, T., *States and Social Revolutions* (Cambridge: Cambridge University Press, 1979).

——'Bringing the State Back In: Strategies of Analysis in Current Research', in Evans, Rueschemeyer, and Skocpol (eds.), *Bringing the State Back In*.

Skolnikoff, E. B., 'The Policy Gridlock on Global Warming', *Foreign Policy*, 79 (Summer 1990), 77–93.

Smillie, I. and Helmich, H. (eds.), *Non-Governmental Organisations and Governments: Stakeholders for Development* (Paris: OECD, 1993).

Smith, F. L., Jnr., 'Carnival of Dunces', *National Review* (July 1992).

Smith, M. J., *Pressure, Power and Policy: State Autonomy and Policy Networks in Britain and the United States* (London: Harvester-Wheatsheaf, 1993).

Smith, S., 'Environment on the Periphery of International Relations: An Explanation', in Thomas (ed.), *Rio: Unravelling the Consequences*.

Sohn, L. B., 'The Stockholm Declaration of the Human Environment', *Harvard International Law Review*, 14 (1973), 423–515.

Soroos, M. S., *Beyond Sovereignty: The Challenge of Global Policy* (Columbia, SC: University of South Carolina Press, 1986).

Speth, J. G., 'A Post-Rio Compact', *Foreign Policy*, 88 (1992), 145–61.

Stein, J. G., 'International Co-operation and Loss Avoidance: Framing the Problem', in Stein and Pauly (eds.), *Choosing to Co-operate*.

——and Pauly, L. W. (eds.), *Choosing to Co-operate: How States Avoid Loss* (Baltimore: Johns Hopkins University Press, 1993).

Stone, P. B., *Did We Save the Earth at Stockholm?* (London: Earth Island, 1973).

Sullivan, F., 'Forest Principles', in Grubb *et al.*, *The Earth Summit Agreements*.

Sununu, J., 'The Political Pleasures of Engineering: An Interview with John Sununu', *Technology Review* (Aug./Sept. 1992), 22–8.

Tanter, R. and Ullman, R. H. (eds.), *Theory and Policy in International Relations* (Princeton: Princeton University Press, 1972).

Thacher, P. S., 'The Role of the United Nations', in Hurrell and Kingsbury (eds.), *The International Politics of the Environment*.

Thomas, C., *The Environment in International Relations* (London: RIIA, 1992).

—— (ed.), *Rio: Unravelling the Consequences* (London: Frank Cass, 1994).

Thompson, K., 'The Rio Declaration on Environment and Development', in Grubb *et al.*, *The Earth Summit Agreements*.

Thomson, J. E., 'State Sovereignty in International Relations: Bridging the Gap Between Theory and Empirical Research', *International Studies Quarterly*, 39 (1995), 213–33.

Thorp, W. L., *The Reality of Foreign Aid* (New York: Council on Foreign Relations/Praeger Publishers, 1971).

Tietenberg, T. (ed.), *Innovation in Environmental Policy* (Brookfield, Vt.: Edward Elgar, 1992).

Tilly C., *Coercion, Capital, and European States, AD 990–1992* (Cambridge, Mass.: Blackwell, 1992).

Tolba, M. K., *Sustainable Development: Constraints and Opportunities* (London: Butterworth, 1987).

—— *Saving Our Planet: Challenges and Hopes* (London: Chapman & Hall, 1992).

Tunstall, M. D., 'The Influence of International Politics on the Procedures of Multilateral Conferences: The Examples of Conferences on Human Environment and the Law of the Sea', unpubl. Ph.D. diss., University of Virginia (May 1979).

Udall, S., *The Quiet Crisis* (New York: Holt, Rinehart and Winston, 1963).

Van Rooy, A., 'The Altrusitic Lobbyists: The Influence of Non-governmental Organizations on Development Policy in Canada and Britain', D.Phil. thesis, University of Oxford (Apr. 1994).

Vasquez, J. A., 'Foreign Policy, Learning and War', in Hermann, Kegley, and Rosenau (eds.), *New Directions in the Study of Foreign Policy*.

Vig, N. J., 'Presidential Leadership and the Environment: From Reagan and Bush to Clinton', in Vig and Kraft (eds.), *Environmental Policy in the 1990s* (2nd edn).

—— and Kraft, M. E. (eds.), *Environmental Policy in the 1980s: Reagan's New Agenda* (Washington, DC: Congressional Quarterly Press, 1984).

————(eds.), *Environmental Policy in the 1990s* (Washington, DC: Congressional Quarterly Press, 1990).

————(eds.), *Environmental Policy in the 1990s*, 2nd edn. (Washington, DC: Congressional Quarterly Press, 1994).

Vincent, R. J., *Human Rights and International Relations* (Cambridge: Cambridge University Press/RIIA, 1986).

Vogel, D., 'The Power of Business in America: A Reappraisal', *British Journal of Political Science*, 13 (1983), 19–41.

——*Fluctuating Fortunes: The Political Power of Business in America* (New York: Basic Books, 1989).

Vogler, J. and Imber, M. F. (eds.), *The Environment and International Relations* (London: Routledge, 1996).

Walker, R. B. J., 'Social Movements/World Politics', *Millenium: Journal of International Studies*, 23/3 (1994).

Waltz, K., *Theory of International Politics* (New York: McGraw-Hill, 1979).

——'Reflections on *Theory of International Politics*: A Response to My Critics', in Keohane (ed.), *Neorealism and Its Critics*.

Wapner, P., 'Politics Beyond the State: Environmental Activism and World Civic Politics', *World Politics*, 47 (1995), 311–40.

Ward, B. and Dubos, R., *Only One Earth: The Care and Maintenance of a Small Planet* (London: Penguin/André Deutsch, 1972).

Watkins, T. H., 'The Perils of Option 9', *Wilderness* (Winter 1993).

WCED (World Commission on Environment and Development), *Our Common Future* (New York: Oxford University Press, 1987).

Wendt, A., 'The Agent–Structure Problem in International Relations Theory', *International Organization*, 41 (1987), 335–70.

——'Bridging the Theory/Meta-theory Gap in International Relations', *Review of International Studies*, 17 (1991), 383–92.

——'Anarchy is What States Make of It: The Social Construction of Power Politics', *International Organization*, 46 (1992), 392–425.

——'Levels of Analysis vs. Agents and Structures: Part III', *Review of International Studies*, 18 (1992), 181–5.

——'Collective Identity Formation and the International State', *American Political Science Review*, 88/2 (1994), 384–96.

Whitaker, J. C., *Striking a Balance: Environment and Natural Resources Policy in the Nixon–Ford Years* (Washington, DC: American Enterprise Institute, 1976).

Wicker, T., 'Waiting For an Environmental President', *Audobon* (Sept./Oct. 1994).

Wildavsky, A. (ed.), *The Presidency* (Boston: Little, Brown, 1969).

——'The Two Presidencies', in Wildavsky (ed.), *The Presidency*.

Wilson, G. K., *Interest Groups* (Oxford: Blackwell, 1990).

Zacher, M. W., 'The Decaying Pillars of the Westphalian Temple: Implications for International Order and Governance', in Rosenau and Czempiel (eds.), *Governance without Government*.

Zimmerman, J., *Contemporary American Federalism* (Leicester: Leicester University Press, 1992).